W9-AVG-416

STUDIES ON THE CHINESE ECONOMY

General Editors: Peter Nolan, Sinyi Professor of Chinese Management, Judge Institute of Management Studies, University of Cambridge, and Fellow of Jesus College, Cambridge, England; and Dong Fureng, Professor, Chinese Academy of Social Sciences, Beijing, China

This series analyses issues in China's current economic development, and sheds light upon that process by examining China's economic history. It contains a wide range of books on the Chinese economy past and present, and includes not only studies written by leading Western authorities, but also translations of the most important works on the Chinese economy produced within China. It intends to make a major contribution towards understanding this immensely important part of the world economy.

Published titles include:

Bozhong Li
AGRICULTURAL DEVELOPMENT IN JIANGNAN, 1620–1850

Alfred H. Y. Lin
THE RURAL ECONOMY OF GUANGDONG, 1870–1937

Nicholas K. Menzies
FOREST AND LAND MANAGEMENT IN IMPERIAL CHINA SINCE THE SEVENTEENTH CENTURY

Ryōshin Minami
THE ECONOMIC DEVELOPMENT OF CHINA

Peter Nolan
STATE AND MARKET IN THE CHINESE ECONOMY

Yuming Sheng
INTERSECTORAL RESOURCE FLOWS AND CHINA'S ECONOMIC DEVELOPMENT

Hong Wang
CHINA'S EXPORTS SINCE 1979

Wang Xiao-qiang
CHINA'S PRICE AND ENTERPRISE REFORM

Shangquan Gao
CHINA'S ECONOMIC REFORM

Xiaoping Xu
CHINA'S FINANCIAL SYSTEM UNDER TRANSITION

Malcolm Warner
THE MANAGEMENT OF HUMAN RESOURCES IN CHINESE
INDUSTRY

Tim Wright (*editor*)
THE CHINESE ECONOMY IN THE EARLY TWENTIETH CENTURY

Yanrui Wu
PRODUCTIVE PERFORMANCE OF CHINESE ENTERPRISES

Haiqun Yang
BANKING AND FINANCIAL CONTROL IN REFORMING PLANNED
ECONOMIES

Shujie Yao
AGRICULTURAL REFORMS AND GRAIN PRODUCTION IN CHINA

Xun-Hai Zhang
ENTERPRISE REFORMS IN A CENTRALLY PLANNED ECONOMY

Ng Sek Hong and Malcolm Warner
CHINA'S TRADE UNIONS AND MANAGEMENT

Studies on the Chinese Economy
Series Standing Order ISBN 0–333–71502–0
(*outside North America only*)

You can receive future titles in this series as they are published by placing a standing order.
Please contact your bookseller or, in case of difficulty, write to us at the address below with
your name and address, the title of the series and the ISBN quoted above.

Customer Services Department, Macmillan Distribution Ltd
Houndmills, Basingstoke, Hampshire RG21 6XS, England

Reworking China's Proletariat

Sally Sargeson

First published in Great Britain 1999 by
MACMILLAN PRESS LTD
Houndmills, Basingstoke, Hampshire RG21 6XS and London
Companies and representatives throughout the world

A catalogue record for this book is available from the British Library.

ISBN 0–333–71985–9

 First published in the United States of America 1999 by
ST. MARTIN'S PRESS, INC.,
Scholarly and Reference Division,
175 Fifth Avenue, New York, N.Y. 10010

ISBN 0–312–22047–2

Library of Congress Cataloging-in-Publication Data
Sargeson, Sally.
Reworking China's proletariat / Sally Sargeson.
p.   cm.
Includes bibliographical references and index.
ISBN 0–312–22047–2
1. Labor—China—Hang–chou shih—Case studies.   2. Business
enterprises—China—Hang–chou shih—Case studies.   3. China–
–Economic policy—1976–   4. Proletariat.   I. Title.
HD8740.H36S27   1999
331'.0951—dc21

98–40506
CIP

This book is printed on paper suitable for recycling and made from fully managed and sustained forest sources.

10   9   8   7   6   5   4   3   2   1
08   07   06   05   04   03   02   01   00   99

Printed and bound in Great Britain by
Antony Rowe Ltd, Chippenham, Wiltshire

For Max

Contents

Preface

Who speaks? For what, and to whom? (Said, 1989, p. 212)

China's proletariat, defined in the abstract by its structural position and structured relations with another class, cannot speak of its experiences or ideas and neither, given the constraints imposed upon China's media and intellectuals, and the usurpation of workers' voices by the trade union adjunct to the party-state, can its experiences and ideas be retrieved from the public realm. But the proletariat is composed of many speakers: speakers who are simultaneously subjects of the Maoist discourse of class and of the post-Mao discourse of national economic growth, and agents with their own stories to tell – stories which, in my view, are much more compelling than the ideological stories which have 'told' them.

Yet how can we listen to, and read these stories? How is it possible to discern the ways in which capitalist production relations impact upon identity formation and the expression of certain sorts of consciousness? And, just as problematic, how might these be represented in a text? Ethnographers' approaches to people and their discursive productions and exchanges will obviously affect the sense they make of things and the story they tell (Geertz, 1973, pp. 19–20). A note on my research methodology is, therefore, in order.[1]

Between 1992 and 1993, I spent one year amongst contract and temporary workers in enterprises in Hangzhou, the capital of Zhejiang province, talking to them about the ways in which their lives, ideas and identities are being reworked by China's economic reforms. I had three specific methodological objectives in undertaking this inquiry. First, inspired by calls for anthropologists to adopt multifaceted, multi-locale perspectives on macro-processes (Marcus, 1986, 1989), I aimed to conduct research in a variety of sites with a range of people who were engaged in China's market reforms. But in order to come to grips with the experience of wage labour in capitalist production and find out whether this classic locus of class brought that concept to the fore, I particularly wanted to spend time with non-tenured employees in China's new profit-driven firms. Therefore, work places were foregrounded in both the research process and the text.

The second objective derived from my belief that people's common-sense notions about the logic of the social order are produced dialogically in everyday conversation and activity (Volosinov, 1973; Benson and Hughes, 1983; Bakhtin, 1986; Boden and Zimmerman, 1991). Hence, much of my time in the field was spent observing relations in the work place, which people associated with one another, what they discussed and, even more importantly, when and how they discussed it.

My final, closely related methodological objective was to try to participate in, and so come to some understanding of, the life-worlds of workers. I wanted to live amongst, and work alongside, workers. The focus of my questions and the language in which they were posed were to be shaped by my informants' own topics of conversation and vocabularies (Tedlock, 1987). For these reasons, this book presents quite different views of space, social relationships, ideas and values from those which are represented in Chinese government, media, and sociologists' accounts. Here, the local is a domain in which 'outsiders' are un-knowing and powerless. Here, the state (which in other studies looms as an omnipresent authority) manifests largely as a source of irrational, oppressive regulations, and the bastion of corrupt officials. And here, workers' right to choose their own end-of-year gift, the amount of meat in their meals, and their connections with village or departmental heads, all figure as marks of social distinction.

DELIMITING THE 'FIELD'

Before going to Hangzhou, I was not at all sure that my research project would be approved, much less whether my methodological objectives could be achieved. On my previous visit to Hangzhou in 1989, I had been accommodated in a University guesthouse. In work places, I had been restricted to conducting formal interviews and distributing a survey questionnaire. Everywhere, I had been frustrated by gatekeepers who interposed themselves between myself and potential informants in order to control and monitor opinions which did not conform with authorised accounts. I did not know whether I could get long-term, unaccompanied access to work places. Even if that were possible, I did not know whether workers would feel that they should try to give me the 'right' answers to questions, or try to speak, as official documents do, on behalf of the entire work force, nation, or race (Pieke, 1992, pp. 487–506).

My fears were unfounded. To my delight, when my son Max and I arrived back in the Hangzhou suburb of Qiushi, we found ourselves living in an ordinary flat just down the street from our previous residence. The apartment block accommodated twenty-three Chinese families, comprising retired grandparents, electricians, factory workers, teachers, switchboard operators, army personnel, clerks, sales staff, more than a dozen school children, and an impressive variety of small, very short-lived, pets.

To the south, our tiny balcony overlooked identical concrete apartment blocks, a public bathhouse, a village-owned hotel, a rapidly shrinking patch of tea-trees, and a proliferation of construction sites. To the north, on the pavement alongside a busy road, squatted the bike repairers and shoe menders who, in the year to come, would provide me with an unending commentary on the doings of the street. Amongst them flowed itinerant sellers of toffee haws, socks, and greeting cards. Shops bordered the pavement: a large general store, small noodle and *jiaozi* (dumpling) restaurants, fruit and magazine stalls, tailors, hairdressers, and a telegraph office whose equipment was almost always under repair. Behind these was the post office where our old friend Haiyan worked. Diagonally opposite on the other side of a T-intersection, the main gate of the local landlord, boss, and investment banker, Zhejiang University, loomed through a permanent haze of dust and traffic fumes.

Within a few weeks of our arrival, our neighbours had come to inspect and discuss us representatives of what Trouillot (1991, pp. 38–9) calls, the totalised western 'other'. They had familiarised themselves with westerners' generic sleeping and eating habits, attitudes towards the forthcoming Olympic games, religious beliefs, and opinions about marriage, divorce, pre-marital sex, the care of aged parents, and child-rearing. They instructed me to stock up on electric fuses, hang out my washing early in the morning, and wear long underwear until the weather improved. As the months passed, we spent more and more time in our neighbours' homes. I began to take turns with other families escorting the children to and from kindergarten, and was sometimes given the weighty responsibility for doing neighbours' daily market shopping.

My neighbours also quizzed me about my research topic. They disapproved of both the topic and my intention to spend long periods of time in work places talking to non-tenured workers. Workers in non-state enterprises were, they explained, often unsophisticated, of rural origin and, hence, not well educated; not at all the sort of people with whom 'their' foreign friend should interact. If I insisted upon conducting research into these 'backward' people, then they, the worldly, urban, and literate, would find suitable specimens for me to interview, and would act as cultural translators.

Fortunately, by the time my neighbours had decided to take charge of my research, I had already begun networking amongst the very people they found unacceptable. A friend had introduced me to Aihua, who agreed to wash and clean for us one hour each day. Aihua, her husband and their immense circle of relatives, friends, and past and present fellow workers who were staying in Hangzhou or were travelling *en route* to jobs in Shenzhen, Nanjing, Beijing or Xiamen, provided me with countless more introductions and an inexhaustible source of talk.

I had also begun strolling along the streets of Qiushi, and stopping to introduce myself and my research interests to anyone who looked in the least interested. This scandalously direct approach elicited a range of responses. One small group of middle-aged saleswomen in a department store immediately turned away and muttered that they had no time to chat either during or after work.[2] On the other hand, a young male hairdresser from a village in western Zhejiang responded as though he had always wanted just such an opportunity to unburden himself of his opinions on every conceivable subject. I left his shop after a couple of hours with a pad full of notes and lungs full of smoke and hairspray, and returned on many occasions. Throughout the year, many of the people I had met plied me with hospitality, introduced me to their family and friends, interrogated me about 'the west', demanded to know what others had been saying to me, and offered opinions as to their veracity. In addition to making these neighbourhood contacts, one hot morning in early June I met the general manager of the Laolian Company in his office one block away from our apartment. He gave me tea and fruit, introduced me to his staff, and gave me permission to visit the company workshops whenever I wished.

When my research proposal was formally approved in June, a university colleague arranged interviews with several enterprise managers to help me find other research sites. At the end of each of these interviews I requested that I be able to come back regularly to observe the work place and speak with employees. Four managers agreed. However, it soon became evident that not all enterprises could provide me with the access I required. For instance, after several visits to one silk factory I had managed to spend only a few hours talking alone to workers. When I repeated my request to the manager that I be left alone on the shop floor, he expressed anxiety over the potentially sensitive political nature of my research and said he could only allow me to remain unaccompanied in the silk painting workshop. As this was the most agreeable workshop in the factory and all the painters there were tenured workers, I declined his invitation. I narrowed my observation activities to three joint venture enterprises which employed contract and temporary workers, and which gave me completely unrestricted access to the shop floor and freedom to speak with all staff and workers: the Laolian workshops which produced transducers, laboratory equipment, and computer software, a factory assembling electronic components and greeting cards, and a western-style bakery. Together with our neighbours, Aihua's network, and an ever-expanding circle of local acquaintances, the workers in these enterprises delimited the 'field' of my research in Hangzhou.

ASYMMETRIES OF POWER AND PRESENCE

The term 'field' in anthropology, Roger Berger (1993) reminds us, is laden with connotations of positivism, Imperialistic power, and racial and class privilege. In the 'field', anthropologists have licence to map geographical locale, and investigate and comment upon the material culture, kinship structures, beliefs and odd customs of the native population. Like the natural scientists they once imitated, anthropologists' collection and recording of data about places, people, and behaviour implies a discovery of previously unknown 'facts', authorises their representations of the 'field', and marks their claim to a professional turf. In Berger's view, as indeed in many other critiques of anthropology (Thomas, 1991), the 'field' does not participate in its own mapping. The anthropologist sets the boundaries of the subject 'field', decides upon research methods, and determines what is, and is not of significance.

However, when I wrote, above, that my neighbours and acquaintances, Aihua's friends, and workers in three enterprises delimited the 'field' of my research, I was signalling active intervention. In Hangzhou, the public dissection and regulation of our lives, attempts to supervise my research and reinterpret other informants' words, and the neighbourhood's on-going meta-commentary on the course and content of my research, all forced me to reconsider assumptions about cultural integration and the unidirectional operation of power relations in the 'field'. In return for some measure of acceptance in Qiushi, I was required to relinquish my privacy, silence, and autonomy in decision-making. My neighbours not only told me how to discipline my son and suggested questions I should ask of informants the following day, they also insisted, in turn, that I advise them on their family relations and problems at work. Every worker I interviewed commented upon the appropriateness of my questions to them, asked questions of me in turn, and remarked upon the usefulness of my research topic and the validity of my data.

As for power, that too was by no means a simple configuration. In China in the early 1990s, white-ness and western-ness were consciously being rejected as indices of superiority. The economic decline of many western countries, and emergence of China as an economic, military, cultural/intellectual, and sporting giant, were popular topics in the mass media and in private conversation (Barmè, 1995; Song, Zhang and Qiao,

1996). This global shift in power found expression in a generational metaphor: I was told on several occasions that though I was able to enjoy the privilege of going to study Chinese workers in the early 1990s, I should expect that my son would become the subject of their children's research, and that his country would be the destination for their investments, aid, and tourism. As a white foreigner – the archetypal outsider – with few material assets, little social expertise, and almost entirely bereft of cultural capital, I was conscious of my impotence, rather than of a power granted by race, education, wealth, or 'observer status'. Indeed, one of the terms for 'foreigner' in Mandarin, *lao wai*, is used in colloquial speech to describe a novice or someone who lacks specialised knowledge.

But ethnography also provided rationale and method for engaging in a mutual sense-making project (Fabian, 1990, pp. 764–5). Research became an epistemological exchange which, over time, breached prejudice and charted points of common conceptual ground. True, my foreign-ness was never forgotten and my ability to understand was always questioned. What did change was that I became placed at the end of a recognised continuum of comprehension, rather than in a space of alterity and irretrievable ignorance. This subtle shift was brought home to me one morning at the bakery. As we perched on upturned crates enjoying shafts of wintry sunshine, young Wang joked about my never-ending questions, and commented: 'A foreigner couldn't possibly understand it all, because Chinese society is so complex. Even we Chinese don't understand most of what goes on, so how will you?'

Dorinne Kondo (1990, pp. 7–8; see also Said, 1993, pp. 159–96) remarks that ethnographies tend to follow the temporal conventions of the novel, by narrating the researcher's journey through time from their initial feelings of strangeness and confusion, towards comprehension and the resolution of problems. That structuring convention contributes to the production of portraits of coherent, intelligible social orders where, in fact, there are none. This book does not trace an 'awakening' to China's unitary social structure and workers' interpretation of that structure, so much as what Whitaker (1996, p. 8) calls my 'publicly displayed learning' about contract and temporary workers' understandings of how their lives and their social worlds are being reworked by economic reforms.

NOTES ON THE TEXT, NOTES ON FIELDNOTES

The text is dialogical, to the extent that all informants volunteered to participate in its construction. It is also dialogical in that their conversations and stories have been told back to them, to be confirmed, amended, or refuted. I have tried not to deny specificity, difference and self-interest among the people with whom I spoke. I have, on their advice, accepted contradictions and shifts in their speech as evidence of the contextual nature of their selves and the complexity of their history and contemporary political-economic environment. But it is difficult to qualify a whole year of talk in the light of the last and the next informants' words. Inevitably, the informants, quotes and events have been selected, and the analysis herein is the product of one author.

My fieldnotes were all written 'in' the field, rather than being 'of' the field (Sanjek, 1990, pp. 94–108). In subject and density, they chart an ever-increasing familiarity with the local economy, people, and work place politics. The notes dated two days after my arrival in Hangzhou contain short descriptive passages and lists of individuals' and enterprises' names. One year later, they conclude with a single-spaced six-and-a-half page transcript of workers' gossip about managers.

While on the shop floor, I usually handwrote notes in English. If someone used an unfamiliar or particularly pithy expression, or spoke Hangzhou dialect rather than Mandarin, I wrote in Chinese characters or pinyin and asked the informant, friends and neighbours for an explanation. These fieldnotes soon became a collective project amongst my informants:

'What does that say? Is it what I just said? Read it back to me.'

'Can you really read that scrawl? Why don't you write it in Chinese?'

'Hey, did you hear what she just said? You should write *that* down!'

When I inadvertently left my notepad behind in enterprises, it was brought to me immediately after work or set aside in a safe place to await my return. My favourite notepad spent two nights locked in a drawer at the bakery, then was returned spotted with butter stains and redolent of warm sponge cakes.

In relatively quiet settings such as my apartment, offices and dormitories I asked people if they would allow me to tape conversations. Taping initially induced feelings of self-consciousness in people, and was disruptive of conversations that rambled over much longer time spans than did my 90-minute cassettes. However, tape transcripts are much richer and more nuanced than fieldnotes. Because I privilege speech as a research source, after quotes I distinguish tape transcripts from fieldnote entries.

SALLY SARGESON

Notes

1. Martyn Hammersly (1990, p. 609) takes ethnographers to task for producing work which does 'not make explicit the values, purposes and relevances upon which it is based'.
2. Just as these department store saleswomen rejected my overtures, so too did many other middle-aged urban women. I was told their shyness might have been born of Cultural Revolution paranoia, disapproval of my failure to adhere to norms of female propriety, or their limited exposure to the outside world of travel, strangers, and (even stranger) foreigners.

Acknowledgments

The writing of this book was made possible by a number of agencies. An Australian Postgraduate Research Award and a scholarship from the Asia Research Centre at Murdoch University allowed me to undertake research for the doctoral thesis on which this book is based. Library research on the topic was facilitated by receipt of a Fulbright Postgraduate scholarship to Harvard University. Travel and a year's residence in Hangzhou were funded by an Australian Award for Research in Asia from the Australian government, and a travel grant from Murdoch University's School of Humanities. Accommodation in Hangzhou was provided by Zhejiang University.

Wang Wei, Zhang Jian, Zheng Wei and Li Min of the Foreign Office and Economics Department of Zhejiang University secured approval from the State Education Commission and Zhejiang province's Public Security Bureau for me to conduct research. They helped me arrange dozens of interviews with enterprise managers and Union spokespeople, and supported my request that I be given unrestricted access to work places. Most important of all, they positively encouraged me to develop my own contacts among enterprise workers.

In Hangzhou, three enterprise managers generously gave me permission to enter and leave their factories at any time and speak individually to their employees. I spent more than 300 hours with workers in each of these enterprises, and many more hours socialising with them outside the work place. I am also immensely grateful to the dozens of academics, officials, entrepreneurs and workers in Hangzhou who discussed their lives and thoughts with me, and, in doing so, overturned many of my preconceived ideas about work, consciousness, and identity. I would particularly like to thank Lijun and Aihua for having shared their space, time, cares, and friends with me, providing me with more hilariously drunken meals than I care to remember, and teaching me more about their respective 'Chinas' than I ever hoped to know.

Tim Wright stimulated my interest in China's political economy, and provided invaluable comments on early drafts of the book. Dick Robison, Carol Warren, Annemarie Medcalf, Jocelyn Grace, Jo Brown, Tamara Jacka, Gerard Greenfield, Zhang Jian and Vedi Hadiz supplied the intellectual and moral support, jokes, gossip, and coffee that are essential in maintaining the sanity of those of us unhinged enough to even contemplate writing books. Roger Frey sometimes managed to get me to forget about the book. And when that was no longer possible, he formatted it.

Above all, Max's humour, imagination and patience made my life as a writer worth living.

SALLY SARGESON

Part I
Theorising China's Proletariat

In identity there is struggle, in particularity there is universality, and in individuality there is generality. To quote Lenin, 'there *is* an absolute *in* the relative'. (Mao, 1965, p. 343)

1 Introduction

You must be brave to be a *dagong*. One day's pay for one day's work. No old age welfare, no social guarantees, and the level of reward is set solely by the boss. For that, you must do whatever the boss orders, exactly as they wish. If you complain, act rashly, take sick leave, then you lose your rice bowl … It is common practice all over the world to work an eight hour day. Even primary school children know their parents work eight hours! How, then, is it possible for bosses not to know? Yet bosses extend the working day as a means of extracting surplus value from the *dagong*. ('Suan, tian, ku la', 1992, pp. 48–52)

Dagong, wage labourer, to work for wages; *hetong gong*, contract workers; *linshi gong*, temporary workers; *nongmin gong*, peasant workers; *wailai gong*, immigrant workers. These terms, to be overheard daily at bus stops, noodle stalls, on factory floors and television news broadcasts throughout China today, illuminate one of the most important, but neglected, consequences of the economic reforms undertaken in China since the end of the Maoist era: the reworking of China's proletariat.

I use the word proletariat advisedly.[1] The aggregate characteristics of the workers mentioned above accord well with classic Marxist descriptions of capitalist Europe's early industrial work force (Marx, 1954, pp. 305–14; Marx and Engels 1986, pp. 40–3; Engels, 1987, pp. 65–7; Lovell, 1988). They are also in keeping with the Chinese Communist Party's (hereafter CCP's) concept of the proletariat (Han, 1986; Wang, 1987). Many of these workers have been dislodged from the countryside by a combination of overpopulation, underemployment, and rural officials' and entrepreneurs' monopolisation of capital and resources. Others are the offspring of urban workers who lack the capital and contacts essential to enter higher education, succeed in private business, or find a job in the privileged, 'iron rice bowl' spheres of administration or state-owned enterprise. Propertyless, and lacking alternative means of subsistence, they have no option but to compete to sell their labour power to the owners and managers of industry in order to earn a livelihood. Once employed, they are told what to produce, and how it must be produced. Their job security is conditional upon the good will of their employers, enterprise requirements and profit margins, and their own productivity. Their products are sold for profit, which is reinvested in further production and accumulated by those who own the enterprises in which they labour.[2]

3

Statistics give a crude indication of the rapidity with which this proletariat has re-emerged. In 1978, some 49 million Chinese workers were employed in industry, commerce, construction, transport and services in enterprises which were not state-owned. By 1995, their numbers had increased to 167 million, or approximately 60 per cent, of China's non-agricultural work force (*Zhongguo tongji nianjian 1995*, hereafter *ZGTJNJ 1995*, pp. 84–5). The vast majority of these workers were contract and temporary employees. The enterprises in which they worked, owned by individual capitalists, company share-holders, local governments and cooperatives, produced two-thirds of China's industrial output and generated more than half its export income.

Common expressions point to the existence of a proletariat. Theoretically informed definitions describe its relations with other classes in society. Statistics indicate that it comprises a large, growing segment of China's work force. Nevertheless, it is denied its name. In the 1990s, the Chinese term *wuchan jieji*, proletariat or, literally, propertyless class, is very rarely heard or seen. The more commonly encountered synonym,[3] *gongren jieji*, or working class, is used in the media in a sense which occludes contract and temporary workers, for it typically refers to permanent state-sector workers. Indeed, *jieji* is usually only appended to *gongren* on the occasion of Labour Day speeches, or when Party and Union spokespeople appeal publicly to their imagined worker constituents. Even members of this ex-nominated proletariat have discarded the Marxist lexicon. They refer to themselves simply by the words which appear at the beginning of this chapter: labourers, temporary workers, immigrant workers. As a group which stands in relation to other groups in society, they describe themselves as ordinary people, or small people.

Whilst Marx's nouns have been abandoned, however, when describing their situation workers continue to use a verb critical to his theorisation. One of their definitive features, they say, is that they are exploited, *boxue*. The verb is used in a unique context. By exploitation, workers mean the extraction of surplus value from wage labourers by their employers. The definition is consonant with Marx's theorisation. However, although workers identify their bosses as exploiters, they also state that they are exploited by state officials, city people, locals, networks, and even clans. These words point to relations of ownership, employment, and accumulation between the proletariat on the one hand, and entrepreneurs, bureaucrats, territorially constituted groups, informal social organisations, and kin corporations on the other.

The formation of China's proletariat, the composition of that proletariat, and its discursive construction prompt me to pose a series of questions: questions about the naming of workers, and workers' naming of their exploiters, about connections between workers' experiences of wage work and their changing identities, attitudes and patterns of behaviour, and about the terms and modes of interaction between workers and other social groups. More broadly, what conclusions might we draw about the causal connections between China's transition from a socialist, centrally planned economy to a capitalist market economy, and the economic situation, culture, and politics of China's proletariat?

CLASS BY ANY OTHER NAME

Why, when a proletariat is in the making, do official and popular discourses eschew the classic terms which denominate it? Is it because, as Kuhn (1984), Taylor (1989) and Chu (1957) suggest, historically, Chinese people viewed society as being hierarchically stratified first by noble birth, and then by education and occupation? In the early twentieth century the words used to describe Marx's social categories were borrowed directly from the vocabulary of hierarchy. The compound *jieji* originally referred to ranks on a scale, degrees of aristocracy, and merit grades in officialdom (Kuhn, 1984, pp. 17–19). In the third decade of this century, it could denote caste as well as class (Mathews, 1931, p. 84). At the same time, lack of property, *wuchan*, was just as likely to be used to characterise all labourers, the multitude or masses (*qunzhong*), as to refer to a class (Mathews, 1931, p. 1068). Accordingly, there was, and still is, no conception of groups in Chinese society being separated and set in opposition by the ownership of property and exploitative production relations.

A simple comparison suggests this explanation is not entirely adequate. In England up until the nineteenth century, the word class commonly denoted estates located in an aristocratic hierarchy, the possession of social and cultural capital and groups defined by relations of deference. According to Raymond Williams (1976; see also Ossowski, 1963), the word still encapsulates concepts of social hierarchy, education, prestige and 'breeding'. But despite its aristocratic freight, academic and popular usages of the English word class simultaneously imply Marxist categories defined by property ownership, relations of exploitation, and modes of surplus appropriation.

Besides, the Chinese verb to exploit, *boxue*, does not draw upon the same vocabulary of hierarchy as does the noun for class, *jieji*. The compound *boxue* is composed of the character *bo*, to flay, peel or strip, and *xue*, to pare, scrape characters from a tablet, or seize territory. By the turn of the century, it carried connotations of fleecing an opponent in the market place or the reduction of wages, as well as the use of property and wealth to gain an economic advantage (Mathews, 1931, p. 733; Hu, 1960, p. 104). In this respect, the meaning of the word was closer to the Saint-Simonian idea of exploitation as coerced extraction – an experience with which oppressed people everywhere are familiar – than to ideas either of feudal tribute or of surplus appropriation (Carver, 1987; Cunliffe and Reeve, 1996).

Moreover, after the Communist victory of 1949 and establishment of the socialist party-state, class and exploitation were intentionally invested with new meanings. An explicitly Marxist definition of exploitation became the main criterion for class categorisation of the populace (Hinton, 1966; Selden, 1979, pp. 218–25). In the course of classifying members of their communities during land reform and participating in the public rituals of retribution known as 'speaking bitterness', class became a moral benchmark and a criterion by which land, resources, and power were redistributed (Anagnost, 1994). After the abolition of private ownership of the means of production, class designations remained a standard by which the party-state evaluated behaviour and consciousness, and allocated political positions, jobs, goods and services (White, 1976; Wortzel, 1987). As such, class labels became both the subject and the means of struggle amongst people throughout the country (Chan, 1982).

According to the class code by which people's relationships, attitudes, and actions were evaluated, the working class was publicly applauded for its advanced political thought and behaviour, and rewarded by the party-state's provision of secure employment and subsidised housing, health care, and food. Simultaneously, at school, at work and in urban neighbourhoods its members were subjected to intense indoctrination intended to instil in them precisely the sorts of thought and behaviour the party-state conceived to be politically advanced. All this, together with the operation of an extensive surveillance system and penalties for poor political thought and attitudes towards work, ensured workers' observance of socialist 'proletarian' norms, adherence to an homogeneous 'proletarian' identity, and orthodox expressions of socialist 'proletarian' consciousness (Schurmann, 1960; Howe, 1973; Walder, 1986).

Were the terms proletariat and class corrupted by the party-state's creation of precisely those distributional patterns, behavioural norms and disciplinary systems? Were they eventually rendered meaningless because of their cooptation by ambitious class careerists, the increasingly apparent inability of the Communist Party's version of socialism to deliver on promises of economic development and political democratisation, or as a result of the ferocity and arbitrariness of the so-called class warfare that occurred during the Cultural Revolution? Such interpretations are supported by evidence of the growing apathy and cynicism of the population which can be found in fiction, autobiographies, and films set in that period.[4]

Perhaps, as Anita Chan (1993, pp. 50–1) argues, class denominations were finally made obsolete because China's post-1978 leaders viewed class rhetoric as a political impediment and an obstacle to economic growth. Certainly, along with Maoist polemic, Marxist terms were culled from official documents and speeches issued throughout the 1980s and 1990s. The only element retained from that discourse was an enthusiasm for anything which would foster 'the development of productive forces'.[5]

Taken together, these ideas go further in explaining the demise of the name for China's proletariat. Still, they do not suffice. While it is undeniable that dominant groups in society appropriate to themselves the authority to define and name things and, as in the case of China, monopolise the means for communicating names (Williams, 1976; Bourdieu, 1991), the implicit logic underlying the foregoing explanations is that Chinese workers were the passive recipients and carriers of an alien discourse foisted upon them by an ideologically zealous political elite. This implies that the lexicon of class either never had any referential validity or explanatory power for people, or that it lost whatever coinage it once possessed when it was misused by Maoist careerists, then discarded by post-Mao leaders. The masses, always obedient, followed suit.

This line of reasoning neglects the everyday, interactive contexts in which the meanings of words and names are continually being contested and transformed, even those words which at some point become part of a hegemonic discourse. Meanings alter over time. That truism is demonstrated by the history of the changing meanings of *jieji* and *boxue*. Moreover, changes are as likely to be propelled by collective critique as by the dissemination of propaganda. People draw upon personal experiences of the world and employ common sense to assess the validity of terms given them (Heritage, 1987; Scott, 1990; Shotter, 1990; Huspek, 1994). Authoritative meanings of some terms in a corpus might be conserved in aphorisms, some will be abandoned, and some transformed as they are borrowed into other contexts, employed rhetorically in such a way as to call attention to an unfulfilled meaning, or used to satirise the messages they once conveyed or the individuals or groups who propagated those messages (Douglas, 1975; Harré, 1978; Humphrey, 1989). In short, people exercise agency in, and through, their creative use of language.

We know that names for class were once in common usage in China. In examining the experiences, attitudes and behaviour of members of China's proletariat, we need to consider why they have discarded, transformed, or retained terms to suit their *own* communicative purposes, rather than assume that they have simply followed the dictates of their political leaders. Was class jettisoned because it simply had no referential validity for the lived experiences and identity orientations of workers? Why is exploitation still part of current speech? And why do workers describe themselves as small people, exploited by officials, members of local urban communities, and social networks?

THEORISING THE PROLETARIAT: IDENTITIES, CONSCIOUSNESS AND BEHAVIOUR

Posing questions about the naming of China's proletariat opens up an even wider field of inquiry: how do those contract and temporary workers who stand at the forefront of capitalist processes of production and accumulation live, understand, and describe their work situations? How have their experiences of wage work and production for others' profit informed their senses of identity, and their interpretations of relations among workers, and between workers and their employers? And, if class does not figure as a point of identification, are there alternative identities and organisational foci which might provide a forum for workers' activism?

These questions are central both to theories of class, and to the history of Chinese labour. Two contrasting theoretical perspectives characterise much scholarly research into the relationship between wage work and workers' collective identities, consciousness and behaviour. The first of these derives directly from Marx. The second is informed, rather more circuitously, by the ideas of Weber and Durkheim. The assumptions, causal connections and political prognoses which distinguish these approaches are evident in the work of the three scholars who, more than any others, have shaped Western views of the formation of China's proletariat through the twentieth century: Jean Chesneaux, Elizabeth Perry, and Andrew Walder.

Generations of Marxist scholars have privileged employment in capitalist industry as the experience which, above all others, awakens a consciousness among workers of class as a primary aspect of their identity. The concentration of workers in industries, control of their labour and the appropriation of their surplus product by the owners of those industries supposedly represents a crucial moment in the emergence of a proletariat. It establishes the objective conditions and antagonistic structured relations which will be formative of classes: ownership and control of the means of production by capitalists, the mode in which the labour process is controlled so as to extract surplus from workers, the realisation of profit and the accumulation of capital by owners (Przeworski, 1977; Wright, 1982; Bodemann and Spohn, 1986; Marx, 1986; Aronowitz, 1992).

The working class is called into being by capital, but as a 'class in itself' workers are not yet conscious of their class position and interests. Residential and work place proximity and the collective social nature of their labour leads them, piecemeal, to realise their common plight, aspirations, and collective identity, and develop collective strategies to improve their lot (Merriman, 1979; Katznelson, 1986; Ollman, 1987). In studies which follow Marx's early work, participation in collective struggle in the face of repressive productive and political regimes is the alchemy which sparks an appraisal by workers of their objective situation, and development of appropriate forms of activism. In Leninist analyses, the intervention of socialist intellectuals inspires workers to transform their wage concerns into an objective, scientific understanding of issues of class (Lenin, 1971, p. 186; Calhoun, 1982, pp. 222–5). Both approaches hold that class-conscious political activism marks the emergence of the proletariat as a 'class for itself' (Poulantzas, 1974, p. 17; Thompson, 1980, pp. 887–915; Burawoy, 1984, 1985, 1989).

The essential nature of the proletariat *qua* proletariat will determine all aspects of its members' activities:

> It is not a question of what this or that proletarian or even the whole proletariat momentarily imagines to be the aim. It is a question of what the proletariat is and what it consequently is historically compelled to do. Its aim and historical action is prescribed, irrevocably and obviously, in its own situation in life as well as in the entire organisation of contemporary civil society. (McLellan, 1977, p. 135)

Thus, in the course of struggle, the proletariat gains a unity of identity and purpose which allows it to perceive, and reject its segmentation and ideological representation as an atomised work force of individuals, members of trades, clans, religions, or races (Stedman Jones, 1983, p. 42; Ollman, 1987; Wright, 1987; Miliband, 1991). All is transformed by the ineluctable, abstract logic of working for and against capital.

This presupposes a sequential development from a lower, subjective state of consciousness to a more objective appraisal of its state (Marshall, 1988). In Hegelian terms, class consciousness resolves subject/object, truth/falseness, and in-itself/of-itself dichotomies (Marx and Engels, 1947, p. 47; Warminski, 1995). It is, therefore, a state which, once reached, is complete. Ira Katznelson (1986) points out that although these progressive assumptions are rarely stated, they clearly inform Marxist labour studies.

Indeed, while Katznelson applauds E. P. Thompson's work for having inspired a generation of social historians who are sensitive to the mediation of structures by historically and culturally constituted agents, he remarks that Thompson also theorises class formation as a process of 'making' and 'becoming' which, ultimately, will be a finite movement towards 'truth'.

Jean Chesneaux's *The Chinese Labor Movement 1919–1927* (1968) provides the most commanding, and faithful, application of Marx's ideas to the early history of China's industrial work force. According to Chesneaux, in the 1920s, China's proletariat had already achieved a critical mass which was concentrated geographically and in industrial sectors. Chesneaux concedes that as a proletariat, it had certain weaknesses, for, in loyalty to Marx's progressivist bent, Chesneaux's 'revolutionary work force par excellence' would have been experienced, urban, skilled, male, and employed in large scale 'modern' industry. The more educated workers were, the more likely that they could come to a 'correct' understanding of their objective situation. The bigger and more mechanised the industries, the better the odds that collective action would occur. China's industrial work force, however, was young, geographically mobile, and unskilled. These anomalies were compounded in specific cities such as Shanghai, where the work force comprised a large proportion of recent peasant immigrants and females, and Tianjin, where most workers were employed in small, poorly capitalised workshops.

Chesneaux argues that, despite these handicaps, the proletariat had begun to forge a distinct collective identity as a result of its experience of capitalist employment relations:

> the Chinese industrial proletariat in the twenties was completely differentiated, because of its new economic status, from the social classes from which it had been recruited: the poor peasants, the skilled craftsmen, and the urban populace. It had undergone a qualitative change. Common experience of industrial work had welded its composite elements together to form a new social force that was quite alien to older Chinese traditions. (p. 142)

The growing maturity of the Chinese proletariat was demonstrated, Chesneaux argues, by a heightened consciousness of class as expressed in specific forms of political organisation and activism. It had achieved a sufficient degree of consciousness of its position and interests as a class that it had begun to agitate against its capitalist employers, the nascent bourgeois state, and Imperialist aggressors. Increasingly, the traditional patterns of association and bourgeois-dominated 'labourite' organisations were replaced by well coordinated, truly representative unions affiliated with socialist parties. Strikes were no longer precipitated solely by clashes on the factory floor and dissatisfaction over wages. Instead, workers began to agitate over matters of real class import, such as working conditions, job security, the bosses' lack of respect for their dignity, and, most important of all, the desire for radical political transformation:

> economic struggles, however important, could never be an end in themselves. They were more in the nature of a prepatory stage for later action, during which class consciousness was awakened and forces were organized, than of a direct solution to the basic problems of the Chinese working class; and the labor movement was hardly ever deflected by these economic issues from taking part in the political struggle. (Chesneaux, 1968, p. 386)

However, contrary to Chesneaux's confident pronouncement, and despite the organisational efforts of unions and socialist parties, common experience of industrial work did *not* weld composite elements of the work force together to form the quintessential proletariat. Regionalism, and gender and status prejudices persisted in China's early capitalist work places. Labour organisations were coopted by criminal gangs and bourgeois parties, and the proletariat remained politically divided and weak. In short, China's workers, like workers almost everywhere, remained obstinately different from the homogeneous, politically active proletariat envisioned by Marx.

While Marxist scholars have looked to participation in capitalist production as the causal factor in the creation of a unitary proletarian identity, consciousness and behaviour, liberal researchers of labour history tend to search outside the work place to detect forces shaping the status hierarchies and occupational competitions which distinguish work places and differentiate workers; they discover these in the historical development of national polities, forms of social organisation, expressive/symbolic systems, and religions.

Workers' interpolation into capitalist production is not presumed to give rise to a distinctive proletarian identity, and a politic designed to eliminate positions given by relations of ownership and employment. Instead, on the one hand, work encourages a rational systematisation of pre-existing culturally and socially ascribed identities and political affiliations (Durkheim, 1933, pp. 147–50, 175–90; Calhoun, 1982, pp. 222–33; Sabel, 1982; Marshall, 1988). On the other hand, dissimilarities are sharpened by workers' sensitisation to new status, prestige, and income differentials. Collective activism comprises reformist activities intended to improve the relative position of particular groups of workers.

Embedded in many such approaches are developmental and essentialist assumptions which, whilst based upon an alternative explanatory schema, echo those purveyed by Marx. Differences of identity, particularly those derived from community structures, patterns of belief and socialisation, give rise to particular 'world views' and forms of activism (Lockwood, 1966; Sabel, 1982). As the working class becomes better educated and 'more modern', its members create formally constituted organisations to represent their interests.

These ideas inform several studies which trace the fragmentation and political weakness of the Chinese proletariat to its organisation by territorial, ethnic, and criminal consortia (Chan, 1975; Honig, 1986, 1992; Rowe, 1989). Place of origin associations and criminal gangs organised the recruitment of workers and channelled particular groups into occupational niches. Within factories, industrial relations were mediated by patronage networks, and disputes often took the form of competition between ethnic and place of origin groups. Outside the work place, workers deferred to the leaders of native place associations, guilds, and gangs. They lived, socialised, and were protected by same-place communities, real or fictive kinship groups, and religious associations. The divisive effects of these organisational and cultural patterns were compounded by differences established by workers' sex and skill. Hence, the argument runs, primordial patterns of identification and organisation precluded a consciousness of working-class interests and the possibility of class organisation (Honig, 1986, 1992).

In *Shanghai on Strike*, Elizabeth Perry (1993) has contested the suggestion that those affiliations inhibited workers' organisation and consciousness. Drawing on the work of Weberian scholars like Craig Calhoun (1982), as well as phenomenological theories which locate changes in consciousness in the generic sphere of social action (Perry, 1993, p. 8), Perry demonstrates instead that intra-class divisions and organisation on the basis of place of origin and trade frequently served as a vehicle of Shanghai workers' activism between the 1920s and 1940s: 'the fragmentation of labor can provide a basis for politically influential working-class action, not only in support of one or another political party, but even in the emergence of new political regimes' (1993, p. 2).

Perry is ambivalent, however, about whether the experience of employment in capitalist enterprises was a major catalyst of labour militancy and class consciousness. Her ambivalence is prompted by recognition that workers' activism was not always generated by tensions over the labour-capital relationship. Identification with place sometimes overrode class solidarity, and disputes were often precipitated by competition among workers from different regions (1993, p. 30, 250). If, Perry suggests, class consciousness is 'an awareness of exploitation by owners and a propensity to redress grievances through independent collective action' (Perry, 1993, p. 47), then some strikes in Shanghai were in fact 'unconscious', whilst others were paradigmatic instances of class-conscious activism.

In accounting for this variation, Perry fixes upon artisanal status as the single most important factor determining Chinese workers' achievement of class consciousness and ability to organise collectively to negotiate solutions to their grievances (1993, pp. 61, 251–52). Artisans such as metal workers, carpenters, mechanics, and weavers were knit together by tighter bonds of community, cooperation, and pride in their craft than were less skilled proletarians such as dock workers, silk spinners, and tobacco packers. Artisans had a higher level of literacy, were imbued with the 'democratic culture' of their guilds (p. 51), and were 'susceptible to the appeals of radical student organizers' (p. 252) and the call of nationalism. They joined 'modern' political organisations, including the Nationalist and Communist Parties. They were more affluent, and hence less compelled by the necessity to earn each day's livelihood.

Despite a disclaimer to the contrary, the discrepancies Perry detects between these urbane artisans and the masses of semi- and unskilled workers designated as proletarians are imparted in the familiar tropes of modernity (defined by literacy, rationality, pluralism and democracy), and tradition (illiteracy, irrationality, uniformity, hierarchical authority) (Gramsci, 1971, pp. 5–13; Torgovnick, 1990, p. 18). Proletarians were distinguished by their affiliation with village and kin group rather than with the new republican 'nation' or their trade. They performed 'traditional peasant marriage practices', in contrast to the 'love matches' and common-law unions formed by skilled, educated workers (Perry, 1993, pp. 59, 187). They clung to the dress codes and amusements of their native rural areas, rather than follow their artisan contemporaries in adopting sophisticated, individualising fashions. They were 'closer to … the "lumpen" beggar, night soil carrier, prostitute, or docker than to the carpenter or the mechanic' (Perry, 1993, p. 55, 59, 186–7). In the cities, they fell prey to the brutal authoritarianism of gangs. Their obedience to gang 'chieftains' was symbolically expressed in initiation rituals and expressions of 'filial' obedience, which were qualitatively different, we are led to believe, from the ceremonial enactment of deference received by guild heads from artisans, or by artisans from their apprentices (1993, pp. 51–2).

Given the distinctions drawn between Shanghai's artisans and proletarians, it is not surprising that their experiences and perceptions of capitalist production and the strikes they initiated are also said to be different in kind. This, despite Perry's acknowledgment that in Shanghai's BAT factory in the 1920s, strikes staged by proletarians outnumbered those staged by skilled workers; they targeted issues ranging from job insecurity to Imperialist aggression, and they were well organised.[6] The empirical anomaly requires explanation:

> How, then, do we account for the strike propensity among unskilled workers, whose mobility, and exclusion from guild membership would seem to have undercut their potential for group cohesion. Is this simply a case of anomie, in which rude peasants unaccustomed to urban norms engage in spontaneous violence against the restrictions of city and factory life? (1993, p. 50)

Rhetorical speculation slips into assertion: in the following pages, the activism of proletarians is dismissed as the rage of rural-primitives suddenly subjected to modern disciplines and employers' threats to reduce wages. Unaware of their common class interests and hence incapable of overcoming their fragmentation, their protests remained limited in aim, scope and effect. In contrast, because of a cohesiveness given by their craft pride, education and liberal forms of association, skilled workers were able to transcend 'traditional' affiliations, perceive their 'true' position and common interests and establish effective political organisations. Class consciousness precipitated artisans' strikes, but not proletarians' strikes.

In both Chesneaux's and Perry's accounts, the proletariat is compelled to act as it does because of what it is. Both also imply that workers' achievement of class consciousness is evidence of a developmental process which is expressed, and can be detected, in three trends. There is, first, a recognition of objective class position and interests. Second, there is the formation of formally constituted, disciplined, inclusive labour organisations. And third, those organisations adopt recognisable political strategies. They call and coordinate strikes with the aim not only of improving the pay and conditions of workers, but also to attain long term objectives such as participation in political decision making. But where Chesneaux identifies a unitary, organised, politically effective working class, Perry sees a class energised by, and organised around, internal divisions. Skilled workers were politicised by their experiences of work and struggle. In contrast, proletarians remained unconscious and incapable of contesting the terms of their exploitation.

Whereas Chesneaux and Perry focus upon factors contributing to workers' class consciousness and activism before the revolution of 1949, Andrew Walder (1983, 1984, 1986) sets himself the task of accounting for the absence of those very things in the post-revolutionary work force. Drawing upon both Marxist and Weberian perspectives, Walder argues that

Chinese workers' identity, consciousness and behaviour were shaped by the all-encompassing ideology, policies and economic activities of the socialist party-state. Thus, the focus of analysis shifts from relations between capital and labour, or primordial association and proletarians, to relations between boss-state and public sector employees.

The party-state which came to power in 1949 claimed to be the 'historical agent' of the working class. Thus authorised, it dictated the nature and scope of activities of every formal organisation and association. The All China Federation of Trade Unions (ACFTU) – many of whose leaders had been members of the pre-revolutionary working class – became a regulatory arm of the party-state (Wilson, 1986; Chiang, 1990). The state's central planning apparatus controlled the utilisation of raw materials and investment capital, all aspects of production in state-owned enterprises, population movement, job allocation, and the distribution of food and consumer goods. Workers came to rely upon state, enterprise, and their immediate superiors for the determination of social goals, the organisation of all forms of social activity, and the satisfaction of all their needs and wants. The urban work force was divided by the ownership type of enterprises and individuals' status as permanent, contract, and temporary employees. Within work places, workers were further fragmented by the extent to which they were integrated into the patron-client networks which underpinned the Communist Party's control of enterprises, and management's control of the production process.

Walder argues that in splicing the material interests and status aspirations of urban workers to their employer enterprises, and by suppressing all ideas and vehicles for resistance, the party-state created a compliant, cliental work force. The causal connection is demonstrated by data on demographic changes, employment trends, and increasing competition for secure, well paid jobs in the state sector, by interviews with workers about the exercise of state authority in work places, and by the implied non-existence of collective activism for, despite the occurrence of many thousands of labour disputes and myriad acts of protest, the only labour unrest which emerges from these studies involved antagonism between ordinary workers and worker 'activists' loyal to party-state and management (1986, pp. 166–70).[7] Thus, Walder is able to submit that because Chinese state sector workers never experienced exploitation, and never engaged in the collective organisation and struggle which Marxists point to as critical moments in the cognitive and political maturation of the working class, the revolution rendered workers *un*conscious, and 'ushered in the *unmaking* of the Chinese working class' (Walder, 1984, p. 41). The same teleological assumptions which underpin Chesneaux's and Perry's discussion of class consciousness as a process of experiential learning and enlightenment lead Walder to proclaim the post-revolutionary work force a developmental failure.

Writings about the past help us make sense of the present. Chesneaux, Perry and Walder alert us to the operation of factors which, in the pre- and post-revolutionary periods, influenced Chinese workers' responses to the experience of wage work, and their identities, consciousness, and relations with differently categorised workers as well as with employers and other social groups. The key variables they identify are experiences of, and agitation against, exploitation, identities and patterns of organisation centred on work, place of origin and socially accredited skill, and governance by a paternalistic socialist party-state.

At the same time, however, their studies highlight inconsistencies between the assumptions, causal relationships and prognoses implicit in both Marxist and Weberian approaches, and the messy realities that have characterised the recent history of Chinese labour. In particular, these inconsistencies cast doubt on the Marxist idea that class identity overrides other criteria of identification, as well as the liberal argument that pre-existing identities are not radically transformed by production relations. They raise questions as to whether, and why, differences of identity and interest among workers preclude class consciousness and collective activism. And they call into question the idea that the achievement of class consciousness is a finite process of maturation which eventually results in workers coming to an identical understanding of their objective situation, organising inclusive, independent labour unions, and staging strikes in pursuit of broad, class objectives. These assumptions have led us to neglect formative links between the development of capitalism and non-class forms of identity, organisation and activism. One of the aims of this study is to illuminate those links.

A NAVIGATION AID

This book has utilised ethnographic methodology and cross-disciplinary theories to examine the ideas, attitudes and actions of the proletariat that has been reworked by the economic reforms undertaken in China since 1978. It concentrates on that unnamed, but quintessential segment of the proletariat which comprises contract and temporary workers. In examining contract and temporary workers' experiences, understandings, and attitudes toward wage work, the book develops a simple, argument. Capitalism in China is being created on the basis of place, power and particularism. So, too, are class relations and class consciousnesses expressed in struggles which centre upon place, power and particularism.

The book begins with a lens wide enough to encompass the national political-economic changes associated with economic reform, then focuses in on a region, a suburb, and enterprises located in that suburb. The central segment of the book analyses working conditions and relationships within enterprise work shops. It then opens out again to examine patterns of social interaction and the production of meanings in workers' residential neighbourhoods.

Part I situates China's proletariat, first, in the context of China's socialist market economy. It explains how changes in the aims, functions and ideology of the state, the nature and activities of enterprises, and the form and operation of labour markets and mediating, regulatory and representative institutions have created conditions conducive to the exploitation of Chinese workers. The chapter concludes by identifying commonalities and differences between the industrial relations environments of the pre-revolutionary period and Maoist era, and that of the 1990s. The second chapter describes the socio-spatial dynamics that have given rise to place-based, class-structured communities in north-eastern Zhejiang and Hangzhou, and introduces the location and enterprises in which field research was conducted in Xihu district. The histories of these enterprises demonstrate the ways in which capital, control over businesses and jobs have been allocated through local social networks.

Part II analyses contract and temporary workers' experiences and understandings of waged work through a detailed investigation into employment relations, production processes, and pay systems in the case study enterprises. This analysis elucidates why workers describe their own and their exploiters' identities in terms of place, power and particularism, and frame their acts of resistance accordingly. Chapter 4 demonstrates how labour market conditions, recruitment practices and the terms of employment of workers reflect, and give further substance to, distinctions based upon rural and urban residence, membership and non-membership of local communities, and social connections. Chapter 5 explores spatial signification in the work place. It depicts the ways in which managerial controls and patterns of production and extraction are expressed and enforced in the design of enterprises, and describes workers' reactions to these regimes. The means by which surplus value is secured by employers in the labour process and in the payment of wages to workers are the subjects of Chapters 6 and 7. Managers who purportedly adhere to the dominant meritocratic ethos propagated by the reformist state are shown to manipulate identities and relationships established by place and particularism in order to assert and maintain control over production processes. But, as certain disputes illustrate, those methods of control can also be strategically deployed by workers to contest the terms of their subjugation and exploitation.

Part III connects workers' experiences and understandings of waged work to their construction and representation of collective identities, discourses about values and morals, and patterns of social interaction in their neighbourhoods. It analyses workers' perceptions that place, social networks based upon power and wealth, and communicative acts of consumption are central elements in the construction of capitalist relations of production in China and their own experiences of exploitation. They are also shown to be primary points of identification and resistance. The book concludes by responding to the questions posed in this introductory chapter, and reflecting on the theoretical implications of the reworking of China's proletariat.

2 Reforming the Proletariat

The year 1978 marked the beginning of a decisive transformation in the nature of China's economy, from one characterised by central planning and the operation of collective institutions and state-owned enterprises, to a market economy dominated by various types of non-state firms. In 1978, the CCP and central government began to approve experiments in household contracting of agricultural production, establishment of special economic zones intended to encourage exports and the import of technology and capital, market exchanges, and private commerce. Initially, the country's leaders argued that all these activities would remain under the aegis of the state's planning organs, and state-owned enterprises would continue to predominate: the economy therefore remained socialist. In the mid-1980s, the radical changes wrought by reform were acknowledged by state spokespeople who began to refer to China's socialist 'commodity economy'. In the 'commodity economy', the party-state exercised control over markets which, in turn, helped to guide the activities of enterprises which enjoyed varying degrees of autonomy (Hannan, 1995; Survey of World Broadcasts (hereafter *SWB*), 13 February 1993). At the 14th Party Congress held in 1992, the economy was redefined as a 'socialist market economy' (Zhongguo gongchandang, 1993). Since then, the party-state has attempted to eliminate price controls and give full play to markets in production factors, products and services, guarantee the private ownership rights of investors, establish an independent commercial banking system, and liberalise trade (*China News Digest*, hereafter *CND*, 10 January 1994, 27 March 1995; Yabuki, 1995; Gao, 1996).

Economic reforms have changed the political-economic environment in which China's proletariat lives and labours and, in doing so, have reformed the proletariat itself. Workers' roles, their public image, and their relations with their employers have been dramatically transformed. They have become the producers of private profit, rather than of social wealth. Officials, industry leaders and the state-dominated media have ensured that workers, once represented as the vanguard of the socialist revolution, have been discursively recast as the recalcitrant bearers of an out-moded leftist ideology. As such, they have become the object of policies, re-education campaigns, and new disciplinary systems designed to make their attitudes and behaviour compatible with the needs of the 'socialist market economy'. And owing to the ever-present possibility of a reduction in income or summary dismissal, workers have been rendered vulnerable to employers' intensification of productivity pressures.

Yet reports on the consequences of economic reform have a tendency to overemphasise the impact of policies designed by the party-state and implemented at its direction by lower level bureaucrats and entrepreneurs. Concurrently, they neglect the means by which various sections of society have taken advantage of, or resisted implementation of new initiatives, and thereby altered the course of reform. To some extent, this chapter is guilty of producing another top-down view of the reform process. It notes changes in the ways economic activities are being governed, and in the economic activities of different levels of government. It traces links between the state's reform policies and the development of new enterprises which are characterised by capitalist relations of production, where surplus value is extracted to be realised as profit and invested in further accumulation. And it explains how party-state policies and management strategies have altered the economic, politico-legal, and industrial relations contexts in which enterprises employ wage workers. However, this top-down perspective is moderated later in the book, where the focus shifts to the many ways various social actors utilise localism and particularism to adapt reform policies to their own ends. Such opportunism is no less characteristic of the activities of local governments eager to maximise their revenue from local enterprises, than it is of business investors seeking local government protection and reliable employees, or contract workers struggling to gain some measure of job security by developing connections with their boss's family.

GOVERNING REFORM

The major objectives of the economic reforms undertaken by the party-state since 1978 have been to increase gross national product (GNP), raise the standard of living of the Chinese people, and, concurrently, popularise the continued rule of the CCP (Gao, 1996). These objectives and the activities directed toward their realisation are expressed in an ideological discourse about the pursuit of national economic growth (Friedrich, 1989; Giddens, 1991; Miller and Rose, 1993). National economic growth is demonstrated, and economic reform is concurrently justified, in the universal language of ever-increasing numbers: increased numbers of employees, improved per capita productivity relative to capital investment and energy usage, larger state revenues, higher wages, and expanded household consumption of major commodities.

The central party-state and local governments[1] have played critically important roles in defining and constructing the conditions of a socialist market economy so that profits, and growth, can be secured. The central government, persuaded by the apparent failure of central planning to raise productivity and generate national growth, as well as by the arguments of neo-liberal economists that a separation of state and market and competition between firms would invigorate China's economy, has ceased directing most economic activities. Instead, it now uses macro-economic levers to try to guide the pace and direction of growth. This has resulted in a transfer of economic decision-making and responsibility for profits and losses from the central government to local governments, investors, and enterprise managers. None of these changes has proceeded smoothly or without resistance from those parts of the central party-state which have had to relinquish control, or from lower levels of government, enterprises, and social groups which fear that they will be disadvantaged by market competition.

In order to achieve quantifiable growth, much of the Chinese economy has been oriented towards production for profit through exchange in markets. Hence, the main economic focus of the central party-state is the design of policies and creation of institutions to support business activities and markets. Tariff cuts and currency reforms have assisted the expansion of domestic export manufacturing and technology transfers (Kueh, 1992; Lardy, 1992; *SWB*, 31 January 1996). Some of the legal and institutional conditions necessary for private and collective capital investment and accumulation have been established. There has, for instance, been the enactment of laws guaranteeing security of property rights, laws pertaining to the establishment of share-holding and joint ventures and a stock market, the provision of investment-related tax exemptions and permission for repatriation of profits for foreign firms, and the development of new banking and credit facilities and futures markets (Thomas, 1993; *Beijing Review*, hereafter *BR*, 15 August 1994; Murray, 1994, pp. 269–90). Market competition has been underwritten by the elimination of some import quotas and most domestic subsidies and fixed prices, and new laws which govern contracts (White, 1993; Murray, 1994).

In addition to establishing an environment conducive to private activity in the market economy, the central party-state has introduced policies and regulations which are intended to make state-owned enterprises contribute to China's economic growth by becoming more independent, productive, and responsive to market signals. State enterprises are being transformed into joint stock companies which retain after-tax profits, and make their own investment decisions. Heavily indebted firms are increasingly being forced to shed surplus employees, declare bankruptcy, or sell assets. The introduction of contractual employment and establishment of social insurance systems are expected to ease the heavy welfare burdens of state enterprises.

Whilst labour is not mentioned as a separate item in the party-state's macroscopic agenda, transformation of the position, role, and productivity of the Chinese work force is clearly an essential precondition for establishing a 'socialist market economy' (*Guangming ribao*, hereafter *GMRB*, 26 March 1993; Zhongguo gongchandang, 1993; *Zhongguo laodong bao*, hereafter *ZGLDB*, 29 December 1992). It is proposed that all production factors be transformed into commodities, and enterprises be given the means by which to ensure that those factors can be used in the most productive manner possible. Accordingly, the party-state has devised measures which are intended to create a market in labour power and grant enterprises the tools with which to enforce productivity increases and limit wage costs. As I examine these changes in some detail below, it is sufficient here just to draw attention to the main policy initiatives. The state has encouraged workers' geographical and job mobility. It has simplified hiring and firing practices, eliminated life-long employment in state firms, and supported enterprise-based, productivity-linked pay schemes (*ZGLDB*, 26 January 1993). It has also drawn up a national labour law to regulate relations between employers and employees, and has encouraged local governments to establish arbitration committees to oversee labour disputes.

These practical initiatives have been underpinned by promotion of an ideology appropriate to market-led growth. In a logic and vocabulary informed by neo-classical economic theory, state-owned media and cultural organs have began to argue that competition and rational endeavour on the part of both individuals and enterprises will result not only in national economic growth, but also in higher personal incomes. Merit, which was once bestowed symbolically for employees' political consciousness, will be earned in the market place in the form of money. Teachers, media producers, and the leaders of mass organisations are cultivating new attitudes and knowledge which are considered to be economically serviceable: self-reliance, individualism, competitiveness, entrepreneurial drive, awareness of contractual obligations, acceptance of meritocratic principles, and technical, marketing and legal expertise (Rofel, 1989b; *Xinhua*, 10 April 1996). In this vein, workers are told that 'in liberating their thought, they must completely eliminate those old fashioned, leftist ideas which are obstructing the development of the productive forces and affecting China's progress' (*ZJRB*, 19 May 1992).

Given the central party-state's assumption that the separation of government and business is a precondition for assuring market-led growth, it is ironic that the dismantling of most of the central planning apparatus and devolution of decision-making and management to firms has had the effect of dramatically increasing both the economic interests and the economic functions of local governments. In the planned economy, local government revenues and official salaries were principally fixed by centrally determined budgets and wage grades. Then, in addition to their administrative duties and management of local infrastructure and services, local governments were responsible for local economic development and provision of employment opportunities and welfare for local residents.

Now, the motivation for, and substance of, their activities have changed, for the income of both local governments and officials is directly linked to expansion of the government's revenue base (Oi, 1992; Wang Shaoguang, 1994; Zhang, 1996). This has resulted in a proliferation of local governments' and officials' entrepreneurial and rent-seeking activities (Qian and Stiglitz, 1996; Kwong, 1997). Local governments now negotiate and retain a share of tax revenue from local enterprises. They have the authority to grant tax exemptions to enterprises which meet national and local criteria, thereby enticing investors to their localities. They may, within specified limits, approve direct foreign loans and investment, and may engage in, and administer, foreign trade (*BR*, 30 October 1995). Local governments and their component parts own real-estate property and power and water supplies, from which they receive rents. They also hold property rights in collective, share-holding, and joint venture firms, in which capacity they operate in a manner which some scholars have compared to the roles played by boards of directors and majority shareholders in capitalist corporations (Oi, 1990, 1992; Nee, 1992). Local governments also have the discretionary power to impose charges, levies, and registration fees on most kinds of economic activity occurring within their jurisdiction. In addition to accruing revenue from these sources, individual officials extract private rents from their control of access to publicly-owned resources, energy, credit, housing, job vacancies in government-invested firms, and licences for everything from the right to establish an investment company to the issue of building permits (Bruun, 1989; Cheng Shu, 1992; *Gongren ribao*, hereafter *GRRB*, 13 September 1992; *Hangzhou ribao*, hereafter *HZRB*, 7 September 1992; Zhang, 1993).[2] One of my neighbours in Hangzhou quipped that, as a consequence, 'Nowadays every official in China has made licensing their business!' (see also Wang Shaoguang, 1994, p. 97). Recognition of the increased scope of local government entrepreneurship has prompted universities and colleges to offer courses in Business Management, Economics, and Commerce specifically designed for, and timetabled to suit the convenience of, officials.

Individual officials' economic activities have been expanded and protected through familial and social ties (Yu, 1990; *CND*, 9 February 1998). There is evidence of nepotism and intermarrying amongst the families of officials in key economic departments, and of retired officials and their relatives moving into businesses where they can utilise their connections with members of the bureaucracy to maximum benefit (Oi, 1989a, 1989b; Nee, 1991, pp. 267–82; Kane, 1992; *ZGLDB*, 5 November 1992). By these means, ex-officials and members of officials' families have become disproportionately active in such crucial and lucrative areas of the economy as banking, technological development, foreign trade, and real estate. A study of 35 foreign sector managers conducted by Margaret Pearson (1992) found that most were the children of officials.

This transformation of local government activities has resulted in new patterns of competition and cooperation. Different levels and departments of government now compete for dominion over the most lucrative spheres of administration, and for precedence in initiating and overseeing projects which offer income-earning opportunities (*Nanfang zhoumou*, 13 February 1998, 27 February 1998; Wang Shaoguang, 1994). In addition to these struggles over turf, Luo Xiaopeng (1994, p. 125) charges that local governments 'form a conspiracy' to defend their sources of income against extractions of tax by the central party-state.

On the other hand, given their common business interests, it is not surprising that close cooperative links have been forged between local governments and entrepreneurs, especially those in the collective, foreign-invested, and private sectors. The owners and managers of firms frequently receive local government assistance in securing tax holidays, scarce resources, energy supplies, bank credit, highly skilled staff and labour, and even monopolies in local markets (Nee, 1992; Zhang, 1993). In return, in order to ensure the viability of their enterprise, business people must invest large sums of money and extended periods of time cultivating their connections with selected government departments and officials. Cheng Shu quotes one private entrepreneur's explanation for the care with which he managed his relations with local government officials: 'You have to wait until all those connections are secured, become familiar with all the "immortals" on the street, before the money you earn is your own affair' (1992, p. 162). The strength of these business links have prompted Dorothy Solinger (1993, p. 258) to remark that officials and business people have begun to form a stratum or class which has become 'inextricably entangled'.

The entanglement of local governments and local business has important implications for regulation of the complex new forms of property right which have emerged over the past decade (Lee Kuen, 1993; Walder, 1995; Li, 1996). It is common knowledge that in the 1980s, local governments and private business people intrigued to assign collective status to private ventures so that they could benefit from preferential taxes, safeguard against shifts in policy towards private business, and deflect consumer concerns about quality and community concerns about growing inequalities of ownership and income (Young, 1991, pp. 117–18; Odgaard, 1992, pp. 230–1). When the leasing and sale of public enterprises was approved, local governments' award of contracts to lease, manage and purchase collective enterprises was often made subject to the payment of fees and bribes, or informal provision of services (Jiang, 1990; Oi, 1990). In the early 1990s, the transformation of many collectives into share-holding cooperatives allowed local governments, individual officials, and managers of collectives to increase their ownership of firms at the expense of local communities' lawful property rights and customary rights to employment and income (Sargeson and Zhang, 1997). These transfers of public property into private hands are routinely condemned in the media (*Zhongguo gongshang bao*, hereafter *ZGGSB*, 22 June 1992; see also *ZGLDB*, 11 June 1992). Nevertheless, under the umbrella of local governments, the transfers continue.

The many antagonisms which have been generated by recent reforms of property rights and industrial relations all require adjudication. That function, too, is performed by organs of local government, and the decisions of those organs are enforced by yet other sections of local government. Of particular significance in the settlement or repression of conflicts are the lowest cells of the judiciary and newly formed district government arbitration commissions, labour bureaux, industry and commerce departments, tax departments, public security bureaux and police, branches of the ACFTU and, with decreasing effectiveness, neighbourhood committees.

In response to public criticism that there is a clear conflict of interest between their own business activities and their management of the public sector and protection of the public interest, local governments have embarked on campaigns to educate and placate their constituencies. What is good for the business of local governments and entrepreneurs is represented as being good for the local community. What is good for the local community is represented as being good for national economic growth. At the lowest levels of administration, village and township leaders spend a considerable amount of time and money appraising the populace of the benefits to be gained from acceding to their business plans (Wang Shaoguang, 1994; Sargeson and Zhang, 1997). Nevertheless, protests against government corruption, nepotism, and injustices continue to increase in number and scale (*Zhongguo laodong tongji nianjian 1996*, hereafter *ZGLDTJNJ 1996*, 1996, p. 551; *Far Eastern Economic Review*, hereafter *FEER*, 26 June 1997, 18 December 1997).

Changes in the roles of governments and the pursuit of market-led economic growth have profoundly influenced workers' perceptions of the contours of power relations in society, and their own situation as employees. In particular, workers have become highly sensitive to the function of new policies, ideological discourses, and government interests in specifying the accumulation of private profit rather than creation of social wealth and an equitable society as a desirable national goal, and in redefining labour as a de-politicised factor of production instead of the political force it theoretically represented in the pre-reform era. At the same time, they are conscious that at a local level the merging of public administration and business, and the close connections which have been forged between governments and entrepreneurs, have profoundly altered the conditions under which they live and work. As I shall show in later chapters, their perceptions of this local nexus of power and wealth inform workers' description of officials and business people as bosses, big people, the higher ups, city people, and clans.

ENTERPRISES IN THE REFORM ERA

A second set of shifts which occurred as a result of the economic reforms undertaken since 1978 concerned the nature and operation of enterprises. These shifts involved a multiplication of types of enterprise ownership, changes in the objectives and activities of firms, and a transformation in the relative economic importance and geographical distribution of various kinds of enterprise.

At the onset of the reform era, state enterprises were expected to remain predominant in the economy and continue to function as a linchpin of the urban employment and welfare systems. Certainly, scholars who examined state enterprise management in the 1980s found that managers' behaviour had not changed. They continued to subordinate the pursuit of profit to other aims, such as providing jobs for employees' dependents and satisfying the consumption demands of staff and workers (Walder, 1989a; Huang, 1990). The central party-state promoted growth of non-state firms partly in an attempt to expand employment opportunities and satisfy pent-up consumer demand by supplementing state firms' production of goods and services (White, 1993, pp. 60–6; Sabin, 1994).

By the mid-1990s, the relative importance of state firms in the economy had declined dramatically, and so too had their mode of operation altered. Non-state firms predominated by number, size of work force, and value of output in China's economy. The owners and managers of these non-state enterprises stated that their primary objective was to raise productivity and increase profit, rather than to provide employment opportunities or play a supplementary role in the economy. And similar attitudes were being expressed by state sector managers. In a study of fifteen state and collective firms, Lin (1992) found all enterprise managers aimed for higher enterprise profits and personal incomes. This transformation can be explained by the introduction of leasing, contracting and share-holding systems which provided clear profit incentives for state sector managers, and security deposits which acted as disincentives to poor performance (Liu Jisheng, 1992; Groves *et al.*, 1995; Zhao and Nichols, 1996). The sometimes contradictory means by which owners and enterprise managers pursue profit, and the ways in which workers experience, perceive, and respond to these strategies, will be a recurrent theme throughout this book. To provide a context for that analysis, it is worth outlining the structural changes wrought by the diversification of ownership types.

Statistics give a crude indication of the changing importance of various types of firms. In 1978, state-owned industrial units produced more than three-quarters of China's total industrial output value (*ZGTJNJ 1993*, p. 23). In 1995, their contribution to the value of total industrial output had fallen to approximately one-third (less than was produced by collectively-owned rural firms). Conversely, the industrial output value of the collective sector had risen from just over 22 per cent in 1978, to around 40 per cent in 1995 (*ZGTJNJ 1995*, p. 375; *ZGTJNJ 1996*, p. 401). Non-state firms were at the forefront of China's export boom and were also responsible for generating more than two-thirds of the total value of domestic retail sales (*BR*, 4 January 1993; *ZGTJNJ 1995*, pp. 17, 525). Present trends suggest that in the near future, the non-state sector will continue to experience high growth rates.

A number of new types of firms had been created, and these, in turn, had combined to develop yet other enterprise forms. Whereas at the beginning of the reform era, Chinese businesses could be defined by ownership as state and collective (comprising the public sector), or privately and individually owned (the private sector), by the mid-1990s this classificatory system was no longer adequate. In addition to the original state, collective and private categories, enterprises were being categorised as wholly foreign owned, joint or cooperative ventures between foreign and domestic firms, joint or cooperative ventures between firms of different ownership types or between firms and institutions, township and village enterprises (hereafter TVEs), joint stock companies, limited liability companies, and share-holding firms (*ZGTJNJ 1993*, p. 4).[3] Many collective and private enterprises had begun to adopt share-holding systems similar to those pioneered in provinces such as Zhejiang, where TVEs introduced combined public and private share ownership (*Zhejiang dianshi tai*, 20 February 1993).[4]

Collectives are firms which have been established by various levels of government, or by institutions, state-owned enterprises or groups of individuals. But, as I have pointed out, the formal appellation collective ownership does not indicate actual property rights. An unknown number of collective enterprises are, in reality, private enterprises (Bruun, 1989, pp. 128–30; *ZGGSB*, 22 June 1992; *ZGLDB*, 11 June 1992). Others, such as two village factories I observed, were originally founded as collectives, but property rights in the firms have effectively devolved, in the first instance, upon a manager and his family, and in the second, to a small network of people associated with an institution (see also *GRRB*, 17 February 1993). Collective ownership is not commonly given substance through workers' collective participation in management or the redistribution of profit to communities.[5]

Collective firms were the most numerous, employed the largest number of workers, and produced the highest value of output of all firms outside the state sector in the early 1990s. And of all collective firms, TVEs were especially significant along the wealthy eastern seaboard (*CD*, 15 February 1997). An illustration of the irregular geographical distribution and economic weight of TVEs is provided by their prominence in the coastal province of Zhejiang. There, between 1978 and 1991 the proportion of total industrial output value produced by TVEs increased from 23.4 per cent to 66.3 per cent, a much higher amount than that cited above for the whole country (Chi and Rong, 1992, pp. 29–30).[6] Even within Zhejiang, however, the distribution and importance of TVEs was skewed. TVEs located in the province's north and east were more numerous, had higher output value and were more profitable than those located in the interior of the province.

While foreign invested firms still represented a relatively small percentage of all enterprises in China, they nevertheless had begun to assume considerable economic importance. In 1992, foreign-invested enterprises earned 20.4 per cent of China's total export earnings of US$85 billion (*BR*, 8 March 1993, p. 37). Although the most common path for foreign investment was the creation of joint ventures with domestic firms, in the 1990s there was a significant increase in the numbers and scale of wholly foreign-owned firms. The bulk of overseas investment ostensibly came from companies registered in Hong Kong and Macau. However, it is impossible to disaggregate the actual countries of origin of much foreign capital or to disentangle property rights in foreign and joint venture firms. In order to benefit from the same terms and incentives that were offered to foreign investors, many Chinese firms have moved off-shore and re-invested in China as foreign-owned and joint venture companies. The latter are commonly referred to as 'fake foreign joint ventures' (*jiayang hezi*). In the case of Hong Kong and Taiwanese investments, capital often has been lent, or given over to the management of mainland relatives, who act as *de facto* owners, co-owners, resident-managers, and go-betweens with local governments, up-stream firms, and customers (Smart and Smart, 1992). Control over the product and profits of these firms is the basis upon which these people have forged connections with local officials and expanded their spheres of economic and social influence (Wank, 1995)

Private and individual businesses also proliferated and increased in scale. During the 1980s, because of government interference, the difficulty of arranging credit, fierce market competition, the common practice of registering expanding private businesses as collectives, and the windfall gains to be made from tax holidays and government incentives to new businesses, the majority of privately owned firms tended to be small and be short-lived (Gold, 1989, pp. 176–9, 183–91; Young, 1991; Nee, 1992). However, since Deng Xiaoping's 1992 speech encouraging 'big leaps forward and creative experiments' in economic reform (Yabuki, 1995, p. 290), there has been less necessity for private enterprises to dissemble about their ownership status or the scale of their operations. By 1995, private and individual enterprises in China employed approximately 56 million people (*ZGTJNJ 1996*, p. 110). And in Zhejiang province, they produced a larger proportion of industrial output value than did state owned firms (*ZGTJNJ 1995*, p. 379).

Despite the relatively small average size of their operations, profits realised by private business people have been high. In 1991, 26 per cent of all bank savings deposits belonged to private business people (*China Daily*, hereafter *CD*, 8 December 1991, p. 3; *Xinwen huabao*, hereafter *XWHB*, 10 August 1992). One year later, when the average urban per capita annual income was less than 2000 yuan, it was widely publicised that there were more than one million millionaires and dozens of billionaires amongst China's private entrepreneurs (*XWHB*, 10 August 1992; *Yangcheng wanbao*, hereafter *YCWB*, 11 March 1993; *BR*, 15 February 1993). To many of the workers I spoke with in Hangzhou, this accumulation of private wealth was made possible by the creation of new types of relations between officials and bosses on the one hand, and bosses and workers on the other. They agreed with Cai Tirong (*Foreign Broadcasting Information Service*, hereafter *FBIS*, 31 May 1990, p. 42; see also *GMRB*, 11 May 1992) that, in both private and foreign-invested firms, 'relations are those between employers and employees. They are relations of exploitation.'

The proliferation of collective, foreign, joint venture, share holding, and private businesses in China, and the employment relations which characterise these businesses, has been of immense significance to workers' experiences and understandings of work, and to their identification of various groups in society. Once, workers were told that China's socialist economic system and their position as the leading class in society would be safeguarded by the predominance of state ownership in the whole economy. Yet in the 1990s, three-fifths of China's non-agricultural work force was employed in non-state enterprises which hired workers to produce goods and services which were sold for profit in international and domestic markets. Many earlier analyses of attitudes towards people engaged in foreign-invested and private business emphasised popular condescension and mistrust for people involved in a marginal, 'low status', sphere of the socialist economy.[7] Once the non-state sector came to represent the largest part of the Chinese economy, old status considerations began to give way to a heightened awareness of material inequalities between social groups and regions, and to the localistic and particularistic processes by which businesses were being established, and private wealth was being accumulated (*Joint Publications Research Service*, hereafter *JPRS*, 26 November 1991, 40–6; *XWHB*, 10 August 1992; *GRRB*, 9 February 1993).

REFORMING LABOUR: CREATING THE CONDITIONS FOR EXPLOITATION

Economic reforms have profoundly altered relations between employers and employees, as well as amongst workers themselves. For the majority of workers, these changes immediately involved commodification of their labour, contract rather than permanent employment and the associated spectre of job insecurity, and a further weakening of workers' representative organs. The long term significance of these reforms is that China's proletariat is being reworked as a cheap, 'manageable' work force that will produce profit for investors and enterprise owners.

Marketing Labour

China's labour force today is characterised principally by two features. First, there are significant disparities between urban and rural areas in levels of unemployment. Second, nationally there is an enormous surplus of unskilled and semi-skilled labour. In 1994 the officially acknowledged unemployment rate among urban residents had risen by 1 per cent since 1985, but still remained very low, at 2.8 per cent (Renmin Ribao, hereafter *RMRB*, 11 May 1995; *ZGTJNJ 1995*, p. 107). In addition to those urban residents who were without jobs, there was a chronic problem of underemployment in state enterprises, with a potential redundancy rate of over 20 per cent (*FBIS*, 7 November 1991; Jefferson and Rawski, 1992; *ZGLDB*, 20 November 1992). Estimates for people registered as residents of rural areas indicated that up to one-third of the adult work force, or approximately 200 million people, were surplus to agricultural requirements and were underemployed or unemployed (*FBIS*, 15 May 1991; *BR*, 3 January 1994, p. 16). Projections indicated that over the next three decades, China's economy would need to employ an additional 280 million people (Shen and Spence, 1993).

Until the early 1990s, Party documents avowed that in a socialist society labour power was not a commodity. The politically explosive term 'labour market' was eschewed in favour of neutral references to the 'allocation' of labour resources, or markets in 'labour services' (White, 1989, p. 159; *ZGLDB*, 1 December 1992, p. 2). However, awareness of the massive unemployment and underemployment problem facing China, and of the part played by labour intensive, export-oriented manufacturing in sparking growth in other Asian economies, informed the central party-state's plans for fostering economic growth in China. Key elements in these plans included the development of a genuinely competitive labour market as a means of boosting employment and productivity, repressing wage and consumption levels, and attracting investment into export-oriented industries. A report prepared by the Chinese Economic System Reform Research Institute makes the links between a labour market, productivity pressures, and wage restraint explicit:

> To check fundamentally the expansion of consumption funds and the continuous rise of the aggregate wage level, we must utilize our 'unlimited supply of labor' ... by prudently and gradually breaking down barriers to job mobility, encouraging a flow of workers between different ownership systems and between the cities and rural areas, and, in general allowing the surplus labor force to enter into market competition. Forming a labor market and labor mobility will not only create a direct check on wage increases through employment competition. It will also help lower people's expectations and self-evaluation, thus indirectly checking wage increases through weakening the 'upward emulation' mentality. (1987, pp. 19–20; see also *ZGLDB*, 13 October 1992, 27 October 1992; *South China Morning Post*, hereafter *SCMP*, 16 March 1993)

To facilitate labour mobility and the operation of a labour market, the government introduced identity cards, approved temporary residence permits and the transfer of personnel dossiers, and even gave consideration to dismantling of the residential registration system (*CND*, 27 April 1994). It reduced the job allocation role played by state labour bureaux, and authorised the operation of private job agencies. Direct hiring by firms was encouraged. In addition, police and labour bureaux were advised to turn a blind eye to the appearance of spot labour markets in China's large cities (*ZGLDB*, 7 January 1993). In the media, people who competed openly for jobs were applauded for their 'progressive thinking', their rejection of the tradition of laziness induced by decades of access to 'iron rice bowls', and their responsiveness to material incentives (*GRRB*, 9 July 1992). Conversely, those who railed against the labour market as a capitalist tool were said to be old fashioned, ignorant, and to require 'patient ideological and political education' (*HZRB*, 28 May 1992)

Given the government's blessing and the lure of wage-earning opportunities, geographical and job mobility amongst the least and most skilled sections of the work force increased dramatically in the space of one decade. Many unemployed rural residents travelled to urban centres in search of work.[8] At the beginning of the 1990s, there were between 70 million and 80 million immigrant rural workers in China's towns and cities ('Chengshi liudong renkou wenti tantao', 1990, pp. 73–5; Solinger, 1991, p. 10). Most of these semi- and unskilled people were employed in urban manufacturing, transport, and service enterprises (Gu, Zhu, and Deng, 1989, pp. 24–8). Many others, not accounted for in these estimates, had migrated to work in TVEs located in urban hinterlands. At the same time, highly qualified youngsters gravitated to cities in the east and south to take up well paid jobs in non-state enterprises. Surveys indicated that foreign and joint venture firms had become the preferred choice for skilled young job-seekers, rather than the state enterprises which had been favoured in the past (*GRRB*, 9 July 1992, p. 4; see also Casati, 1991; *GMRB*, 13 May 1992; Zou, 1992, pp. 60–1). Moreover, those who found employment in non-state firms continued to show high rates of job mobility (Dai and Li, 1992; Jefferson and Rawski, 1992, pp. 46–7; *ZGLDB*, 20 February 1993).

Indeed, by early 1994, many of the government's objectives in fostering a labour market were being met. Over half of all China's 'labour resources' were finding jobs through rapidly growing local labour markets which, particularly in economically developed areas, were impelled by supply and demand signals (Meng Xin, 1990; Knight and Song, 1993; *BR*, 3 January 1994). Employment in manufacturing had grown at a significantly higher rate than had the size of the labour force (*ZGTJNJ 1995*, p. 96). Foreign investors had flocked to eastern China in order to take advantage of abundant labour and low production costs (Smart and Smart, 1992; *BR*, 26 July 1993, p. 14; Zhu, 1995). And, as Flemming Christianson (1992) demonstrates in an analysis of the Jiangsu labour market, the in-house employment of surplus rural workers combined with the subcontracting of tasks to rural enterprises kept wage levels low amongst unskilled employees, and allowed state enterprises to expand production without incurring extra expenditure (see also Korzec, 1992).

Labour markets were not, however, characterised by free and equal competition and the uninterrupted play of market forces. On the contrary, markets which should have functioned as a rational allocative mechanism were being administered in such a way that they maximised benefits for those actors considered by local governments to be economically and politically significant: foreign investors, profit-oriented domestic enterprises, and local workers. Municipal governments repressed wage levels to retain and attract investors, and repelled immigrant workers so as to maintain 'social stability' amongst the urban populace. Lower level governments intervened in enterprises' recruitment decisions to ensure that local residents got priority in employment, and imposed wage ceilings on collective and share holding enterprises to protect their own revenue (Zhang, 1993). In addition to the effects of government intervention in distorting markets for labour, the following section demonstrates that modes of enterprise recruitment and the terms of employment offered workers were heavily influenced by China's residential registration system, localism, gender, social and ethnic prejudices, and the operation of social networks.

Contractual Employment: 'Freedom, Equality, Property and Bentham'

> Freedom, because both buyer and seller of a commodity, say of labour-power, are constrained only by their own free will. They contract as free agents, and the agreement they come to, is but the form in which they give legal expression to their common will. Equality, because each enters into relation with the other, as with a simple owner of commodities, and they exchange equivalent for equivalent. Property, because each disposes only of what is his own. And Bentham, because each looks only to himself. (Marx, vol. 1, 1954, p. 172)

An essential foundation of China's labour markets was provided by the central party-state's definition and regulation of contractual employment – almost in the same mystifying terms so bitingly satirised by Marx – as an equal, voluntary exchange between individual buyers and sellers of labour power. Contractual employment, according to spokespeople for the government and ACFTU, was intended to provide workers with the freedom to shape the course of their lives by responding to the opportunities and material incentives provided by the market economy (Rofel, 1989; Hong Kong Trade Union Education Centre, 1990; *GRRB*, 3 June 1992; *Xinhua*, 10 April 1996). Indeed, the ACFTU argued that contractual employment and workers' individual autonomy in the market place actually buttressed the proletariat's political ascendancy: 'In reality, contract jobs help guarantee the position of workers as masters, because if workers' remuneration is not equitable then they can negotiate, and if negotiations are unsatisfactory then they can leave' (*ZGLDB*, 1 December 1992; see also *GRRB*, 9 February 1993). This view of contractual employment was a key component in the state's ideological re-working of the proletariat from a cohesive political agent to an atomised population of objectified, self-interested, utility-maximising individual producers. Of course, contractual employment was simultaneously critical to the state's pursuit of economic growth, not least because it provided mechanisms by which unemployment might be reduced, wage and welfare costs minimised, labour productivity and discipline improved, and enterprise profits increased (White, 1989; Jackson, 1992; Korzec, 1992).

In October 1986, state enterprises were instructed not to grant new employees permanent positions. All recruits were supposed to be hired on contract for fixed terms, unless exceptional circumstances prevailed (*FBIS*, 1 October 1991; *GRRB*, 26 February 1993; Xia, 1992).[9] Labour contracts were to be entered into willingly by both parties, and to specify production targets and working conditions, duration of contract, wages, bonuses, and benefits, punitive sanctions for violations of discipline including conditions for dismissal, and any other relevant conditions.[10] Despite injunctions to the contrary, some state enterprises and institutions unilaterally began to remove the tenured status of old employees (*Shehui kexue bao*, hereafter *SHKXB*, 16 April 1992; *ZGLDB*, 4 June 1992, 8 August 1992).

Among workers employed on contract in the state sector, there was a formal distinction drawn between workers who were employed either as contract system workers (*hetong zhi gong*) or as contract workers (*hetong gong*).[11] Contract system workers had urban residential registration. They were employed within the state plan and received the same wages, paid holidays, and social security benefits as tenured employees.[12] Contract workers, on the other hand, were usually registered as rural residents. They were employed outside the plan and were not eligible for the same social security packages as tenured and contract system employees, though they were eligible for compensation for injury and some sickness benefits. Temporary workers (*linshi gong*) could be urban residents, but the great majority were rural residents. Although temporaries in the state sector were supposed to be employed with a contract only for short periods of time (Zhongguo renmin gongheguo guowuyuan, 1989), several workers in state institutions and enterprises I interviewed had been employed without contracts and paid on a daily rate for more than five years.

However, by the mid 1990s, the majority of the non-agricultural work force were not employed in state enterprises, but rather worked in TVEs, urban collectives, and share holding, private, and joint venture firms (*ZGLDTJNJ 1996*, pp. 17, 38, 404–5). The vast majority of these workers belonged to what Robert Parker (1993) refers to as a contingent work force. Many particularly in private firms and TVEs, have no employment contracts. One survey of 450 joint ventures in Shanghai found that, of 38 844 employees, 9820 had no contracts, and 3224 were illegally employed (*Wen hui bao*, 4 October 1995). Another Shanghai survey found that more than 20 per cent of the 3700 labour contracts examined did not conform with national regulations (*ZGLDB*, 14 May 1992). Even when employment contracts were legally binding, contract terms were often ignored by employers. In urban collectives and joint ventures, contract employees were entitled to similar compensation and benefits as those in the state sector, but in many cases these were not provided. Researchers in Guangdong complained that in TVEs and foreign invested firms, legally binding contracts had been terminated at the convenience of employers without advance warning or wage compensation for employees. Even in the case of industrial accidents, workers sometimes did not receive compensation (*Asian Labour Update*, no. 19, 1995).

The confusion caused by many enterprises' failure to give legally binding contracts to employees and to abide by the terms of contract regulations is compounded by popular terminology which tacitly acknowledges the contingent nature of contract employment. In Hangzhou, the terms most frequently used to describe an employee's status were regular (or real) worker (*zhengshi gong*), and temporary worker (*linshi gong*). These terms were commonly used in all enterprise types. Tenured and contract system workers were always referred to as regular workers. But so, too, were some contract workers. Indeed, 'regular' and 'temporary' were even used to differentiate between employees who had signed identical contracts. Clearly, these titles did not refer to a formal contractual relationship. Instead, they pointed to the informal practice of discriminating between contract employees on the basis of local residence and social connections, since the distinguishing characteristic of 'regular' contract workers was their membership of the local community or their influential social connections, and the relative job security which they derived from these. In contrast, 'temporary' contract workers either were not long term residents of the locality or lacked useful contacts. As they had no standing in the local community, they were unlikely to be employed for a significant length of time.

The practice of discriminating between non-tenured workers on the basis of community membership and connections was particularly prevalent in smaller collective firms which Alan Gelb (1990, pp. 281–2) describes as following a 'communal' model. However, I found that workers employed on contract were also treated with partiality in quite large state and joint venture enterprises. For instance, in one large state-owned Hangzhou silk factory, the personnel manager told me that contract system and contract workers who perform well could be given second contracts of 20 years or more. When I remarked that such long term contractual employment seemed little different to the system of tenured employment which it was intended to supplant, the manager responded that this method of rewarding employees for 'diligence and hard work' was one of the advantages of the way their factory had implemented the new employment system. Yet despite the manager's effusive praise for the strength, hard work, and punctuality of immigrant contract workers in comparison with local contract system workers, not one immigrant worker had ever been offered anything more enduring than a five year contract. Only Hangzhou residents had ever been granted the security of a 20-year contract.

According to Michael Korzec, these sorts of prejudicial practices have resulted in a statistical lacuna: 'it is no exaggeration to say that a sizeable part of the Chinese labour system is, quantitatively and qualitatively speaking, *terra incognito*' (Korzec, 1992, p. 35). One thing, at least, is clear. Non-tenured employment had steadily increased in all enterprise types. The rate of increase of contractual employment varied between types of enterprises and between provinces. Whereas in 1990 only 12 per cent of the nation's urban labour force were contract system and contract workers, by 1996 this percentage had risen to 41 per cent, comprising some 61 million employees (*ZGTJNJ 1995*, p. 99; *ZGLDTJNJ 1996*, p. 38). Contract system and contract workers generally represented 40 per cent of employees in state owned enterprises, 37 per cent in urban collectives, and 63 per cent in joint venture and foreign firms (*ZGLDTJNJ 1996*, p. 38). In highly market-oriented provinces such as Jiangsu and Shandong, significantly higher proportions of the work force were employed on contract, whilst inland provinces consistently have lagged behind the national average.

By far the greatest expansion in non-tenured jobs has occurred in TVEs. Between 1979 and 1997, the number of employees in TVEs alone had increased from 29 million to approximately 130 million (*ZGLDTJNJ 1996*, p. 406; *ZGTJNJ 1995*, p. 85). These people were invariably employed either on contract or as temporary workers, irrespective of their status as local 'regulars' or immigrant 'temporaries'. In the Hangzhou hinterland, most employees in TVEs signed contracts.[13] But, as in many economically developed areas along China's seaboard, the great majority of workers were immigrants to whom job contracts granted precious little job security (Interview, head of Xihu District Statistical Bureau, 23 November 1989; Interview, Deputy Director of Zhejiang Province Economic Planning Commission, 4 December 1989; *Qianjiang wanbao*, hereafter *QJWB*, 24 December 1992).

Reforming Work Place Relations

The leaders tell us we should learn from the west, that not everything from outside is bad. Sure, that's true. But there should be a limit! China is a socialist country. We should be more discriminating than this! (Fieldnotes, 10 January 1993)

Under the socialist, centrally planned economy, state sector managers were required to at least make a pretence of encouraging workers to participate in enterprise management, planning, and the resolution of problems. That pretence is no longer necessary. Now, all enterprise decision-making is made by entrepreneurs, managers, and technocrats. So, too, have activities on the shop floor itself come under their control. Workers' 'enthusiasm for production', once ineffectually encouraged by political appeals and symbolic rewards, is now genuinely prompted by productivity-related wage payment and the threat of dismissal. Cao Xiaofeng gives voice to the dissatisfaction felt by workers about their weakened position, and the correlated empowerment and aggrandisement of managers:

On the one hand, there are the plant managers and managers with a range of rights and powers, and on the other hand there are workers who should passively obey. The workers are blatantly excluded from participation in enterprise management, and in fact have lost their position as masters of the enterprise. Simultaneously, the direction of public opinion has become seriously biased, excessively propagandising the position and role of plant managers and management. The terms 'entrepreneurs', 'excellent entrepreneurs', and 'star entrepreneurs' have come into use, but the position of the broad masses of workers and their role in reform has neither been fully evaluated nor appropriately affirmed. (*JPRS*, 16 August 1991, p. 77; see also *ZGLDB*, 26 May 1992; *GRRB*, 26 February 1993)

The speed with which employment relations have been transformed in all sectors of the Chinese economy is remarkable. Studies undertaken by

Andrew Walder (1989a), Gordon White (1989) and Michael Korzec (1992) show that through the 1980s, relations between managers and workers in the state sector had not fundamentally altered, although labour relations in foreign-invested and private firms had begun to resemble those in capitalist economies. But by the 1990s, even some state firms were characterised by the same authoritarian management styles, long work days, productivity-linked wage payments, and surveillance and discipline systems as had only operated in 'Shenzhen type' firms in the previous decade (Zhao and Nichols, 1996).

Chinese media audiences have been alerted to the extent and consequences of this transfiguration by the coverage given to cases such as that of Zhang Zhiping, who appealed against her summary dismissal from her tenured job in the state-owned No. 14 Nanjing Plastics Factory in 1992. Journalists reported that the factory's managers had attempted to meet export deadlines by imposing compulsory overtime on workers, and applying a range of bonuses for productivity and penalties for poor performance. Any workers perceived by management to be 'slackers' or, like Zhang, to be unproductive and disruptive, were dismissed on the spot without compensation. Although news articles and television documentaries generally presented Zhang in a sympathetic light because of her poor health, they concluded that labour discipline should be upheld at all costs:

> The manner in which Zhang breached labour discipline was very serious and had to be dealt with. The way in which Zhang was handled by the factory was of secondary importance, a matter of method. The primary issue must be clarified. In the course of reform, it is necessary to protect the interests of workers. But it is of even greater importance to protect the interests of the whole collectivity of workers. And it is in the interests of the working class to deal strictly with those workers who breach labour discipline. (*HZRB* 12, September 1992)

The disempowerment of workers relative to their employers has been effected partly through the purposive creation of a labour market and implementation of contract employment, for, in contrast to the minimal effect upon management-labour relations of the Soviet Union's economic reforms (Burawoy and Krotov, 1993, pp. 85–7), in the context of China's massive labour surplus, these measures have allowed managers to impose despotic controls over workers (Lee, 1995).

However, it has also been facilitated by the state's failure to protect workers' rights by legislation and the provision of regulatory, mediatory and representative institutions. The party-state's stance toward the non-tenured work force has been ill defined both in theory and in law. In 1993, enterprise employees who were registered as rural residents were not considered to be members of the working class. Many national regulations which pertained to contract and temporary employment were relevant only to workers employed in state-owned or collective firms in urban areas, and there had been very little effort by the central government to oversee the conditions of temporary workers in urban non-state firms and TVEs, or arbitrate disputes involving temporary employees (*ZGLDB*, 26 May 1992, 29 December 1992). There was no fixed minimum wage. Workers did not have the right to strike or withhold their labour unless the work place was believed to be unsafe.

Whilst many of these theoretical and legal inconsistencies were remedied with the implementation of the national labour law in January 1995, reports indicate that in practice little changed (Economic Intelligence Unit, hereafter *EIU*, 29 May 1995). Regulations which now govern the working conditions of all contract and temporary employees, such as laws specifying the length of the working week, and minimum wages, working age, and safety standards, continue to be ignored with impunity (*Asian Labour Update*, no. 18, 1995).

The flouting of national regulations and standards has been able to occur for two reasons. Above, I mentioned that lower levels of government are reliant upon local enterprises for their revenue, and officials often cooperate closely with local business people. Consequently, they are sensitive to the possibility that rigorous implementation of national laws relating, for example, to minimum wages or safety standards might lower enterprise profits or drive future investors away (*SWB*, 17 December 1994). This has resulted, on the one hand, in the promulgation of local counter-regulations, and on the other, in a lack of political will to oversee implementation of the national labour law. Chinese lawyers have complained that local and national regulations are often in conflict, and that overlapping government jurisdictions have created confusion (Chen and Qian, 1992; *ZGGSB*, 18 June 1992; *ZGLDB*, 26 May 1992; *GRRB*, 5 March 1993). In cases where local enterprise owners or managers have infringed national laws, local governments have sometimes been reluctant to intervene to protect the rights of workers. There have also been occasions when local labour bureaux and arbitration committees have acted in collusion with employers (*Baokan wenzhi*, hereafter *BKWZ*, 24 November 1992; *ZGLDB*, 16 May 1992; *GRRB*, 5 March 1993). By design or oversight, offices responsible for labour relations and occupational safety have been understaffed and hampered by a lack of resources and legal expertise (*Fazhi ribao*, hereafter *FZRB*, 8 October 1992; *ZGLDB*, 7 January 1993).

Indeed, contract and temporary workers have sometimes purposefully been kept ignorant of their lawful rights: local labour bureaux in Guangdong did not distribute copies of the labour law to all the enterprises for which they were intended, personnel managers did not distribute copies of the law to workers, and activists who used the law as a text in literacy classes for immigrant workers were imprisoned by public security officials.[14]

A second reason why non-tenured workers have been susceptible to despotic management practices is related to the fact that they have no effective organisational focus or mediatory or representative institutions. Labour bureaux and arbitration committees will only accept requests for assistance or intervention from groups of employees who have legally binding contracts. But as I have explained, many workers do not have contracts and many contracts do not fulfil legal requirements. Independent trade unions are prohibited, and people who have established autonomous labour organisations have been imprisoned (Hong Kong Trade Union Education Centre, 1990). *Ad hoc* efforts by contract and temporary workers to undertake independent collective action to improve their lot repeatedly have been crushed by enterprise security staff and police, and denounced by labour bureaux and ACFTU spokespeople for threatening economic and social stability (*SWB*, 3 April 1996)

Despite being workers' only legal representative body, the ACFTU is – by its own admission – often unable to defend or advance the interests of its constituency (*GRRB*, 24 February 1993). ACFTU officials join workers in bemoaning the fact that they are hampered by their conflicting obligations to uphold the state's reform policies and employers' interests (Leung, 1988; Wu and Guo, 1989; *FBIS*, 16 May 1990, 20 July 1991). The union has been accused of being unwilling to represent workers because its leaders are corrupt (*CND*, 19 January 1998). And finally, even if it had the capacity and will to fulfil its formal function, it would be impeded by the fact that its access to the work force has declined at a proportionate rate along with the shrinking importance of the state-owned sector in the economy. In some state enterprises, ACFTU branches have been disbanded or merged with the Party organisation (*GRRB*, 5 March 1993). Where union branches have existed, contract workers have been unaware that, by law, they could ask it to intercede on their behalf in industrial disputes (Leung, 1988, p. 205; *ZGLDB*, 27 August 1992; *GRRB*, 9 February 1993). Few temporary employees enjoy membership of the union, much less an understanding of its role. Union membership is especially rare among employees of TVEs and private businesses (*GRRB*, 15 July 1992).[15] The other bodies which are supposed to oversee workers' interests, enterprise-based workers' congresses, have similarly been accused of being unrepresentative and powerless (Li, 1989; *ZGLDB*, 20 August 1992).

In addition to their insecure labour market position, their ideological redefinition, and their weak legal and institutional position, the position of workers has been undermined by enterprise owners' and managers' individual efforts to secure higher outputs, enterprise profits, and personal incomes. Media representations of Chinese workers' anachronistic, egalitarian ethos has legitimated employers' introduction of methods designed to ensure that workers use every moment on the job in the most productive manner possible. Crudely coercive techniques for improving output have involved the use of electric prods by line supervisors, draconian piece rate systems, and prohibitions on workers using the toilet, drinking, or talking during working hours (*GRRB*, 26 February 1993; *Asian Labour Update*, no. 18, 1995; Lee, 1995). A Shenzhen survey of firms' in-house regulations found that one factory specified 521 separate punishments for workers' infringement of workplace regulations (Lin, 1991). More sophisticated, hegemonic, methods have been developed by western managers who say they are keen to disabuse their employees of the notion that working in foreign-invested firms resembles "Dallas"-style soap operas, where businessmen schmooze, philander, and do pretty much everything on the job except their jobs' (Engen, 1994, p. 79). The journal *Training* reports on the implementation of a variety of motivational techniques, including one firm's creative appropriation and inversion of a metaphor of national struggle and socialist redemption: a Johnson and Johnson subsidiary in Xi'an attempted to boost employees' enthusiasm for work and increase productivity by inviting them on a 'capitalist camping trip' along the route of the Long March (Engen, 1994; see also Wang Zhongmin, 1994).

Taken together, the central state's policies, the strength of labour market pressures, local government practices, media representations and managerial strategies have had the effect of profoundly altering the relationship between employers and employees in Chinese enterprises. As a consequence of economic reforms, Chinese workers must now accept directives from the owners and managers of firms, for their employment security and wages are conditional upon their obedience, productivity and enterprise profitability. This marks a radical departure from the industrial relations environment of the Maoist era, and a convergence with the conditions facing wage workers in capitalist economies.

On the other hand, one enduring feature of relations between Chinese employers and workers in the reform era is the continued significance of localism and particularism. It is still the case that the characteristics of local economies and the cast of social networks influence the behaviour of local governments, individual officials, entrepreneurs, and workers. Membership of communities shapes opportunities in the labour market and the award of labour contracts. In urban firms, local managers and employees systematically discriminate against immigrant workers, whilst some rural enterprises have become 'single surname factories' where managerial hierarchies mirror degrees of kinship (*ZJRB*, 26 October 1992; *GRRB*, 17 February 1993).

Expressions of localism and particularism are not simply cultural legacies that have been transmitted, unchanged, across generations. Instead, the reform process has given new substance to these types of relations and their attendant practices. The ways in which controls have devolved upon local governments and the consequent enmeshment of governments and business, the ambiguities attending property rights which have allowed local officials and entrepreneurs to assume control of public resources, investment funds, and enterprises, and the semi-marketised nature of the economy which encourages people in search of scarce things (such as jobs), to have recourse to their social networks, all have been dialectically constituted by reform policies as well as by customary practice.

However, if economic reform is being enacted in culturally distinctive ways, I would nevertheless emphasise that for entrepreneurs and employees alike, the ultimate aims are the same as for their peers in capitalist societies. That is, in the case of enterprise owners and managers, to profit by appropriating workers' surplus product. Both the impersonal contractual relations and local and particularistic relations they maintain with workers, and the coercive and hegemonic managerial methods they utilise in the work place, serve the objective of maintaining control over the labour process in order to maximise output, generate profits, accumulate capital, and thereby increase their incomes. For their part, non-tenured wage workers are conscious of the fact that their continued employment and any improvement in their wages and working conditions will depend not only upon productivity and profitability, but also upon maintaining 'good relations' with their superiors. Workers' appeals to managers on the basis of common membership of a community or their social connections are designed to facilitate precisely those 'good relations'. Yet as I demonstrate in the following chapters, employees are concurrently aware that the localist and particularistic dimension of work place relations in particular, and of implementation of economic reform in general, are fundamental to their reconstitution as wage workers, processes of exploitation, and the formation of new social groups.

Economic reforms have altered the parts played by the main actors in China's economy. The central party-state has begun to operate in much the same fashion as a capitalist state, attempting to manipulate macro-economic levers in order to promote national economic growth. Local governments and officials, no longer beholden to the dictates of the central state, have extended their economic activities and social and political support networks. In the process, they have become self-interested entrepreneurs. As entrepreneurs, however, they have the advantage of simultaneously acting as overseers of the community interest and public property, and as arbiters and enforcers of economic laws. Enterprise owners and managers, possessed of an array of property rights and the means for controlling labour, have metamorphosed in the public media into the heroic agents of economic growth, struggling against an obstructive, antediluvian working class. In terms of their everyday management of production, exchange and investment, they act as capitalists. Workers, represented as an over-abundant factor of production which requires ideological re-moulding, have become the object of political and managerial strategies and technologies specifically intended to increase individual productivity and enterprise profitability. In short, economic reform has created the ideological, political, economic, and institutional tools by which China's proletariat is being reworked. I turn, in the next chapter, to the socio-spatial relations which have facilitated this transformation.

3 Placing the Proletariat

In China, place tends to be represented and imagined as the site of socially homogeneous, politically united communities. Place has been made the locus of collective economic activity and social agency, a primary source of identity, and a nostalgic focus. In all these contexts, the carefully crafted 'taken-for-grantedness' of place serves an ideological function (Lefebvre, 1976; Giddens, 1991). The rhetoric of place legitimates cultural hierarchies, political domination and economic advantage within localities, and encourages competition between people from different localities (Rodman, 1992; Beynon and Hudson, 1993; Ching and Creed, 1997).

Place has been a crucial factor mediating the design, implementation and consequences of economic reforms in China. Consider, for a moment, the ways in which place has affected the activities of governments and firms, and the experiences of workers as indicated in the previous chapter. Coalitions comprised of local government officials and business people cooperate to increase their control over local collectively-owned resources and firms. They restrict the exaction of taxes by the central state, and access to scarce materials and markets by non-local entrepreneurs. They compete against similar coalitions from other places for credit, investments, and central government funds and subsidies. And together, they appeal to residents' pride in place when they promote the idea of investing and consuming locally. Local residents similarly call upon employers to 'Hire locally!' Workers who come from the same place as their bosses claim to be more trustworthy than immigrants, and therefore deserving of preferential treatment. Enterprise owners and managers raise the threat of losing contracts and jobs to firms in other places when pushing their employees to raise productivity and product quality. The discourse of place is also invoked by families when they are encouraging overseas relatives to fund business ventures which will develop their *lao jia*, or 'old home'.[1]

A corollary of the fact that place universally affects the implementation and consequences of reform is that the actual content of reform varies considerably between provinces, cities, and districts, as well as between workers from different places. Even within villages, the impact of reform differs between groups of workers who are defined by socio-spatial criteria. Everyday conversations on the effects of reform are delivered in anecdotes about the activities of, or competition between, the residents of a particular place. Conversely, conversations about places tend to revolve around money: where money is being made, by whom, and how. In short, the ideology, politics and economics of place have shaped the conditions which have given rise to a highly differentiated proletariat, and continue to shape the conditions under which the members of this proletariat work, live, and think.

This chapter describes how place is created by, and creative of territorially-based, class-structured communities at three levels of a descending regional scale: north-eastern Zhejiang, Hangzhou, and the Xihu suburbs of Qiushi and Jinshagang. These places have, through history, become characterised by their unique economies, identity stereotypes, patterns of administration, residence, kinship and ritual. Nativist sentiments and local social networks have, in turn, been critical in facilitating the establishment and operation of the three case study enterprises in Xihu district. They are also decisive in recruitment and the labour processes which characterise the case study enterprises, which figure as the subjects of following chapters.

LOCATING THE PLACE OF IDENTITIES

Place of origin is still one of the primary indicators of identity in China, conjuring images of particular livelihoods, shared rights and obligations, language, beliefs, food, manners and morals. But identities based upon place are as multi-layered as onions. They can be pared back from those generic identities circumscribed by dialect or traditional geographical marketing regions, through administrative definitions such as counties or cities, to the idiosyncratic identities created by, or attributed to, villages or urban neighbourhoods. Cohen argues that this magnification involves not only a change of scale, but also of kind and of import:

> As one goes 'down' the scale, so the 'objective' referents of the boundary become less and less clear, until they may be quite invisible to those outside. But also as you go 'down' this scale, they become more important to their members for they relate to increasingly intimate areas of their lives or refer to more substantial areas of their identities. (1985, p. 13)

North-Eastern Zhejiang

For many centuries north-eastern Zhejiang has been acknowledged as one of the most highly developed areas in China. It has been renowned for the fertility of its soils and waters, its position at the terminus of the Grand Canal, the harbours which link the province with China's entire eastern seaboard and ports throughout Asia, its industry, commerce, and banking, and for the consequent wealth, urbanism, and sophistication of its people. Today, the average annual per capita income of the population of north-eastern Zhejiang still is much higher than the national average, with urban residents enjoying a standard of living which is equivalent to that of Beijing's citizens. The value of total social product in Zhejiang has increased at a rate faster than that of all provinces and cities except Guangdong (*ZGTJNJ 1995*, pp. 36–7, 288). Yet unlike the foreign-funded, export-oriented manufacturing basis of Guangdong's economy, growth in Zhejiang has been impelled principally by local investment in collective, private and joint venture firms producing and processing for domestic as well as export markets (Chi and Rong, 1991; Deng, 1989, pp. 326–30, 425).

Residents of the cities and towns of north-eastern Zhejiang have long benefited from processing and trading the products of the province's south-west, and from educating and employing the population of that poor region. Urban residents of the north-east claim nationally renowned scholar-bureaucrats, artists and twentieth-century revolutionary leaders as their nominal forebears. And they point to their illustrious ancestry as evidence that they not only are more worldly, creative, and cultured than people from other parts of the province, but also those who come from other cities in eastern China (Leys, 1977; Schoppa, 1982; Cole, 1986). This sense of cultural superiority informs interregional interactions. Notwithstanding Shanghai's huge size, wealth, and social heterogeneity, on the streets of cities in north-eastern Zhejiang people regale one another with jokes which rely upon a negative assessment of the character of Shanghai natives (see also Cheng, 1996). Central and provincial government plans to forge a 'Shanghai economic zone' by promoting economic cooperation between cities in the lower Yangtze (*FBIS*, 1 July 1991, 23 November 1991) have been impeded by inter-provincial rivalry, and a lack of enthusiasm on the part of Zhejiang business people who condemn the scheme as an attempt on the part of Shanghai to colonise and exploit adjoining regions.

Within the north-eastern part of Zhejiang, there is a hierarchical categorisation of places along an urban–rural continuum. Zhejiang urbanites' disparagement of the province's rural inhabitants is acute. And the poorer the rural region, the more are its residents disdained. Yet cultural valorisation and the ordering of places in an urban–rural hierarchy is not wholly predicated upon wealth; rather, it is founded upon a binary representation in which rural is associated with nature and fecundity, primitive simplicity, unchanging traditions and technology, manual labour, dirt, ignorance and superstition, and a lack of self-discipline. Urban supposedly represents the polar opposite of those qualities: it is marked by cultural sophistication, political power, dynamic modernity, mental labour, cleanliness, educated secularism, and self-restraint. Whilst this dualism is, in part, a product of Imperial history, in the following chapter I argue that state intervention and institution-building in the countryside after 1949 invigorated, rather than dispelled, Zhejiang urbanites' dislike of rustics.

In addition to an entrenched bias against rurality, among themselves natives of cities in north-eastern Zhejiang also distinguish character traits which have been given substance by past political and economic practices, as well as by the changes wrought by economic reforms (Edmonds, 1990, pp. 261–79). In their dealings with one another, business people from cities such as Ningbo and Huzhou banter about their respective dialects and cultural idiosyncrasies. Workers remember and re-enact segmentation based upon the exclusive trade practices of pre-revolutionary guilds and territorial discrimination by place-of-origin associations. In the country-side, inter-village rivalries and snobberies stemming from events occurring in the previous century which were embalmed by Maoist policies of local self-sufficiency and population immobility have been reinvigorated (Skinner, 1965, pp. 385–6; Ding, 1989, pp. 26–9; Liu, 1989, pp. 20–5). Thus, territorial prejudices abound. People from the Shaoxing area claim that Hangzhou people fear their sharp tongues and shrewdness in business and politics; Hangzhou people disparage those from Jiaxing as crude country bumpkins and, in turn, are reviled by Jiaxing natives for their arrogance; Ningbo residents insist they are more skilled in commerce, banking and technology than are Hangzhou people (a pretension which is, of course, hotly contested in Hangzhou). These essentialist stereotypes of place have sometimes been accorded the status of sociological 'facts'. A recent article on Ningbo by Lo and Song baldly asserts that 'Ningbo has a breed of inge-nious people with a special talent for business' (1992, pp. 153–8).

Hangzhou

'Shang you tiantang, xia you Su Hang'
('Above there is heaven, on earth there is Suzhou and Hangzhou': Chinese proverb)

Hangzhou is a commonplace town in exquisite surroundings. (Leys, 1977, p. 95)

Hangzhou, the capital of Zhejiang province, is described in markedly dif-ferent ways by diverse groups of inhabitants and visitors. Its most frequent representations in the local media are as an economically successful, culturally sophisticated city which is justly famed for its history and scenic beauty. Administrators focus upon other characteristics: Hangzhou city is inhabited by more than one million people who live in six government districts. Economists remark upon the unusual ownership and sectoral mix of Hangzhou's economy. Despite the injunction, during the Maoist period, for all cities to engage in heavy industrial production rather than focus upon the production of consumer goods, and despite the channelling of investment into huge, state-owned industries, Hangzhou's economy remained founded upon light industrial production and processing and component assembly in small, mostly collectively owned firms. These characteristics are commonly summarised in the phrase '*qing, xiao, ji, jia*' ('light, small, collective, processing') (Deng, 1989, pp. 326–30). With reform, these features have become more pronounced, as the older industries located within the city limits decline in significance relative to non-state firms in satellite cities and suburban villages. TVEs predominantly centred in the southern part of the municipality, now produce almost half the city's industrial output value. Steel, petroleum products, chemicals, pharmaceutics, machinery, electronic appliances, textiles, shoes, processed foods and alcohol, and commerce and tourism are the source of Hangzhou's considerable wealth. In the municipal government's vision for Hangzhou's future, the city will also become a technology centre (*FBIS*, 20 May 1991, 23 September 1991; *HZRB*, 15 May 1992).

The advent of reform and the shift in Hangzhou's economic centre of gravity from centre towards periphery and from public to private has affected the way in which local urban residents perceive their city and themselves. To many of the people who work in the declining smokestack industries and live in the city centre, Hangzhou has become an increasingly fragmented, unsafe, and de-valued home. Urban residents' once well remunerated and highly sought after jobs now seem comparatively poorly paid, less secure and, consequently, out of favour. Only *nongmin gong*, or peasant workers, are eager to replace them. Suburbs which once were remarkable principally for their architectural, economic, and social homogeneity have been fractured by economic reform, industrial restructuring and the redeployment and dispersal of working class residents. Inner city neighbourhoods are being bisected by road widening and urban renewal projects which have thrown up luxury hotels, real estate offices, neon-lit video-game parlours, and department stores.

Reforms have brought people from the margins of territory, society and the socialist class imagery into the midst of the old city suburbs: private business people and brash speculators who come from other provinces or even other countries, rowdy construction gangs who travel from one urban project to another, and immigrant rural workers who are even more mobile than the business people and construction gangs, and thus considered to be even more dangerous. The sense of disintegration and devaluation felt by Hangzhou's long term residents is exacerbated by the fact that many of the customers who throng the expensive new shops, restaurants, and karaoke bars which have proliferated in the city centre are upstart 'peasant' entrepreneurs.

On the other hand, to the once denigrated 'peasants' who reside in suburban villages on the outskirts of Hangzhou, the city centre and the distinctions it once enshrined have lost much of their importance. The city is no longer the best site for high-value production, or the only venue for well paid employment and conspicuous consumption. In the past, village residents were eager to gain jobs in urban enterprises in return for having their land requisitioned by state institutions and urban enterprises. Now, they themselves have become employers, recruiting immigrant labourers to fulfil subcontracts from struggling state enterprises, or undertake parts fabrication, assembly and processing for domestic and international markets. People have even begun to remark on a new phenomenon which challenges the old hierarchy of urban and rural places: some ambitious urbanites have sought employment in collective village enterprises or marriage to rich 'peasants'.

Visitors to the city also see it from radically different perspectives. To the hundreds of thousands of domestic and international tourists who come each year to see the lake, temples and gardens, Hangzhou is a beautiful, historic, religiously significant city. Compared to other famous resorts and east coast cities, Hangzhou is a relatively cheap place to holiday, hold conferences or stage exhibitions. According to business people who have wearied of the high rents, extortionate bribes, and escalating wages that must be paid in Shanghai and Shenzhen, it is also a good site in which to have things manufactured or processed.

In contrast, however, to the favourable impressions Hangzhou usually makes on tourists and business people, to the hundreds of thousands of people from poor rural areas who have come to this regional metropolis to search for work or scavenge for a livelihood, the city is inhospitable and working conditions are harsh. Nevertheless, they continue to come because it also seems unbelievably affluent: 'It's like a gold mine! Everyone here is rich. They throw food and money away!' (Fieldnotes, 6 February 1993).

Xihu Counterpoints: *jumin, nongmin*, and *waidi ren*

Xihu district encircles the famous lake from which it takes its name: Xihu, or West Lake. Both district and lake are located to the south west of the

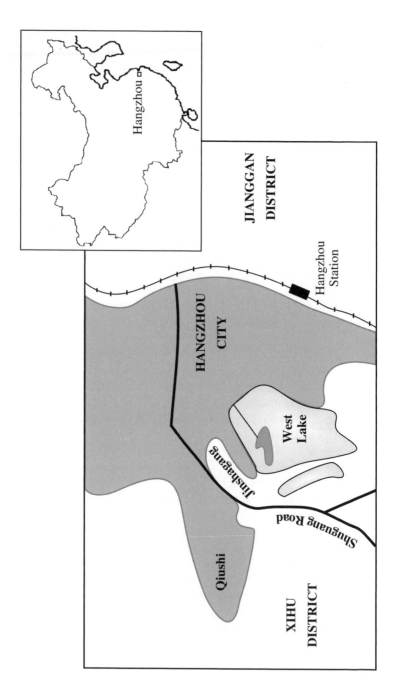

Map: Hangzhou City, showing the location of Xihu district

centre of Hangzhou. Altogether, Xihu covers an area of approximately 228 square kilometres. In 1992 the district had a registered permanent population of 329 887 people (*Xihu qu jingji tongji nianjian 1992*, p. 1).[2] Although most of the district area is classified as rural, and one-third of the population has rural registration and resides in 'villages', in reality Xihu confounds such definitions. The great majority of people in Xihu live in densely populated suburbs fringing Hangzhou's municipal boundary, and are employed in non-agricultural work. Nearly three-quarters of total output value in Xihu now comes from industrial production (particularly machinery, cement, electronics, and plastics), as well as construction, transportation, and commerce. Industry has grown very rapidly. In 1992, the output value of 'village' industries was 42 per cent higher than that in 1991 (*Xihu qu jingji tongji nianjian 1992*, p. 4). As Xihu's industries have grown and diversified, they have also changed ownership. In 1992 all but two of the industrial enterprises in Xihu were registered as collective enterprises, and more than 85 per cent of these were TVEs. By mid 1996, two-thirds of all collective enterprises in Xihu had become share-holding cooperatives or limited liability companies, or had been sold or leased to private business people (Sargeson and Zhang, 1997).

Residents of Xihu identify themselves, and are responded to, according to place. Place does not simply signify current residential address. It also makes reference to families' geographical origins, residential registration, patterns of livelihood and levels of income and consumption, social and kinship organisation and cultural practices. Concurrently, place figures as an idiom through which discourses of collective identity and exploitation are expressed. In particular, place is strongly indicative of the relationships which obtain between three distinctive populations in Xihu: the *jumin* of Qiushi, Jinshagang's *nongmin*, and the immigrants known as *waidi ren*.

Qiushi and Jinshagang are adjacent suburbs of Xihu district. At a glance, they appear to be separated only by Shuguang Road. But their separation is actually effected by much more subtle factors than a tree lined strip of macadam. Qiushi is an urban dormitory suburb which has been constructed over the past few decades upon land once belonging to Yuquan village. Jinshagang is classified as a rural village.

Qiushi's permanent residents have been administratively classified as *jumin*, or urbanites. Their primary point of identification is the province's premier tertiary education institution, Zhejiang University. Most of the households in Qiushi have at least one, and often two tenured wage earners who are, or once were, employed by the University or one of its many subsidiary institutes or enterprises: trade and technology companies, consultancy businesses, factories, shops, a hospital and clinics, kindergartens, restaurants, canteens and entertainment venues. The University also is the host of the local branch of the ACFTU, and the nexus through which elections to political posts and various social activities are organised. Most Qiushi residents have higher middle school or tertiary educational qualifications, and have been allocated to their jobs at the University and its enterprises by government labour bureaux. Many were not born or raised in Hangzhou. As a consequence of their high educational standards and varied backgrounds, conversation between Qiushi residents is usually conducted in Mandarin, with only older local residents speaking Hangzhou dialect.

Due to their employment by the University and its subsidiary enterprises, in 1992–93 most Qiushi residents received stable incomes which fell into the relatively narrow range of 200 to 450 yuan per month. In addition to these modest salaries, they also received heavily subsidised health insurance and pension entitlements. A few managers of lucrative businesses established by the University received more than 1000 yuan per month.

The social uniformity established by similar educational background, common employer, and comparable income levels is reinforced by housing patterns in Qiushi. Until the early 1990s, Qiushi residents paid a minimal rent of between 5 and 18 yuan to live in tall, monochrome concrete blocks of one to five room apartments owned by the University. Economic reform has brought the development of a real estate market, and a partial redefinition of the paternalistic relationship between the University and its employees. In 1993 limited titles to two new blocks of apartments were sold to employee-applicants on the University housing waiting list. The purchase price for housing averaged 13 000 yuan for a two room apartment, which was well below the current average market price for urban housing.[3] At the same time, all occupants of publicly owned housing in Hangzhou were advised that they would have to either purchase their apartments in the near future, or pay for life-long leases on their apartments for sums averaging around 3 000 yuan (*HZRB*, 8 February 1993). Ever-conscious of China's galloping inflation rate and eager to capitalise on the scarcity of housing, many people in Qiushi chose to purchase their apartments.

The diverse regional backgrounds of residents, self-contained character of apartments, absence of common space, and relatively high incidence of intra-suburban mobility as households move to newly constructed or larger apartments, precludes the development of neighbourly familiarity. Any sense of community which exists derives largely from employment in a large state work unit and common feelings of intellectual superiority and middle class respectability, rather than from long term residence, propinquity, and relations of reciprocity.[4] On the other hand, individualism and rivalry is generated by rigid status hierarchies and the way in which money, resources and opportunities are distributed within this same work unit. One young man provided me with the following illustration of the expressions of hierarchy and rivalry he had encountered in his Qiushi home:

> When my father's friends visit, the ones who haven't been overseas won't say hello or goodbye to me unless I have greeted them or said goodbye first, because I am younger than they are. Although I'm an adult, they still think of me as a child, so I have to pay my respects to them first. The ones who have been overseas and the ones who are really rich, they are more casual, just say goodbye because they have gained so much face they don't need to stand on ceremony. Then, you know my father is a professor. Well, on the floor directly above us lives another professor. He is the head of a research institute, same as my dad. And they are about the same age. That's a problem for them. They never say hello unless they have to pass one another on the stairs. I asked my dad why he doesn't chat to this fellow he has been living and working beside for decades. He said, 'I don't know him.' I think it's hilarious, the way they pretend not to know one another. They are so conscious of their relative position in this strict hierarchy. They all have to queue for promotions, trips away, research funds. Everyone is jealous of everyone else. So they are nice to their superiors. They give them presents, flatter them, pull *guanxi* with them. And they are nice to subordinates, because they patronise them and get presents and flattery from them in return. But anyone on the same level is a competitor. I've often thought about it, this professor that we have lived under all my life that we 'don't know'. (Tape, 30 October 1992)

The domestic life of Qiushi's population is clearly attuned to the dictates of state-fostered modernisation, and the status claims of the inhabitants. Population growth in Qiushi is largely consequent upon the expansion of the University and its enterprises and the construction of University housing. The majority of households are neo-local nuclear families with independent budgets. According to leaders of the neighbourhood committee, the current pattern for Qiushi couples to have only one child predates the introduction of population control policies, and is closely associated with Qiushi women's relatively high educational qualifications and participation in the work force. Less than one-quarter of households include a member of the older generation or a consanguinal relative. Infants are cared for either by grandparents or, because many grandparents do not reside locally, by nannies. Children attend kindergartens and primary schools in the suburb, and many adolescents go to the key No. 15 middle school which is built on land once belonging to Jinshagang. Marriages, house warmings, and funerals in Qiushi are discreet events, in keeping with the modest salaries and respectable demeanour of the inhabitants. The state employment, secular education, and 'modern' outlook of most Qiushi residents probably also accounts for the remarkable absence within apartments of objects associated with religious worship or ancestral rituals.

Qiushi's permanent residents look across Shuguang Road towards the village of Jinshagang with mixed expressions of disdain and envy because, to the chagrin of Qiushi's population, although Jinshagang's residents are *nongmin*, or rural residents, and obviously lack the educational and cultural qualifications of their Qiushi neighbours, they are conspicuously wealthy and occupy a beautiful, spacious, leafy suburb: 'They are rich, over there. The peasants get to live in three storey houses. But look at us intellectuals – we cannot even afford decent apartments, much less three storey houses!' (Fieldnotes 20 October 1992).

In return, Jinshagang residents are antagonised by Qiushi people's superior airs:

> I don't know any intellectuals, we don't have anything to do with them. Well, we do go shopping down near the University because it's so close. But we don't know them. They are all educated while we ... They look down on us, because we aren't educated, are we? To be honest, I loathe them! (Fieldnotes, 13 August 1992)

People in Jinshagang have a lower average standard of education than those in Qiushi, with most young adults only receiving a lower or higher middle school education. Village children generally attend primary schools located in Jinshagang, though a few offspring of the wealthier, socially ambitious villagers pay high fees to attend Qiushi primary school. Similarly, most village adolescents travel to Xihu middle school; only a select few attend the academically prestigious no. 15 middle school which serves Qiushi teenagers.

Differences between Qiushi and Jinshagang populations extend beyond educational levels and social snobbery. Membership of the village of Jinshagang is only attained by birth, or by in-marriage and long term co-residence, familial continuity and extension. A sense of community is fostered by the strength of the local collective economy, regular social and ceremonial interaction, and use of Hangzhou dialect in everyday speech. This sense of belonging to a bounded community is illustrated by the fact that even younger residents of Jinshagang who have no memory of the pre-reform period still refer to their village in the old collectivist terminology as a *dadui*, or production brigade. Economic reform has, however, created social cleavages in Jinshagang. In particular, as I shall show in later chapters, dissatisfaction over the activities and aspirations of the Mao family is slowly growing. The Maos have 'only' lived in Jinshagang for a couple of decades and are still considered by some villagers to be outsiders. Yet through a combination of well-timed political activism, extensive networking, business acumen, opportunism, and the alienation of what some villagers consider to be community property, the Maos have become one of the richest families in the village.

Despite its rural status, few Jinshagang residents still cultivate land. Remnant vegetable patches and tea farms are tended by retirees or those who relish gardening. Many plots of land lie fallow or are being built upon. Most adults in Jinshagang find employment, via the village government and their own contacts, in collectively owned manufacturing, processing, and service enterprises. A smaller number of elderly and middle-aged residents have been given jobs by the University or by urban enterprises in compensation for the requisition of their land.

Growth and diversification of the village economy since the beginning of the reform era has given Jinshagang residents high incomes, and an enviable standard of living. In 1992–93, a few residents such as the Maos enjoyed monthly incomes in excess of 10 000 yuan, and even some young unskilled women earned more than the University professors who lived across Shuguang Road. One revealing indicator of the high average level of household income is that young wage earners generally use the bulk of their earnings as they please. Popular items of consumption amongst the young people I was familiar with included motorbikes, personal television sets (so as to avoid arguments over programmes), and Nike running shoes: all things considered by Qiushi residents to be luxury goods. In addition to enjoying high incomes, village residents also benefit from the village government's use of dividends from local collective enterprises to fund old age pensions, health subsidies, and the education of village children.

A considerable proportion of Jinshagang families' income is channelled into private housing construction. Village housing has symbolic as well as practical significance, for, in contrast to the regularly spaced, grey, publicly owned apartment buildings which mark Qiushi residents as dependants of the state, Jinshagang houses are artefacts which signify villagers' successful entrepreneurship. And that, in the discourse of economic reform, denotes responsibility, independence and modernity. Village houses and the winding paths which connect them also express and sustain community

relationships, activities, and values. The houses are built on land allocated
by the village government to households on a per capita basis, and it is
common for relatives to occupy adjacent or nearby blocks of land. In
1992–93, new houses cost between 35 000 and 55 000 yuan to build. Some
families in the village have used land allocated to their children to build
second houses which are rented out to Hong Kong business people and foreign scholars at the University for approximately 1 000 yuan per month.[5]
Houses are multi-storeyed, free standing, painted in pastel colours, decorated with ceramic tiles, and festooned with television antennae and airconditioning units. The grounds are, by Chinese standards, spacious. In
their courtyard gardens, people gather to wash clothes and prepare vegetables, play *majiang*, eat sugar cane or *guazi*, and chat with neighbours and
passers-by. Some courtyards feature goldfish ponds, flower beds, and displays of potted ornamental trees and strangely sculpted rocks: a dramatic
contrast to the cramped balconies on which Qiushi residents store tools,
dry washing, and raise small pots of chrysanthemums and chives.

Jinshagang residents also differ from those of Qiushi in their domestic
configurations and celebrations. As might be expected of a rich community, there is very little out-migration from Jinshagang. A low rate of population growth comes from in-marriages rather than from births, for as in
most industrialised and densely populated areas of China, people tend to
follow the one child policy (*Xihu qu jingji tongji nianjian 1992*, p. 5).
Marriage is generally virilocal. However, owing to the village's wealth,
local women whose partners are from poorer villages or, occasionally,
even from Hangzhou city, prefer to remain in Jinshagang. Hence, uxorilo-
cality is not uncommon. Village households tend to consist of stem families, and all but a few infants are cared for by resident grandparents.
Jinshagang weddings, funerals, and house warming festivities are much
more expensive, sociable and noisier events than the subdued ceremonies
held in Qiushi. So, too, are Spring Festival and *Qingming* observed with
much more elaborate ceremonial, including visits to ancestral graves in the
hills surrounding Xihu where the generations bow in obeisance, place
huge paper wreaths, and light long strings of red firecrackers.

Despite their manifold differences and the feelings of antagonism
between them, the residents of Jinshagang and Qiushi share an important
characteristic in common. That is, they are the employers, supervisors, and
beneficiaries of a large fringe population of immigrant workers who they,
and the immigrants themselves, refer to as *waidi ren*, or outsiders.[6] The
actual positions in which Qiushi and Jinshagang residents stand relative to
immigrant workers are consequent upon their personal links to local nodes
of capital accumulation. In the case of Qiushi residents, power and money

issue from privileged positions and contacts within an institutional hierarchy which enjoys access to state funds and administratively allocated resources, extensive organisational capacities, and bureaucratically derived property rights in business ventures. In Jinshagang, power and money accrue from membership of an administratively, economically, and socially delineated community in which individuals can take advantage of their connections with village leaders, collectively accumulated capital, and the recent sanctioning of new property relations, business forms and market activities.

Certainly, to the outsiders employed by the residents of Qiushi and Jinshagang, the differences between them seem relatively minor. As the following conversation with two immigrant workers demonstrates, their employers' most distinctive, common trait is that they are all locals. And, as locals, they enjoy ownership and control over property and capital, have the wherewithal to employ outsiders from poorer places, and are, consequently, wealthy:

> Deng: All our friends are *wailai ren*. The *jumin* don't get along with us. They just hire us to work in their enterprises.
> Sally Sargeson (hereafter SS): Why don't they get along with you?
> Deng: Because they have lots of money and we don't.
> SS: Why is that significant?
> Chen: Just because they are rich. They have been to more places than we have, seen the world, so they look down on us.
> Deng: When they speak to us they are really scornful.
> SS: What about people from the villages around here? They are *nongmin* too, like you. How do they treat you?
> Deng: Pretty much the same. They aren't any different to the *jumin*. They are rich too. They are bosses. They won't have anything to do with us. (Tape, 11 January 1993)

In contrast to local residents' occupation of a highly industrialised and commercialised place, and their embeddedness in institutional hierarchy and community, outsiders in Xihu are disadvantaged, and, hence, (dis)placed by the fact that they hail from poor rural areas. Most are from south-western Zhejiang, or from the neighbouring provinces of Anhui and Jiangxi. At home, they lack sufficient land and capital to make an adequate livelihood, or the social connections which could be called upon for assistance in the search for paid employment. The poverty and (dis)placement of these people helps to make Qiushi and Jinshagang the places they are.

Most outsiders in Qiushi and Jinshagang have found employment as factory workers, builders, carters, cleaners and nannies through personal recommendations from people who share their place of origin or other migrant co-workers. Outsiders tend to change jobs with much greater frequency than do locals, and are more inclined to undertake multiple geographical moves. They generally earn between 120 yuan and 300 yuan each month. This is a lower wage range than that earned by both Qiushi's state-oriented employees and Jinshagang's entrepreneurial collective employees.

For outsiders new to the city, finding affordable accommodation and feeding themselves until they find work can be very difficult. Many have no alternative but to sleep in parks such as that near the Hangzhou railway station, or under shop awnings on the pavement, and to eat sparingly until they have a job. If they are fortunate, their employers will provide them with dormitory accommodation attached to their places of employment, for which they pay a minimal rent of 3 to 5 yuan per month. Low rent is virtually the only attractive feature of dormitory accommodation. Factory dormitories are, without exception, crowded, dirty, noisy, and lacking all but the most basic facilities. Outsiders who do not have access to dormitories rent rooms from households in outlying villages. Rent payments by outsiders average between 60 and 100 yuan per month, a much higher proportion of their monthly income than that spent on accommodation by local residents.

Almost all outsiders in Xihu have attenuated family relationships. Those who live in dormitories by necessity live apart from their families. Others are separated from their spouses because they have been unable to find work in the same city. Couples who have been lucky enough to find two jobs in Hangzhou often have to leave their children with relatives in their village because they cannot support the extra costs of food, health care and education in the city. Two couples I knew who had school age children living with them paid more than 2 000 yuan in annual fees to Xihu primary school, several times more than local children were required to pay.

In addition to limitations on their family life, outsiders also suffer from having relatively low levels of social interaction in Hangzhou. They claim that this is because they are saving money for marriage or village house building, because they have small disposable incomes and long working hours, or because there are not many people from their place of origin in the neighbourhood and locals are unfriendly towards them. Given that few are eligible for paid holidays, and they are only granted unpaid leave during Spring Festival or in the event of parental death, they are necessarily deprived of the opportunity of participating in many life-cycle rituals and annual festivals.

The majority of younger immigrant workers I spoke with in Xihu had received a lower middle school education, though a considerable number had completed higher middle school, trade apprenticeships, and diploma courses at night schools. Older immigrant workers tend only to have been to primary school. A few admitted, with great embarrassment, to being illiterate: a result, they complained, of political upheaval, chronic rural poverty, and, in the case of two women, gender discrimination. When outsiders are among people from their place of origin, they speak local dialects. When conversing with Hangzhou residents or foreigners, they speak Mandarin.

These three place-defined groups, *jumin*, *nongmin*, and *waidi ren*, comprise the main populations of Xihu, and it is to relations between and amongst them that much of the following analysis turns. But before proceeding, it is necessary to acknowledge the existence in Xihu of a small, relatively stable population of self-employed people and store keepers who do business alongside the main roads of Qiushi and Jinshagang. Through their business relationships with local governments and institutions, their market activities, and their recruitment of a few employees (usually relatives or outsiders), these people are also implicated in the creation of local economic structures and discourses on identity.

Yet these petty business people are not defined by place to the same extent as the three groups I have described. In fact, in comparison to the relatively clear identity boundaries which mark other inhabitants according to place, they form an amorphous company. In the minds of all the people with whom I talked, the trait which distinguishes them is their individualistic mode of livelihood: they are not knit into place-inflected relations of ownership, wage employment, production, and accumulation. Many are outsiders, and as such share certain characteristics with immigrant workers. Although they tend to have a higher income than do immigrant workers, and come from a wider variety of regions, they still must rent accommodation and frequently live apart from their families. And, like immigrant workers, some complain that they work long hours and have only superficial and limited social networks in the city. Those self-employed and small shop keepers who are local residents live with their families in Qiushi and surrounding villages. While some of these locals have social networks which they use to advance their business activities, they are kept at a distance by many of the more conservative Qiushi locals because of their involvement in petty trade. Most small business people have had a wide range of occupations, some having worked in several different types of enterprises and trades over the past decade. They have travelled widely and speak a number of dialects. Their educational qualifications are similarly varied: they range from a few years of primary schooling through to university degrees.

PLACE AND PARTICULARISM IN XIHU ENTERPRISES

The place-defined identities of people in Qiushi and Jinshagang are partly a product of the way in which economic activities are mediated by localism and particularism. This causal relationship begs closer attention. Precisely how have economic pursuits concurrently encouraged allegiance with places, and allowed some local residents to become the employers and beneficiaries of the labour power of other residents of that place, and of people from other places? A brief introduction to the three case study enterprises which form the empirical focus of this book, the Jinshagang electronics factory, and the Sanxian bakery and the Laolian technology company in Qiushi, shows that they are representative of the whole spectrum of enterprise types which have emerged during the reform era, and are especially characteristic of Zhejiang's economy.

These enterprises have in common, first, the fact that they all were established with a view to the production of goods for profit. They also resemble one another in the extent to which small local groups have taken advantage of pre-existing public organisational and financial resources to develop corporate forms in which they have predominant property rights. For while all three firms were established with some public funds and are nominally collectively owned, in fact individual investors and/or managers play a critical role in all phases of decision-making over production and the disposal of product and income, and claim for themselves a significant share of profits. A third common feature is that the relationships between the enterprises and the government bodies, institutions, and individuals involved in their establishment are legally and financially ambiguous. Fourth, they are vulnerable to extortion by parts of the state. Jinshagang factory, Sanxian bakery, and Laolian company subsidiaries all make regular mandatory payments of graft to local government departments and officials. A fifth characteristic is that all firms are engaged in relatively small, light manufacturing and commercial activities, are highly responsive to market signals, and have experienced rapid growth and branching-off of subsidiaries. And finally, with the exception of a few management staff, all the workers in these enterprises are non-unionised contract and temporary employees whose livelihood depends upon wage employment, and whose employment security is determined by their own productivity and the profitability of the enterprise, as well as by their social connections and residential status. In short, these are precisely the sorts of enterprises in which China's reworked proletariat labours.

The firms are differentiated, of course, by their individual histories. These histories highlight various sources of start-up capital and arrangements for the disposition of profits, dissimilar production processes, and work forces of different sizes, skills, origins, and gender balances. Yet even these singular features illuminate the determinant influence of place and social network in creating China's differentiated proletariat and determining the conditions under which it will labour.

The Jinshagang factory was established by Mao Jinhua as a village-owned collective in 1978. Director Mao gave three reasons for the factory's creation, not least of which was to provide him with a entrée into the brave new world of socialist business. The factory was also intended to generate revenue for the village government, and increase employment opportunities and income for local residents. Mao proposed the idea of the factory to the village leaders, who provided him with an old vacant building. He also arranged with the head of a technical institute to trade the institute's expertise, equipment, and contacts in return for the village's provision of land to construct a dormitory for institute staff. The factory's first products were electronic calculators which were sold on the domestic market. By 1980, competition from more sophisticated and cheaper imports forced it to switch to the manufacture of school laboratory equipment. In 1985, the head of the research institute introduced Director Mao to a Toshiba representative who was searching for a company to take over an assembly contract from a Hangzhou state factory which could not meet deadlines and quality requirements. Within a matter of months, the Jinshagang factory had been supplied with all the necessary equipment and materials, and had sent off its first shipment of components to Japan. Since then, all the factory's products have been exported to Japan.

The collective has expanded rapidly. The Jinshagang factory's Japanese client companies and product lines have expanded and, in addition to a variety of electronic components, it also produces a range of greeting cards and plastic clothes bags. In 1991 a new factory building was constructed, but within eighteen months this already had become too small to accommodate its activities. Two subsidiary factories have been established, and processing work is also subcontracted to another collective's factory in Xiaoshan. The value of collective's assets and circulating capital had increased more than twenty-fold by 1992, when annual sales were worth more than 13 million yuan and net profits were more than 3 million yuan.

As a consequence of this growth, the in-house work force of the factory increased from 25 to more than 600 in the space of seven years. In 1993, some 560 of these employees were unskilled females with lower middle school education. More than 500 were immigrants from rural areas. All were employed on contract.

The collective's profits have been used to establish and develop other businesses. In addition to the Jinshagang factory which is now managed by Director Mao's son, Mao Gang, the collective now owns two restaurants, a transport company, a vehicle accessories factory, and a machinery repair works. As well as controlling all enterprises in the collective, members of the Mao family all have extensive private business interests.

The Mao family have adopted a variety of measures to increase the profitability of Jinshagang factory and, concurrently, increase their own stake in the firm and reduce their obligations towards the village government. First, the factory has altered its nominal ownership status. In early 1993 the factory signed a 'fake' foreign joint venture contract with a Hong Kong businessman, and became a limited liability company. This change of status gave the factory three years' exemption from taxes and administrative fees, and the ability to act independently to control its exporting activities. Mao Gang directly linked these moves to his anticipated personal stake in the enterprise, the rising costs of basic labour intensive processing firms in China, and competition from other low-wage countries:

> If I am to inherit this firm [*sic*] and just continue to sell our processing facilities, I might not be able to keep going. At the moment we are doing fairly well. But compared to other places in south-east Asia – Taiwan, Malaysia – then we can't possibly compete with them because of their high quality, technology. And now, Vietnam and the Philippines represent an even greater threat to our labour intensive industries because they are even cheaper than we are... We need to be able to import and export without interference, manage our own affairs and expand into other areas. We can still offer fairly cheap labour for a few more years if we don't have to pay tax, and that will give us time to grow and diversify. (Tape, 16 February 1993)

Moreover, as a reward for the factory's rapid expansion and its conversion to a joint venture company, Mao Jinhua managed to negotiate a more favourable profit sharing arrangement with the village government. When the factory was originally established, it was agreed that profits would be shared between the collective and village government on a ratio of either 60 : 40, or 50 : 50, depending on the factory's need for more capital investment. But from 1993 the factory began to pay the village government a dividend based upon its 1992 profit share plus a 10 per cent increase over each previous annual dividend. The village government retained the authority to set a limit on the basic monthly wages paid to workers in the factory. That authority is, however, limited by the fact that Mao Jinhua was simultaneously granted the right to use net profit as he pleases. This includes the right to set all bonus payments, including his own and those of his family members. Thus, this change provides the Mao family with a much greater incentive to expand the factory and increase profitability, as Mao Gang acknowledged: 'All I care about now is people's contributions towards our company, towards our economic returns. That's the crucial thing' (Tape, 16 February 1993).

Another means by which the Maos have attempted to secure the future of the collective is by currying favour with officials in crucial posts. A slush fund is used to protect both collective enterprises and the Mao family's private businesses against interference or harassment. Shanghai customs officials, officials in the provincial bureaux administering taxes and export licences, people in charge of several crucial municipal and district government departments, and the village head are feted and presented with gifts bi-annually, invited to participate as silent partners in business ventures, and sometimes provided with free trips overseas.

The development of the second case study enterprise, Sanxian bakery, was also facilitated by local networking. And, like Jinshagang factory, the firm is a 'fake' foreign joint venture. Sanxian was established at the end of 1987 with an initial investment of approximately 650 000 yuan. This was paid in equal shares by the University's collectively-owned Labour Service Company (LSC), and two close relatives of leaders of the University who set up a shell 'briefcase company' in the USA with the specific intention of reinvesting in China as a foreign firm so as to qualify for tax exemption. The two premises the bakery occupies in Qiushi were provided by the LSC as part of its original investment. The sole aim of establishing the bakery was to maximise returns to the investors.

Networks within the University and its LSC also proved critical in the appointment of the bakery's manager, and continue to be important in determining the appointment and job security of employees. Rong Jia, formerly a state enterprise engineer, was appointed general manager. She had no previous business, management, or catering experience, but did have good connections, or *guanxi*, with University leaders and the head of the LSC. Over the period in which I observed the bakery, the total number of employees varied between 25 and 80, with frequent lay-offs and re-hiring in response to seasonal demand and official harassment. All the higher administrative, purchasing and technical staff were local residents who had relatives or friends either in the University, the LSC, or within the bakery's administration. These employees all signed contracts. More than half of the local contract staff were females with higher middle school or college education. In contrast, the majority of bakers were male. They were recruited either on the basis of their personal connections with people in the LSC or bakery administration, or because of their trade skills or strength. Local bakers predominated over unskilled temporary immigrants during slack seasons. But when sales were brisk, outsiders outnumbered locals. Only one-third of the local bakers, and none of the temporary immigrants employed by Sanxian, signed contracts.

It took manager Rong a year to get the necessary approvals from all the relevant government departments before the bakery could begin operation. By that time, all the original investment monies had been used to purchase equipment and pay bribes. In order to provide circulating capital, Rong, on behalf of Sanxian bakery, took out a bank loan of one million yuan. At the end of each year the two Sanxian partners stipulated what they expect as a return on their investment for the following year. In 1992–93, dividends of 70 000 yuan were paid to each of the two sets of investors from after-tax profits of just 150 000 yuan. From the profits remaining, 25 per cent was supposed to be paid into a superannuation and welfare fund, but in lieu of other investment funds this money was used for development. The balance, if there is any (often, there is not), should be distributed as bonuses to employees. Manager Rong's income is negotiated directly with the investors, and she sets all other employees' wages and bonuses.

The bakery's business has expanded, but not as dramatically as that of the Jinshagang factory. It now produces more than twenty-five different kinds of breads, cakes, pastries, and festival specialties such as moon cakes. Products are discontinued if demand drops, and new products are constantly being introduced. The bakery's products are sold in two directly leased shops as well as in department stores and small shops throughout Hangzhou, and in other cities in northern Zhejiang and southern Jiangsu. At festival times, the bakery also takes orders from big work units throughout the area. Sanxian's aggressive expansion into what is seen to be Shanghai's traditional hinterland has boosted the bakery's sales, but it faces constant pressure in maintaining its market niche from two other Hangzhou bakeries which also produce high quality western-style breads and cakes.

Problems posed by stiff market competition have been compounded by the insecurity of outlets, officials' rent seeking, and a lack of capital. The bakery must 'lease' counter space in shops, and the cost of leases is subject to constant renegotiation as shop keepers take note of sales levels. In 1992, officials from the district health department closed the bakery for a week during the busy moon cake season because Rong mistakenly believed that as she had made payments to contacts in the municipal health department it was not necessary also to present gifts to district health officials. The lack of capital impacts directly upon Sanxian's operations, and on the incomes of all who work for the company. Rong frequently complained that despite increases in output, sales, profits, and the numbers of people employed, the company was overly constrained by its heavy debt and the excessive amounts taken out annually by the investors. In the hope of increasing profitability, she set up subsidiary food and entertainment businesses which were recapitalised as joint ventures.

The history of the third case study enterprise, the Laolian company, presents a somewhat different dynamic of enterprise development which is less market driven, and more in tune with depictions of 'communal' enterprises. Nevertheless, here too local social connections were critical to the establishment and organisation of the firm and remain significant in determining employees' security. And as in the case of Jinshagang factory and Sanxian, Laolian's expansion also has been facilitated by diversification of products and the formation of subsidiary enterprises.

Laolian technology company was established in 1988 with an original investment of 210 000 yuan from the State Education Commission which was administered by Zhejiang University.[7] The company's brief was, first, to engage in production and marketing to stimulate the dissemination of technology and, second, to generate profits which could be reinvested in applied research and company expansion. Twelve male academics who are close friends of the man appointed by the President of the University as General Manager were enlisted to get the company running. Premises above the Qiushi produce market were rented from the district government's commerce department. Laolian began producing industrial technology such as transducers and weighing machines, and laboratory, medical, and science teaching equipment.

The general manager was the only employee of the firm who, in 1993, remained a tenured employee of the University. At the outset, engineers and technicians were hired from amongst the managers' ex-students and by word of mouth. Hence, all top posts in the company – managerial, marketing, and technical – were filled by local residents who had long been familiar with one another. More than half of production workers were also local residents who found their jobs through social connections. All locals were contract employees. The only immigrant employee with both a supervisory position and a job contract was a highly skilled engineer.

Company managers were exclusively male, while at all levels below that of departmental manager, there were approximately equal numbers of males and females. Laolian's work force numbered approximately 120.

Although the Laolian work force and product lines both increased, the company has shown a very low profit rate. Indeed, if it were not for the company's quasi-institutional status which ensures it pays minimal taxes, it would have become insolvent. The company pays a 3.27 per cent tax on enterprise profits, returns 20 per cent of after-tax profits to the University, and divides the remainder equally between administration, development, bonuses, and a welfare fund. Total sales in 1991 were valued at 13 million yuan, but this generated profits of only 400 000 yuan. Most sales are made to institutions such as schools and hospitals, and industrial enterprises through trade and technology fairs and orders received by sales representatives. Up to 50 per cent of what might otherwise be profits on sales are eaten up by entertainment expenses and commissions to the official organisers of these fairs, to institutional and company purchasing officers, and to the state-owned companies from which Laolian buys supplies. According to Laolian employees, however, the main reason for the company's lack of profitability is incompetent management and marketing by the old academic cronies of the General Manager. These people receive the same wages as they once drew from the University, but their annual bonus payments are decided amongst themselves. Other workers' wages are fixed by the General Manager, and their monthly bonus payments are set by departmental heads.

Although Laolian has not been particularly profitable, the firm has expanded by taking advantage of its connection with the University to gain access to short-term bank loans. These have been used to turn former departments of the company into independent enterprises. According to the enthusiastic young manager of the newly created software company, the General Manager plans to turn Laolian into a large corporate group. Certainly, that vision looks more feasible from the vantage point of the balance sheets produced by the software company than from the ledgers of the original company. After only one year in operation, the software company's 1991–92 sales totalled 1.2 million yuan, and profits from this were 250 000 yuan: a considerably higher profit margin than that earned by the parent firm. One-fifth of those profits were paid back to the parent company, and half of the remainder was channelled into research. The company also borrowed 700 000 yuan from a provincial technology development fund and the Bank of Commerce and Industry to establish its own independent foreign joint venture in Shenzhen. Yet despite its comparative success and the fact that, like its parent company, the software company is protected by its quasi-institutional status against heavier tax obligations and the rapacity of local officials, it nevertheless faces an uncertain future. There is very strong competition in the computer market from other domestic companies as well as from sophisticated imports, and old technology, poor infrastructure, and regional trade barriers present serious obstacles to the development of all domestic high technology enterprises.

The regional variations and structured inequalities which I have mapped in north-eastern Zhejiang, Hangzhou, and Xihu, and the localistic and particularistic relations which have underpinned development of the three case study enterprises, serve to illustrate why workers in China draw causal links between places, social groups, and money. The advantages or disadvantages which distinguish particular places in north-eastern Zhejiang, and which establish their position in local, regional, national, and global economic systems are, to a large extent, the cumulative consequence of historically formed socio-spatial relations between populations. The recent histories of the case study enterprises illustrate how powerful, place-based groups continue to utilise the rhetoric of place and their social connections to assert control over enterprises, labour and resources, and gain access to economies of ever-increasing spatial scale. Place is integral to the implementation of economic reforms at the local level. Place is also of critical importance to the ways in which workers experience and understand wage work and the emergence of new social groups.

Whilst economic reforms have reconstituted place as a basis for new patterns of social-structural polarisation, however, they have also made organisation and identities based solely upon place less secure. Certainly, the socio-spatial relations which define place-based groups are purposefully being reinforced as those groups seek to take advantage of the economic opportunities opened up by reforms. Even a cursory glance reveals that the case study enterprises are being established by local communities with the aim of generating profits which will be used for the expansion of the local economy and improvement of local individuals' incomes. Yet on closer inspection, it is apparent that these enterprises are in fact founded by, and operated for the benefit of particular individuals, families, or networks within those local communities. And the workers who produce profits in these enterprises either do not belong to that place, or do not belong to those families and networks. In short, the utilisation of place as an ideology and political and economic resource is polarising local societies and differentiating the proletariat.

At the same time, many of the socio-spatial features which once defined a specific place and people's position within that place are being overturned. People from outside the metropolis and the state-owned sector are invading and transforming the material culture, society and economy of the city. Peasants are employing urbanites in their industries. And, in crossing rural/urban boundaries, (dis)placed immigrant workers in cities are threatening old status hierarchies, 'iron rice bowl' jobs, and domestic sanctuaries. The succeeding section brings issues of place to the fore in analyses of recruitment and group stereotyping, work places, labour processes, and the wage labour bargain.

Part II
Experiences and Understandings of Waged Work

4 Recruitment: Segmenting Class

The recruitment of wage labour is essential to the main objective of the capitalist enterprise: that is, the production of profit. According to the managers and workers of the case study enterprises, that global objective is of paramount importance to the reworking of China's proletariat. However, there are a number of factors that affect the recruitment process in China which have important implications for the ways in which contract and temporary workers conceptualise themselves and their position relative to employers, and which thereby inform their understandings of capitalist production processes and the associated formation of collective social identities. State policies regarding different types of workers and jobs, prejudices about rurality and particular places of origin, and informal networking practices are all integral to recruitment and the capital-wage labour nexus in China. Workers' understandings are mediated by their experience of these factors not only in their search for work, but also in the organisation of the work place. Throughout this section, I shall seek to demonstrate that these same factors shape the images workers form of themselves and their employers as sometimes overlapping cross-class groups, rather than as two groups set in opposition by relations of ownership and employment.

This chapter explains how distinctive identities modify, and are modified by, enterprises' recruitment of contract and temporary employees, and, second, shows how these bear upon workers' experiences and interpretations of wage work. In the course of this, it also elucidates some of the ways in which the production and appropriation of profit is founded upon, and gives momentum, to non-class identities and relationships. For while these identities and relationships appear to hinge upon administratively and institutionally defined statuses, place and networking practices, they are at the same time critical to capitalist production relations and are being transformed by production relations as the value of workers' time, and the products of their labour, are measured more and more frequently in money terms.

The discussion is presented in four parts. Part one outlines three common stereotypes which influence employment patterns and the construction of collective social identities. The second part describes how people who are registered as rural or urban residents, or are local or non-local residents, experience competition in the job market in Hangzhou. Part three examines the differentiating effects of connections, or *guanxi,* in recruitment. Finally, I describe the terms under which employers induct workers, fixing some to their jobs, while casting others as easily expendable labour.

STEREOTYPING JOBS AND WORKERS

Stereotypes are exaggerated, 'chronically accessible constructs' about the essential attributes of groups of people (Abercrombie, Hill and Turner, 1984, pp. 242–3; Bierhoff, 1989, pp. 30, 108–9; Hagendoorn, 1993, pp. 33–6). People utilise stereotypes as summary models of reality, referring to them as guides for assessing social situations and choosing appropriate patterns of behaviour.

The allocation of workers on the basis of stereotypical assumptions about group characteristics such as gender or ethnic attributes, and a naturalised hierarchy of the desirability of these assumed characteristics, is a common motif in many national labour markets. Some scholars have argued persuasively that segmentation on the basis of pre-existing stereotypes individualises workers, allows greater managerial control over the organisation and pace of production, and reduces the possibilities for collective labour activism (Phizacklea and Miles, 1980; Gordon, Edwards and Reich, 1982; Willmott, 1987; Collinson, Knights and Collinson, 1990). This has important consequences. It not only allows management to maximise enterprise profitability, but it also gives substance to stereotypical models, thus reinforcing discriminatory attitudes and practices. Stereotypes may also be functional class constructs. Andrew Metcalfe (1990) provides an illustration of this in his examination of the discursive dehumanisation of coal miners by the British and Australian bourgeoisie: a dehumanisation which served to legitimise miners' oppression and exploitation.

While I find these ideas useful, I nevertheless believe that analyses of segmented labour forces must do more than simply reiterate the logical imperatives of capital or the circular consequences of material disadvantage. For one thing, many stereotypes which are instrumental in segmenting the work force are not originally or solely constructed in the work place, and are not simply consequential upon the requirements of capital and management for cheap docile labour. Moreover, while stereotypes can induce self-verifying actions and responses, they are not static. Stereotypes undergo constant, if subtle, change, propelled by the migration of people and capital, and by changes in technology, and political and production regimes (Bierhoff, 1989, pp. 25–6, 121–3; Gallino, 1989; Mennell, 1994). And finally, segmentation of labour forces may be concurrently consequence and cause of political policies and administrative practices. The making and remaking of stereotypes continually modifies the conditions under which people enter and act in the work force, thereby redrawing the boundaries of segmentation and altering social structural dynamics.

In urban China, there are strong assumptions about what sorts of people will occupy particular positions in the labour force. These assumptions not only reflect, but also affect, the ways in which the labour force is segmented. In particular, stereotypical notions influence who will be recruited, the terms under which workers are employed, and their training and promotion opportunities.

The identifying attributes of contract and temporary workers and, following David Knights (1990, p. 308), their constitution as worker-subjects, are shaped by a combination of socially constructed factors. Some of these, such as literacy and technical qualifications, are important in work forces throughout the world. Others which are consequent upon employment, such as income and internal career structures, are specific to enterprises and will be examined in later chapters. But in addition to these, there are three closely interrelated factors which are of unique significance to the social identity of entrants to the Chinese work force, to the way in which competition for jobs is played out, and to the conditions under which they are employed. These are, first, whether workers are registered as rural or urban residents; second, whether they are locals or outsiders and, if outsiders, whether they are negatively stereotyped by their place of origin; and, third, their job status as a permanent, contract or temporary worker. These circumstances have been rendered significant both by old prejudices and by more recent government policies and informal social practices.

Negative Images of *Nongmin*

In practice, as opposed to Confucian rhetoric and romance, rural producers historically have been held to be inferior to most other occupational groups in Chinese society, while literati-officials have stood at the apex of the social hierarchy. In the early Han, the Ming, the late Qing, and Republican periods alike, cities were valued as sites which generated power, status, and wealth (Granet, 1958; Pan and Fei, 1963, p. 12; Chow, 1966, pp. 230–42; Beattie, 1979, pp. 9–21; Faure, 1990).

Despite the CCP's professed aim of improving the condition of peasants and uniting all labouring groups, this urban dominated hierarchy of occupations remained intact through the Maoist period. Indeed, by depicting rural residents as a pre-modern population in need of education, political leadership and government by urban agents, and by channelling resources extracted from the agricultural sector into urban industrial development, Maoist policy and administrative practice actually exacerbated disparities between countryside and city, peasant and industrial worker (Potter, 1983, pp. 474–95; Nolan and White, 1984; Blecher, 1985; Cohen, 1993).

Partly, the persistence of anti-rural bias derives from party-state policies which reified and institutionalised the boundary between rural and urban populations. Since 1958, changing one's place of residence and occupation has not been not sufficient to change one's status as *nongmin*, because this was made an administrative category. Residential registration, called *hukou* or *huji*, was introduced so as to forestall rural-urban migration, guarantee raw material and food supplies to centres of industrial production, and allocate labour in the absence of a labour market (Tien, 1973; Kirkby, 1985; Zhang Qingwu, 1988). According to *hukou* regulations, people who have inherited matrilineally transmitted rural registration are prohibited from entering permanent employment in urban areas, and can only be employed on a contractual or temporary basis in the event that enterprises cannot fill vacancies with urban recruits (Blecher, 1983; Mallee, 1988). *Hukou*, as a formal classificatory system, simultaneously served to consolidate urbanites' belief that peasants were 'backward', and exacerbate rural-urban divisions within the work force.

Now, the *hukou* system is in decline. Less effort is channelled into overseeing registration, few people heed prohibitions on migration, and there have been proposals for the system to be phased out (Ding, 1989; *FEER*, 27 May 1993; *CND*, 27 April 1994). Yet it remains to be seen whether this actually will improve the urban labour market position of immigrant rural workers since it seems more likely that such a move would exert downward pressure on wages for semi- and unskilled urban workers: this trend would increase their sense of insecurity, encourage attempts to strengthen labour market and trade barriers, and add to hostilities towards outsiders.

Placing Outsiders in the Labour Market

Drawing distinctions between locals and outsiders is a persistent feature of social relations in China. William Rowe (1989) notes that in nineteenth-century Hankow, outsiders and lower class ruffians together were represented as a segment apart from respectable local society. He suggests that, along with natural disasters and the increasing ineptitude of the central bureau-cracy, the moral and public security threat represented by outsiders in Hankow actually consolidated a sense of urban community. Appeals to community unity served, in turn, to strengthen the economic and political might of the local elite. Helen Siu echoes Rowe's conclusions when she observes of the Nanxi townspeople in the 1980s: 'In their minds, the "peasants" from the sands are bad enough, and the "outsiders" (*waidi ren*) worse still. It is clear that many town residents feel besieged and threat-ened; but, to an extent, they have managed to keep their work and social life separate from those of the migrants' (1990, p. 77).

The distinction implied in the term 'outsider' is both broader and less flexible than the one drawn between people with whom one is familiar, and those who are outside one's circle of familiars (Gold, 1985, p. 664; Yang, 1989b, p. 40). In Hangzhou an outsider is one who was born and is registered outside the municipality, and who is not fluent in the local dialect. Moving one's registration to Hangzhou, learning the dialect, and living most of one's life in the city, are necessary, but not always sufficient, to become a local. Such a transformation may take more than one genera-tion. Differences between locals and outsiders are routinely invoked in manners, modes of speech, and in daily minutiae such as cooking methods.

With the recent emergence of new peri-urban sites of capital accumula-tion and increased numbers of immigrant job seekers, the actions of local governments, community groups, and enterprises in drawing and redraw-ing the boundaries between local people and outsiders has had consider-able structural effect in the labour market. Irrespective of the ownership status of enterprises, they are popularly thought to be a local community asset. This gives rise to expectations that people who are local residents will enjoy preference in hiring and promotion, the right to exercise super-visory control, and a share in the profits produced by outsiders in 'their' enterprises (*FBIS*, 8 January 1991; Thireau, 1991; *BKWZ*, 3 November 1992; Odgaard, 1992, pp. 170–80; *GRRB* 17 February 1993). Conversely, people defined as outsiders are disadvantaged in the labour market and within enterprises, as Huang Xiaojing and Yang Xiao have remarked: 'Tight employment barriers in all areas of the urban economic structure bar outsiders while guaranteeing employed urban residents a sort of "pro-fessional rent"' (1987, p.148).

Labour market discrimination between people who are registered as urban and rural residents, and between locals and outsiders, is compounded by typecasting about particular geographical places of origin. In her stud-ies of Subei immigrants in Shanghai, Emily Honig (1989, 1992) has shown that entrenched prejudice against Subei immigrants was originally sparked by their conspicuous poverty and different cultural practices. But their poverty and difference were compounded by the channelling of Subei people into unskilled, poorly remunerated jobs and much-hated Japanese enterprises before 1949; and after 1949 by the municipal government's failure to provide them with adequate education and housing and its exclusion of Subei people from political, administrative, and cultural organisations. The stereotyping of Subei people in Shanghai actually was reinforced by labour market segregation and discriminatory administrative practice.

In the 1990s anti-rural bias, local and outsider status and place of origin still sway enterprises' recruitment and promotion decisions, and organisation of the labour process. These identifying factors are also operationalised by job seekers keen to get exclusive information about the availability of work, and preference in hiring and promotion.

Job Status

Finally, I want to emphasise the import of ideas about job status upon the actions of those who are engaged in job-hunting and recruitment. The 1986 decision to grant new employees in state enterprises contractual rather than tenured positions and to encourage contract employment in other ownership sectors has been bedevilled by popular perceptions of contract positions not being 'real' jobs, and peoples' reluctance to be known as 'just' a contract worker (Luo, 1989; *FBIS*, 15 May 1991; Xia, 1992).

These attitudes have a more recent history than anti-rural bias and localism. Since 1949, contract workers have filled the least secure, most onerous and poorly remunerated manual and semi-skilled positions in urban industries (Howe, 1973a; Milton and Milton, 1976, pp. 186–90; Blecher, 1985). Many contract and temporary jobs have been filled by peasants who, for decades, have formed a reserve army of labour that has been used by the party-state to pressure tenured employees to accept poor working conditions and static wages (Howe, 1973b). The characterisation of contract work as temporary, unskilled, poorly paid, and fit only for peasants, subsequently reflects negatively upon the character of people who become contract workers.

When employers operate with a cognitive model of contract workers as being shiftless, poorly educated, and unruly they contribute to the production of a stereotype. They hire people who are considered appropriate for contract work, and may discourage applicants who, in their view, are too good for the job. In Shanghai, Deborah Davis (1990, p. 100) was told by street committee cadres and union officials that urban people who had contract jobs were poorly educated, long-term unemployed youths (see also *ZGLDB*, 18 June 1992, 15 December 1992). As the Chinese government attempts to achieve its aims of transforming the bulk of urban jobs into contract positions and widening the scope of the labour market, these perceptions have shaped spheres of competition in a labour market already compartmentalised by urban bias and localism.

Of course, in keeping with contemporary media propaganda emphasising the importance of open and equal competition to the growth of a national labour market and enterprise profitability, and the profit dictates to which they are now subject, enterprise managers and recruitment staff state that they select workers on the basis of their suitability for the job. But what makes a worker 'suitable'? Managers' primary concern in recruitment might be to assert control over the shop floor, extend their social connections or increase their power in the local community. Similarly, the objectivity of the criteria which influences the selection of employees is frequently spurious. Recruiters choose between applicants on the basis of gut reactions which are, frequently, informed by stereotypes. An examination of the importance of *hukou* in China's labour market substantiates Jenkins' comment that 'The power to make one's models count in the construction of social reality is vital to an explanation of the outcomes in labour markets' (1986, p. 19; see also Coughlan, 1991; Deetz, 1992, p. 22).

COMPETITION FOR JOBS AND THE SIGNIFICANCE OF HUKOU: INSTITUTIONALISING OUTSIDER-NESS

The causal links between social categorisation, the formation of groups, and patterns of group interaction are exceedingly complex. Nevertheless, it seems clear that the act of categorisation may in itself be sufficient to provide the impetus for group formation, and influence both external and internal constructions of group identity (Turner, 1987, p. 28; Rothbart and Taylor, 1992, p. 23). Competition can ensue as soon as people start to define themselves, or are defined as insiders (urbanites or locals) and outsiders. If groups compete over a scarce resource, such as jobs in a labour surplus economy, then solidarity within the ingroup is likely to be enhanced while antipathy towards the outgroup will become more intense (Bierhoff, 1989, pp. 134–41; Maas and Arcuri, 1992; Hagendoorn, 1993, pp. 26–44). With specific reference to immigrant workers, I will consider the operation of *hukou* in delineating separate domains in the Hangzhou labour market, then elaborate upon the way *hukou* stereotypes have affected people's perceptions and behaviour in ways which further impact upon recruitment processes.

Spheres of Competition

The labour market in China is a buyer's market. Competition for jobs is already strong, and will become stronger. Given present rates of population growth, urbanisation, and rural–urban migration, over the next 50 years the size of the work force in urban areas is likely to double to between 640 million and 699 million (*FBIS*, 26 December 1990; Shen and Spence, 1993, pp. 15–16). To provide jobs for such an enormous work force, Shen and Spence (1993) estimate that the Chinese economy will have to sustain an average rate of growth of 9 per cent per annum for the next half century. Yet the intensity of job competition in Chinese cities is largely hidden for, according to official statistics, urban unemployment levels are remarkably low.

There are two reasons why the current unemployment statistics do not give a reliable indication of the numbers of people competing for jobs in urban areas. First, statistics on those 'awaiting employment', refer only to unemployed urban residents. They thus neglect the employment situation of significant numbers of adults who are registered in the countryside, but reside in cities.[1] In cities such as Hangzhou, rural immigrants comprise up to one-third of the total labour force, and this proportion is expected to increase (*QJWB*, 24 December 1992). The omission of immigrants from unemployment statistics is significant because, as a consequence of government policies and local practice, the great majority arrive without any firm job prospects and, when they do find employment, predominate in those sectors in which there are high rates of turnover. Indeed, as I noted in Chapter 2, immigrant workers' job insecurity is inferred by the very terms which people use to describe 'regular' local and 'temporary' outside workers.

The second reason why statistics understate the degree of competition for jobs is that many new jobs are given to people who, on paper, are already employed. Chinese economists suggest that up to one-half of the state enterprise work force are surplus to enterprise requirements and should be made redundant (*FBIS*, 7 November 1991; *GRRB*, 8 June 1992; *JPRS*, 16 February 1992; *ZGLDB*, 20 October 1992; *ZJRB*, 26 October 1992). One way government departments and state enterprises have avoided the potentially destabilising issue of redundancy is by establishing subsidiaries or LSCs with the specific objective of providing jobs for surplus employees (*SWB*, 28 January 1994). In Hangzhou, unemployed informants complained bitterly about the numbers of jobs being created or reserved for enterprises' 'own people'. One obvious effect of this practice is to intensify competition for those jobs which are open to all applicants.

In the context of strong competition for jobs, one of the most salient attributes of job seekers – an even more fundamental factor than their qualifications, work experience, or sex – is their *hukou*. *Hukou* sets the disadvantaged terms under which rural people enter the job market, and allocates them to the least attractive positions both in the economy and in individual enterprises. The importance of *hukou* is evident in the different types of positions which are open to rural and urban registered people, in the ways that the importance of education and sex in the labour market are mediated by *hukou*, and in the manner in which *hukou* inflected stereotypes affect recruitment processes and employees' careers. Because these issues strongly influence workers' experiences and understandings of the labour market, work place relations, and social identities, they warrant closer examination.

All my informants concurred that the only jobs open to rural immigrants were the ones city people refused to countenance:

Li: It's difficult for people with rural registration to get good jobs. We can only get the ones city people don't want.
Small group leader (interrupting from the table behind us): It's ridiculous isn't it? We have the same habits, speak the same language, get the same education, and we can't do the same jobs. If a job is worth having they always say only city people can apply. (Fieldnotes, 29 October 1992)

The majority of jobs undertaken by rural registered workers are short-term positions which lack the benefits which accrue to permanent and contract-system posts. Most contracts expire after two years. But many rural immigrants are not employed on contract. Their resultant insecurity allows employers to pressure them to maximise productivity. Party Secretary Zhao, the boyfriend of one of my neighbours, told me that the state leather factory in which he works only employs rural immigrants as temporaries:

From a formal point of view we should go through the labour bureau to get temporary workers, but if we do that they have to be given contracts. And then if they are contract workers, the factory has to pay for their medical insurance, all those sorts of benefits, almost as much as the regular workers ... The best thing is to hire experienced workers, ones who have already been trained. A lot come from Jiangxi. It's poor there. When they come from poor places like that and don't have contracts they will keep their minds on their jobs ... Now it's just like this: if you want workers, you employ them directly. If you want to sack them, you can just sack them. That's the situation for temporaries. (Tape, 19 February 1993)

In contrast, the contract positions given to urban residents tend to utilise material incentives rather than the threat of dismissal to encourage productivity.

The jobs available to rural immigrants are also considered second-rate because they are labour intensive, dirty, and dangerous. In Hangzhou, immigrant workers are employed in textile and clothing manufacture, chemical and pharmaceutical production, construction, transportation, sanitation, domestic service and foundries (Interview, Xihu Statistics Department, 23 November 1989). A national survey of 50 different occupations ranks these jobs amongst the lowest 10 by prestige score (Lin and Wen, 1988; *CD*, 15 February 1989). Moreover, as the status, conditions and safety pertaining to specific jobs declines, the proportion of immigrant workers employed in them increases. In the mid- and late 1980s when companies engaged in foreign trade, finance and tourism were inundated by young urban job seekers, the city's unprofitable old silk factories could only fill 4 per cent of their recruitment quota from urban applicants. The shortfall was made up by rural immigrants who, within a few years, comprised 25 per cent of the work force in the silk industry (*Hangzhou shi dangqian shiyong nongmingong*; Feng and Jiang, 1987; Wu, 1991; *ZJRB*, 21 June 1992). Another illustration of the structuring effect of *hukou* in the labour market is that tenured urban foundry workers take extended leave during the hot summer months, and their places are temporarily filled by immigrants (Interview, Personnel Department Zhejiang University, 8 November 1989; *CD*, 19 February 1990). Similarly, national reports indicate that the incidence of industrial injuries and deaths amongst immigrant workers in cities is much higher than that amongst urbanites (*ZGLDB*, 26 May 1992, 6 June 1992, 6 February 1993; *GRRB*, 25 February 1993).

Hence, it is apparent that although some media reports suggest rural immigrants are occupying jobs which should be given to unemployed urban youth (*HZRB*, 3 February 1993; *SWB*, 6 January 1994), in actuality urban and rural people rarely compete for the same positions. Immigrants are excluded from jobs which offer security, high pay, promotional opportunities, and status, whilst Hangzhou youths say they would prefer unemployment to working alongside peasants. In short, *hukou* delineates exclusive spheres in the city's labour market.

Segmentation of the labour market by *hukou* is reinforced by the greater likelihood that urban youth will receive a post-secondary education (*ZJTJNJ 1992*, p. 482). Despite the state's policy of positive discrimination with respect to educational funding in rural areas, urbanites' superior education is seen by rural people to be the result of administrative bias. Not only are urban children said to enjoy better secondary schooling but, most importantly of all, they are also thought to be able to enter colleges and universities with lower grades than their rural peers. A young woman, Han, whom I met at dinner at my neighbours' apartment, launched into a litany of complaints when I asked her where she was from and how she had found her job:

> It's been a problem to me all my life, my *hukou*. My mother is registered near Ningbo, so that's where I had to go to school. Then when I did the entrance exams for university, if I had been at a city school, I would have made it. But the marks for us in the countryside were higher than for city people, so I didn't get in. I had to find work. It's always been like that. If you come from the countryside and don't know anyone you can only work as a labourer. A temporary worker in production … If I had an urban *hukou* I wouldn't have any trouble getting a good job, getting into a good unit, even if I didn't have better *guanxi* than I have now, because I'm not stupid. I'm capable and quite well educated. I can use my brain. But as it is I have to think myself lucky that I have a reasonably clean, light temporary job on a production line in a factory in Hangzhou. (Fieldnotes, 5 February 1993)

Rural immigrants who are ambitious enough to try to overcome their *hukou* handicap through further education have to contend with entrenched prejudices and the received wisdom that peasants are fit only for unskilled jobs. Aihua's young cousin, Chunhua, wanted an office job in Hangzhou. To this end, she spent five months in the city taking self-funded night courses in English, typing, and computing to supplement her higher middle school studies. Aihua, wise in the ways of the city, joked about Chunhua's belief that people could compete for jobs solely on the basis of skill: 'She believes the newspaper propaganda! How could anyone be so naive?' Eventually, unable to find a job in Hangzhou despite her hard-won qualifications, Chunhua went back to her village to work in a local factory.

The significance of *hukou* in defining job choices and life chances varies according to sex. Females tend to marry hypergamously, so even though residential status is inherited matrilineally it is considered to be more important for males to have urban *hukou* than for females.[2] Li, an eighteen-year-old immigrant employed at Jinshagang factory, had to weigh up the importance to her brother of purchasing an urban *hukou* against her own chance of furthering her education and thus becoming eligible for an urban job. Like Han, Li had missed out on university entrance by a few exam points. Having spent long, boring hours at a factory desk assembling electric plugs, she bitterly regretted not having won those few points, and vowed she would study harder if she had another opportunity to take the exams. But her parents would have had to provide for her if she continued studying. Although she said that they had always upheld her decisions, she was unwilling to ask this of them because they were struggling to save up 15 000 yuan to buy her brother an urban *hukou*.[3] This was critical to his career and marriage prospects:

> He can get a contract in the unit he is working in now, in the department store, if he has an urban *hukou*. He can work as a contract system worker instead of a temporary, and then he can get bonuses and health coverage, things like that. If he has an urban *hukou* and a contract job it would make him a regular worker ... And then it would be easier for him to find a partner. He could marry a girl from either the country-side or the city. He couldn't do that with a rural *hukou*. (Fieldnotes, 30 January 1993)

Li pondered the situation for two weeks before deciding not only that she would not go home to study, but also that she would not leave the factory at all. I will return to consider the logic of Li's choice when I examine the effects of *guanxi* in the labour market.

Reinterpreting *Hukou*: Rural Immigrants as a Social Problem

It is an almost universal phenomena for recently arrived migrant workers to occupy the least attractive positions in urban labour markets (Roberts, 1978; Cohen, 1988). This fact, together with the ways in which jobs are re-valued and job seekers are categorised, suggests that Chinese government regulations specifying the conditions under which rural residents can be employed by urban units are not the only factors channelling rural immigrants into particular niches in the urban labour force. How is *hukou* rendered so significant?

Rural immigrants to China's cities are described as a serious social problem by government agents and the urban media. Several interconnected streams of public discourse describe this problem group in the same tropes of disorder, danger, promiscuity, and pollution which are applied to the rural population is general. One of the most powerful of these discursive streams depicts a 'floating population' which 'blindly floods' into cities in search of work each spring. These terms, which underline the fact that rural people have left their place of registration and have no pre-arranged job to come to, are repeated at some point in almost all media reports on rural immigrants (*RMRB*, 22 February 1989; Dai and

Li, 1992, pp. 151–2; *HZRB*, 3 February 1993; *ZGLDB*, 7 January 1993, 13 February 1993). But the terms also imply that this movement is something akin to a natural phenomenon which lacks rational intent and organisation (*SWB*, 25 January 1994, 28 January 1994). Thus, migrant workers are not shown to be motivated by an evaluation of their situation in the countryside (which, perhaps, encompasses landlessness, poverty, lack of access to capital, unemployment) as against the possibility of finding work in cities. Nor are they shown to be keen to learn new skills, increase their social contacts, or expand their cultural horizons. Instead, they are commonly compared with vagrants, blown by seasonal winds and unreasoning caprice.[4]

The arrival of these interlopers in the city is represented as disorganising those things which make urban life safe and civilised. Thus, media reports frequently accuse immigrants of imposing an insupportable burden upon urban food and water supplies, overloading sanitation and transportation services, and disrupting the 'orderly disposition of labour resources' (*CD*, 27 February 1989, 4 April 1989; *HZRB*, 3 February 1993; *ZGLDB*, 7 January 1993; *SWB*, 28 January 1994). They are also said to threaten public security. A disproportionate amount of urban crime, particularly theft, is attributed to outsiders. They lower moral standards and spread venereal diseases, because of the poverty which drives them into prostitution, and the sexual promiscuity which results from their 'natural' lack of self-discipline (Interviews with heads of Qiushi neighbourhood committee 24 November 1992, Yuquan police station 23 December 1992; *ZGLDB*, 15 August 1992, 7 January 1993).

Having identitifed outsiders as a social problem, state offices are asked to intercede to remedy that problem. Consider, for example, an article from *Zhongguo laodong bao* (15 August 1992) which focused upon immigrant residents of 'Zhejiang village' in the southern suburbs of Beijing. The author appealed to what were assumed to be the readers' common urban values by dwelling at length upon the chaos and dirt which had come in the wake of the outsiders and rendered the suburb uninhabitable for urban residents. Readers were invited to share the journalist's disgust at the way the suburb's infrastructure had deteriorated to the point that it had come to resemble a village, and the unbridled promiscuity which must have resulted from itinerant men and women sharing cramped quarters. This inevitably would have increased demand for illicit gynaecological clinics. The article concluded by asking readers, 'Is this a healthy development, or a cancerous growth?' The bio-medical rhetoric in which the question was framed simultaneously naturalised urbanites' prejudice against outsiders, and legitimated the radical surgery that was later undertaken to rid the city of this 'cancerous growth'. Much of Zhejiang village was bulldozed.

Similarly, on 15 February 1993, the Hangzhou television station's evening news programme covered the arrival of thousands of job seeking immigrants at the railway station, and their occupation of a nearby dusty park which was used as a venue for informal hiring. For the twenty seconds it took the commentator to announce that the problem was worse this spring than in previous years, the camera panned over the people in the park clustering around the bosses and their recruiting agents, or squatting on top of their belongings, and then closed in for a portrait shot of two bewhiskered old men in ragged blue padded jackets holding their carpentry tools. A reporter then interviewed the Hangzhou railway station master, the head of the police station nearest the railway, and the head of the local district's labour bureau. They all bemoaned the added work load which they had to bear, and appealed to Hangzhou people to be vigilant against the influx of thieves and ruffians in the midst of the 'blind tide'. They also warned people not to employ immigrants: it would be illegal because they had breached *hukou* regulations, and it would be inadvisable because, as outsiders, they might be unreliable or dishonest (see also *HZRB*, 3 February 1993). Not one of the job seekers in the park was interviewed.

This popular media discourse on rural immigrants as a social problem translates at street level into spontaneous acts of vilification and violence. On each of my visits to the railway park to talk with the immigrants camping there, policemen, representatives of the local neighbourhood committee, and local workers yelled abuse at them and warned me to stay away because they were 'dangerous' and 'untrustworthy'. When I took photographs which could be posted home as proof of their safe arrival, I was chastised for focusing upon an 'abnormality' in Chinese society: 'They aren't worth seeing. They're so dirty and uncivilised. Take photographs of your university friends at West Lake instead' (Fieldnotes, 4 February 1993). On my last trip to the park, two men with whom I was chatting and exchanging addresses were attacked without provocation and beaten around the head by police officers. I was told by several people, including one off-duty railway guard, that the beating I had witnessed was a common occurrence:

> They hit peasants all the time. Especially at Spring Festival. There are so many of them, they all crowd into the carriages and the washrooms on the trains and they're dirty. They jostle around and make them feel uncomfortable, so they punch them. Peasants don't know much anyway, don't understand anything about the law, so the police can do whatever

they like to them. Besides, they really do smell bad. (Fieldnotes, 9 February 1993; see also *SCMP*, 9 October 1991)

Rural immigrants are given no voice in the discourses which denigrate them. They can only contest their stereotyping as a social problem in anecdotes which illustrate the extent to which they share in the tribulations of urban residents, and aspire to a common dignity and morality. Yet these same anecdotes illuminate the disempowering effects of their categorisation as an alien 'other' in urban society:

> The police always get tough when they hear our accents. Even when we have done nothing wrong they shout at us and hit us. People like us, we wouldn't dare report anything stolen to the local police because they would treat us as though we are the ones who have committed the crime. They are really frightening. We just have to put up with having things stolen or being beaten up ... I've lost a lot too – bikes, clothes from the washing line, buckets – stolen by vagabonds. You know, some outsiders just stay a month or two then move on. They don't care what people think of them, they have no face, just go wherever they can earn a bit of money or steal something else. They are really bad. So, a few are like that and they are the ones Hangzhou people think are representative of us all. They think we are bad because we are outsiders. (Fieldnotes, 7 February 1993)

Immigrants also contest local residents' belief that outsiders are *nixing*, or 'dirty' in Hangzhou dialect. They point out that their dirtiness results from their employment by locals. Yet their sensitivity to this charge was brought home to me by Yang, the Shaoxing shoemender who, every day, sat and worked on the pavement opposite our apartment, when he and his brother-in-law came to share a cup of tea after work. When I asked him how Hangzhou people perceived rural immigrants, Yang responded:

> They look down on us. How can I put it? It's like this. I've come into your home tonight and everything is really clean. I'll make it all dirty with my dusty shoes and clothes and cigarette butts. That's what Hangzhou people think. As soon as we leave, they would start cleaning up after us. Of course, you know we don't mean to leave a mess behind, because we have been out on the street working and that's how it is ... We have left our footprints on the floor. But the Hangzhou people, they don't like us for that. (Tape 2 February, 1993)

Rurality is, of course, a relative and highly contested term. Rural registered residents of villages adjoining Hangzhou subscribe to the notion of immigrants as a social problem while asserting their own identification with local urban society. In Jinshagang where there has been an expansion of the municipal limits and construction of roads, urban enterprises, and institutions on village land, some villagers have been compensated for their loss of land with urban registration. Most, however, are still rural registered. In the cold factory storeroom in which she is a clerk, Ge said sadly that she rarely has time to go out with her old school friends. She is always doing overtime, while her friends work office hours in the city. When I asked her why she had not gone to work alongside her friends, she answered that they had become urbanites whilst she was still a *nongmin*. Then, perhaps anticipating that this admission might influence my opinion of her, Ge hurried on in a defensive tone:

> I don't really think that it's a problem having a rural *hukou*. I don't feel as though I am disadvantaged. ... Some Hangzhou people still discriminate against us, they think they are better than we are, even people like us who aren't farming but live in the suburbs. We people in Jinshagang aren't any different to city people now ... I don't think any less of myself for having rural registration. I work hard, do a good job, am well educated, earn a good wage. Why should I feel inferior? Of course, it's a different matter if you consider people from poor areas, mountain villages. Lots of Hangzhou people make jokes about people who come from Zhuji or, even worse, Anhui, making them out to be ridiculous. (Fieldnotes, 10 November 1992)

The representation of rural immigrants as a social problem has inevitable repercussions for their participation in the labour market. The ways in which a *hukou* inflected discourse is informally operationalised in the labour market and recruitment sessions concurrently discriminates against immigrant workers and splits the work force, setting urban employees apart from their rural colleagues.

Recruiting Outsiders

The party-state supports the notion that in a socialist market economy there should be fair competition in the labour market. Enterprise owners and managers say they are keen to get the most productive workers available. Nevertheless, *hukou* boundaries and the discursive construction of outsiders as a social problem are deeply internalised and continue to sway decisions by enterprise recruitment officers.

According to Jinshagang's manager, people who seek employment at the factory are evaluated solely according to meritocratic criteria.[5] A test is supposed to determine their level of literacy, comprehension of the factory's quality and discipline requirements, and their willingness to work hard. However, during enlistment sessions for assembly workers at Jinshagang factory, I repeatedly witnessed discrimination against people who had rural registration, and those who came from the poorest, most remote villages fared worst.

For Su, who is the young urban-registered, university educated recruitment officer at Jinshagang, *hukou* is still the most important criteria by which to judge people. He says he consciously has to remind himself that he is surrounded by *nongmin* while he is at work, so he does not make inappropriate jokes. Su defends his prejudices against people with rural registration by stating that regardless of Jinshagang villagers' transfer into non-agricultural employment and their improved living standards, they still exhibit a 'small-peasant mentality'. He claims, with justification, that the dislike he feels for suburban villagers and rural immigrants is shared by many natives of Hangzhou. But, perhaps because many of the applicants he meets at the factory come from poverty-stricken villages in Anhui, Su says that Hangzhou residents direct their greatest contempt at Anhui peasants (see also *ZJRB*, 17 October 1992).

When Su interviews job applicants, his assessment is influenced less by their education or motivation than by his prejudice against *nongmin* generally, and immigrants from Anhui in particular. At the same time, he reveals his attitude by his choice of words, tone of voice and physical movements. When job seekers enter the factory office, they face the open end of a U-shape made up of office furniture and equipment. If they come alone, Su, who sits closest to the door, examines them to ascertain from their appearance where they are from. If they look like customers or Hangzhou residents, he stands to greet them and invite them in to sit down. If they are outsiders, he remains seated and allows them to continue standing. This means that each time anyone enters or leaves the room, the hovering applicant must move into the corner behind the door. The interview is a simple procedure. Su just hands the job seeker a form to complete. He asks very few questions, and rarely looks at the applicant. He also resists any attempts on their part to elicit information about the enterprise, the work they will be required to do, or job conditions. Most people understand his gestures and conversational closures as clear signals of disapproval, and respond by adopting what Huspek (1994) describes as subordinate codes of behaviour and speech: silence, an awkward stand at attention, heads and eyes cast down, and the prefacing of any questions with honorific terms and apologies for their failure to understand.

If there are too many applicants for vacancies, Su chooses between them on the basis of his 'impression':

> Maybe because some people write more clearly than others. I'm not actually sure how I make that decision. If they come from Hangzhou, yes. It's easier to give them jobs then... When they are Hangzhou people, I feel more comfortable talking to them, even if they have rural *hukou*. They are a bit more civilised than the outsiders. (Fieldnotes, 6 November 1992)

Su also explained how he can tell whether people are from villages near Hangzhou, or are outsiders:

> By their accent, and also by their faces, the way they look, clothes. Hangzhou people are very clean. But these outsiders, some of them really stink! They don't wash, or only occasionally. The girl next to me in the office is always complaining about them, saying "Those stinking outsiders!" ...Haven't you noticed? It makes me feel sick sometimes, having to deal with them. (Fieldnotes, 3 December 1992)

Su's preconceptions about immigrant peasants tug him in opposite directions in making recruitment decisions, depending on his own experiences in the factory. When he thinks his talents are being appreciated and he positively values his job, then he favours Hangzhou applicants as recruits. When he is discontented, he favours outsiders because 'they are stupid and uncivilised'. After Spring Festival in 1993, when Su was disappointed with the bonus he received, he began to dissuade locals from applying for jobs by suggesting to them that they take the form home and consider their application carefully: 'the work is tiring and there is a lot of overtime'. Su consciously employs his model of outsiders as inferior people in a strategy of sabotage within the firm:

> In a few months' time they will discover that a lot of these new workers I have been giving jobs to are useless and they will have to send them away. But even if they are completely stupid, they are still too good to work for those people. I suppose in a month or two when I don't feel so angry I will start asking more questions, making sure they can read and write. (Fieldnotes, 2 February 1993)

Although labour market segmentation and the disadvantageous position of rural immigrants stand employers in good stead by providing them with a cheap, flexible, and unorganised pool of labour, rural and outsider stereotypes are not simply recent creations. Rather, old anti-rural prejudices and patterns of localism have been energised by the emergence of a highly competitive labour market during the 1980s and the channeling of *nongmin* into unpopular jobs, the media's and government departments' identification of immigrants as a social problem, and the growth of firms whose labour forces reflect, and are sensitised to, the prejudicial beliefs of recruitment officers. What this means, of course, is that workers come into the work place differentiated by *hukou* and outsiderness. The effects of that differentiation are further compounded by the workings of *guanxi*.

PROLETARIAN CONNECTIONS: *GUANXI*

Guanxi refers not only to social connections or relationships, but more frequently to a field of particularistic ties, the instrumentalist use of contacts and social networks, and informally regulated modes of social interaction and exchange (Liu, 1983b; Gold, 1985; Yang, 1986, 1989b; Yan, 1996). The use of *guanxi* is not strictly synonymous with the exercise of personal power because it is a form of interactive participation. Indeed, the art of *guanxi* may temporarily invert relationships of superiority and inferiority, and introduce new axes of obligation.

Guanxi is significant in recruitment and in influencing non-tenured workers' understandings of social relations in two distinct, but interrelated ways. First, in a job search, people utilise their contacts with those who possess some measure of social capital or familiarity with an enterprise to inform them of vacancies, introduce them to people within the enterprise who can influence recruitment decisions, and pressure potential employers to give them a job. Moreover, concomitant issues which I tangentially refer to here, and will consider in detail in following chapters, are that well connected workers have different duties and receive better treatment than those who are not well connected. Thus, *guanxi* fragments work forces, and structures social relationships outside the work place.

Second, the ability to use one's contacts to secure a desired objective, such as getting a job or an unwarranted promotion, expresses a measure of facility. In this respect, as well as being a means to achieve particular aims, *guanxi* is a mark of the social aptitude, and thus identity, of individuals, families, and groups. Therefore, while *guanxi* is viewed in a utilitarian light by most job seekers, it is also important to keep in mind the way it functions symbolically to distinguish between workers specifically, and groups of people in general.

Recruiting Workers through *Guanxi*

Word of mouth is one of the most common means by which Chinese enterprises find and recruit employees (Yang, 1991; Zhang, 1993). According to the managers of the case study enterprises, hiring workers who are introduced by associates and employees reduces hiring costs and delays.[6] Of even greater importance, though, is the expectation that the reciprocal norms of *guanxi* which are brought into play through informal recruitment practices, and the preferential conditions of employment which are given to familiars, help stabilise the work force and maximise backbone workers' loyalty to the enterprise. The employer, as job-giver, achieves a position of superiority relative to both the new employee and their intermediary contact. For their part, the employee becomes indebted not only to their contact for having introduced them to their employer, but also to their employer for the 'gift' of the job (Jenkins, 1986, p. 136; Yang, 1989b, p. 43).

In fiercely competitive labour markets, job hunters must use all the social connections at their disposal.[7] Workers frequently said that using *guanxi* was the only way to find a position which offered any advantages. Although it has been suggested that males benefit from their use of *guanxi* in job searches more than do females (Davis, 1992a, pp. 1082–5; Bian, 1994), amongst the workers with whom I spoke there was no discernible difference between the sexes. Almost all said that they got their jobs because they were familiar with someone in the firm, or had been introduced by relatives, friends or fellow villagers to staff in the firm. The few exceptions were either people who had graduated from technical colleges and clearly were employed because of their skills, or day labourers who were not even considered to be part of the work force by other temporaries in the enterprise.

Guanxi further benefits local residents relative to outsiders in the search for jobs, and benefits those workers who have good *guanxi* with managerial staff relative to those who only have connections on the shop floor, or, even worse, those who have no *guanxi* in the firm. Owing to the presence of family, old school friends, teachers, and neighbours, and their long term association with a range of local organisations and institutions, local residents have a much wider and better placed network of contacts upon which to call in a job search than immigrants. The route by which Su, the recruiting officer at the Jinshagang factory, found his first job is a well trodden one:

My mother's old secondary school student is in charge of a department in the local government. He has pretty good *guanxi* with our boss, Mao, so every time the factory needs the government's permission to do something they go through this man. When my mother mentioned to him that I wanted a job in the area, something light, he invited me to his office, introduced me to Mao and said I was looking for a job. Mao had to take me on, give me something good. Otherwise our friend would have lost face and the next time Mao wanted a license or something from the government he would have been refused. The guy would have made life hard for him. (Fieldnotes, 10 November 1992)

In addition to having recourse to extensive social networks, local residents also benefit from the obligation informally imposed upon 'their' firms to provide jobs for them, and grant them preferential treatment (Granick, 1991, pp. 272–4; Lu Jianhua, 1991). Thus, because Zhejiang University's LSC is an investor in Sanxian bakery, the bakery is often instructed to employ urban residents who are the spouses or offspring of university staff. Because these people sign a contract with the LSC rather than the bakery, they receive more generous non-wage benefits than their colleagues.

Villagers similarly enjoy preference in recruitment by local TVEs (Gelb, 1990; Meng, 1990; Zhang Gang, 1993). Sometimes, village governments directly allocate local residents to collective enterprises. On other occasions, residents owe their employment to their connections within the village. Jinshagang's store clerk, Ge, has benefited from both these situations. After finishing higher middle school, Ge was assigned by the village government to a job in a collective lathe factory. When the lathe factory needed to reduce its work force, she was paid by the government to spend six months in Suzhou undertaking further training as a lathe operator. Because she did not like working in the male environment of machining and wanted to return to Jinshagang, Ge's parents appealed to their friend, manager Mao, to find her a position in 'his' factory.

Immigrants also use *guanxi* to find jobs. In fact, because they are disadvantaged by their *hukou* and entrenched anti-rural prejudices, tend to be less educated, and are excluded from the preferential hiring schemes just outlined, they appear to be even more reliant upon their connections than are local residents. When Aihua's husband was unemployed for a short period, I asked if he was looking through the job advertisements that appeared in Hangzhou's daily newspapers. She scoffed: 'People like us can't get jobs through newspapers! Uneducated outsiders don't have a hope! We just have to have an introduction. Units that advertise always want higher middle school or technical school graduates with urban *hukou*' (Fieldnotes, 19 September 1992). However, outsiders' utilisation of *guanxi* in job searches tends to be different in scope, and less effective than that of locals. In keeping with their patterns of chain migration, outsiders depend upon advice and introductions from fellow villagers and relatives who have lived in Hangzhou for long periods. And these people tend to be less well placed and less powerful than those called upon by local job seekers.

These difficulties were made clear to me by the tribulations of Yang, the Shaoxing shoemaker. When his wife came to join him in Hangzhou, Yang was unable to find work for her despite asking all his fellow villagers, neighbours and customers if they knew of anyone needing a cleaner, nanny, labourer, or production line worker. After a few months, she returned home, crestfallen. No sooner had she gone than his brother-in-law arrived to look for a job. He grumbled that he had to leave the Shanghai construction gang in which he had been working, because 'I didn't have any *guanxi* with the building contractor. If they don't know you they don't pay much, and they give you all the heavy, dirty jobs.' After spending several days squatting on a stool chatting with locals while he helped Yang straighten umbrella spokes and pull out tacks, he was offered some labouring work with a Shaoxing builder. Yang reflected on the opportunities and costs associated with establishing social connections in the city when he told me the good news about his brother-in-law's job:

> It takes time, getting to know people and getting things set up so you can get by ... People's relationships with one another are all monetary relationships, and we outsiders don't have any money. If you eat dinner at a new friend's house you are costing them money, taking the money from their pockets. Every cup of tea costs money. It all costs money just to be part of it ... But without the connections you can't get by, can't get anything done. (Fieldnotes, 5 March 1993)

Yang's words suggest that social structural inequalities limit the scope of people's *guanxi* networks and, concurrently, are sustained by their utilisation of *guanxi*. These mutual causal effects are spelt out in the complaints of a dispirited young baker:

> *Guanxi!* Younger sister's husband's brother's friend who is an official! That is why some get good jobs and others don't! To get *guanxi* you need to give presents, to give presents you need money, and to earn lots of money you need *guanxi*, see? We haven't got anything. No money, no *guanxi*, and no opportunities. That's why we are temporary workers. (Fieldnotes, 28 July 1992)

Guanxi versus Merit, *Guanxi* as Merit in Recruitment

Although the great majority of my informants supported meritocratic competition in recruitment as an ideal, they also expressed the opinion that in reality *guanxi* is of greater importance in a job search than either educational qualifications or experience. Regardless of intelligence and education, a person with very good connections could always expect to find a good job. This was held to be true in enterprises of all ownership types. Informants who intended to pursue further education so as to be better placed in the labour market said that this step was necessary precisely because they lacked *guanxi*. However, they did not expect further education to wholly compensate for that lack.

Li's decision not to leave Jinshagang factory and return home to study for the university entrance exams provides one example of the way in which *guanxi* influences behaviour in the labour market. Li's resolution was prompted partly by the fact that she felt beholden to her aunt and uncle for having used their *guanxi* with the Jinshagang factory manager to get her a job. They would consider her ungrateful and irresponsible if she left before the expiry of her contract. An even more important consideration, however, was that she doubted whether, even if she did manage to gain entrance to university and complete a degree, she would be able to find a job which offered any more personal satisfaction or opportunities for promotion than the one she already had:

> We just don't have enough *guanxi*... What it comes down to is that a unit might have vacancies for computer operators, technicians or something like that, but they will give the job to a relative or a friend's son, and tell them to do a short course. It won't make any difference even if you are qualified and experienced. It's always the same, *guanxi* and arse licking! (Fieldnotes, 30 January 1993)

Li's claim that the absence of educational qualifications can be overlooked in favour of *guanxi* was substantiated just a few days afterwards in a story told to me by Zhao, Party Secretary at the state-owned leather factory. The daughter of an old friend of their company's general manager had wanted to change work units, and the task of placing her was passed on to the leather factory's manager. Because she had such exalted connections, the manager had to ensure that the contract system job given the woman had reasonably high status and light duties. He sent her to the factory's accounts section. To make room for her, one of the qualified accountants was demoted to the production line. The accountant protested in vain against their unjustified demotion and eventually resigned, while the new 'accountant' was sent to night school for two years to acquire the knowledge and diploma necessary to perform her job.

The fact that *guanxi* mediates the significance accorded education and skill in recruitment, and the effect of intermediaries' prestige in determining the sorts of jobs people get, does not simply discount meritocratic ideals. Instead, as I noted above, it provides a powerful alternative schema for differentiating between the adept and the inept. When people discuss their job options, they constantly affirm the importance of *guanxi*, referring to themselves as being unable to find or go through a back door, having no routes or ways out, and thus being unable to find a good job, or boasting about how they could get a particularly good job because of their *guanxi*. Yet the same people who told me they could not find an agreeable job because they did not have *guanxi* often said they considered personal ability to be the most critical determinant of an individuals' occupational position. Being able to use *guanxi* to find a desirable job is, thus, a reflection of aptitude. This logic was vividly illustrated in a conversation between two young friends, a baker and a carpenter, about the relative importance of factors contributing toward upward social mobility:

> Carpenter: I reckon it's individual ability, that's the most important thing. Other factors are pretty much the same.
> Baker: Yes, I do too. If you are really capable, then you can manage good *guanxi*, all these things can be seen as the result of individual ability, can't they? If you are capable you will have good *guanxi*...
> Carpenter: You definitely need that to begin with, that person like a relative or a friend, or someone who is an official. (Tape, 17 January 1993)

According to this logic, the better *guanxi* networks of local residents as against those of outsiders infers that they are, at least in social terms, more capable. Similarly, amongst both locals and outsiders, those who lack *guanxi* in the work place and are delegated to the hardest, least well paid tasks are there exactly because they do not have the ability to get a better position. This conceptualisation of the labour market outcomes of networking in terms of meritocratic ideals consolidates *guanxi* networks, and justifies structural inequalities which are, in fact, established by much broader political and economic processes. It also inflects non-tenured workers' understandings of collective identities, and the relations which obtain within enterprises, both between employers and employees and amongst an already segmented work force.

SIGNING THEM ON

My focus to this point has been the non-class identities and relations associated with *hukou*, outsider-ness, and *guanxi*, and the ways in which these influence competition in Hangzhou's labour market. This final section considers the motivations for, and structuring effects of enterprise owners' and managers' recruitment of contract and temporary workers and trainees.

Securing Core Workers

The three case study enterprises all offer contracts to their employees. Whilst contract terms and observance of those terms vary markedly, the contracts share one common function in all three enterprises: they are used by management to secure a core work force and ensure that this work force is productive.

At Jinshagang factory, Director Mao said that new recruits were slow and had difficulty meeting quality requirements. Job contracts were specifically intended to ensure that skilled employees would remain in the factory to provide continuity and high productivity. All workers recruited before 1990 signed one year contracts, while those recruited after 1990 signed two year contracts. Once one contract term was completed, employees were not required to sign another, but could continue to work under the same conditions and on the same pay trajectory on a temporary basis. In the Laolian Company, if management wished to retain people after completing a training period of three months, they were offered a contract for two, three or five years. People with highly valued skills or those who had access to sensitive information were pressured to sign long contracts. The shorter contracts were offered to production line workers and young technicians who could be replaced easily. In the Sanxian bakery, contract periods were negotiated between the manager and individual employees. Because the bakery experienced great fluctuations in demand, only key personnel such as accounts clerks, purchasing agents, foremen, and skilled bakers were offered contracts after working for a probationary period of three months. All other employees were temporaries or trainees.

Enterprises' hold over contract workers tends to have real substance. One nation-wide illustration of the utility of labour contracts to enterprises is provided by the effect of their implementation in the notoriously dangerous mining industry. The attrition rate amongst miners dropped from 20 per cent per annum in 1987 to 3.6 per cent after labour contracts were introduced in 1988 (*ZGLDB*, 10 December 1992). The effectiveness of contracts in retaining workers is partly a result of workers' desire for job security in the face of stiff competition in the labour market. In other cases, such as the mining industry, it is a consequence of the clout exercised by large firms within local governments, whose labour bureaux, arbitration committees, and police may compel employees to comply with contract terms.

There are additional measures by which managers attempt to secure a core work force to their enterprises. Payment of a pledge by contracted employees, and non-locals' deposit of their identity card with the enterprise, are both very common practices (Rofel, 1989a, p. 222; Lin, 1991; *QJWB*, 24 December 1992; *ZGLDB*, 5 November 1992). Consider recruits' payment of a pledge when they are contracted to Jinshagang factory. Attached to the job application form is a page which specifies conditions of employment. Recruits sign this page, which then suffices as their contract. The three items listed on the contract concern the pledge, remuneration, and working hours and leave provisions. The first item reads:

> 1. Pledge: in order to ensure continuous and stable production, on entering the factory each employee will pledge a bond of 200 yuan. The employment term is two years. On completion of two years' employment, this pledge will be returned. Those who give up before expiry of the contract term will not have their pledge returned.

As soon as the contract has been signed and the 200 yuan pledge paid, the recruit is taken straight into the workshop to be introduced to the forewoman and group leaders, and start training. Two hundred yuan represents almost a month's wage to workers in the Jinshagang factory. Management and workers both referred to this pledge as a significant factor in 'stabilising' the work force and enforcing labour discipline:

> Ma: Everyone just keeps thinking about their 200 yuan pledge and puts up with whatever conditions they impose on us.
> SS: It's not that much though, is it? Two hundred yuan?
> Ma: Not for local people, it isn't. They wouldn't bother to consider it. But most of the workers here are from very poor places. They have a lot of trouble getting together enough to pay the pledge when they come into the factory. They couldn't possibly leave without it. Two years of this for 200 yuan! If it weren't for that, most people wouldn't stay long. They are counting every hour of that two years. (Fieldnotes, 11 February 1993)

Although the contract states that the pledge will be returned on expiry of the contract, if employees stay working in the factory without a contract the pledge remains with the accountant as a guarantee of good behaviour. No interest is paid when the pledge is returned to the worker.

The pledge is not only used to retain and discipline employees, but also, in violation of enterprises' own regulations, is often withheld as additional punishment if they are fired. Party Secretary Zhao said it is not uncommon for outsiders to lose part or even all of their pledge if they are dismissed from the leather factory:

> If they say they want to leave we don't have to return their pledge, but if we tell them to go we should give it back. So sometimes they have this annoying attitude, you know, that they are pleased we are getting rid of them because they have learned all they need to know to get higher pay somewhere else, or they start making demands ... if they look really smug or get abusive I deduct money from their pledge. They get really angry then, so I tell them to piss off immediately. (Tape, 19 February 1993)

It is also quite common for enterprises anxious to secure skilled personnel to refuse to relinquish employee's personal dossiers, thus making it difficult for them to be recruited into other work units (*GMRB*, 7 September 1992; Pearson, 1992, pp. 66–9). The Laolian company adopted this strategy to try to dissuade a production engineer, Gu, and foreman, Zhen, from terminating their contracts and establishing a private firm which would, of course, have competed for Laolian's customers. The company said the dossiers would be released only on payment to the firm of 3000 yuan (a condition which was not written into the employees' contracts). Gu told me that as they were determined to leave, they had no option but to pay the ransom:

> It's not legal, what they did. But to take them to court would consume a lot of time and effort. Zhejiang University is behind Laolian, and it's a big unit with plenty of pull. It would really be a hassle. We would have to buy lots of presents, lick arses, write letters to departments. I don't have enough *guanxi* to carry it off. I'm not a local. And Zhen doesn't have many connections. It's easier just to wear it ... They tried to talk us out of leaving. They even offered me a raise and to get my girlfriend's *hukou* transferred here and find her a job. They offered us all sorts of things to stay, saying it would cause a lot of inconvenience if we left ... (laughing) Our inconvenience! (Fieldnotes, 15 February 1993)

Guanxi also helped to tie workers to their jobs. Workers employed on the basis of personal recommendations become subject to norms of reciprocity. Their primary obligation is to repay the generosity of their employer-patrons. Their intermediaries become the guarantors of their observation of their terms of employment, for they too are beholden to the employer for having responded positively to their intercession. Among workers already differentiated by *hukou*, localism and place-inflected stereotypes, recruitment through *guanxi* intensifies the construction of cross-class allegiances.

Although contracts, pledges and dossiers fix workers to the enterprise, they actually provide employees with very little job security. All the workers I spoke with insisted that only good *guanxi*, together with workers' productivity and enterprise profitability, provided any measure of job security. Conversely, they believed that if a worker lacked *guanxi*, when enterprise profits or individual output declined, their contract would be terminated. In light of that belief, it is not surprising that many workers saw little advantage to be gained from signing job contracts. Indeed, they could see reasons why a contract might disadvantage workers. It could tie them to an abusive employer or oppressive working conditions, and reduce their manoeuvrability. Young skilled workers are particularly reluctant to sign contracts because, in the context of a growing economy and buoyed by the knowledge that employers place a premium on youth and strength, they prefer to keep their exit options open. If contracts are mandatory, then well-educated young urbanites like Qi prefer those with short terms, a preference which, coincidentally, tallies with the interests of management:

> Qi: After graduation I worked in a bank. It was a horrible situation to be working in, with everyone bored and mistrusting everyone else. So I left and went to work for a computer company in one of the development zones. But it wasn't a very good company. No future. While I was there I was on the lookout for another job ... So then I went to Xerox.
> SS: Do you have a contract with Xerox?
> Qi: Yes, one year. Everyone has to sign a contract for one or two years.
> SS: Don't they give long term contracts?
> Qi: No. If you haven't done a good job they want to get rid of you. And for people like me, I wouldn't want a long contract either. I want to be able to move if I can find a better job. (Tape, 4 February 1993)

Temporary Measures

A critical component in the reworking of China's proletariat has been the transformation of labour into an easily expendable resource. Job contracts go some way towards achieving this aim. But in addition to a core work force, many enterprises also require workers for a few days, weeks or months so they can meet fluctuating demand at minimum cost. Hence, temporary employment has become increasingly common. In the Sanxian bakery during the slack summer season, temporary workers are all dismissed. Then when the weather cools and demand picks up, the bakery again advertises vacancies. These temporary employees are paid a monthly wage and bonuses. During the busy moon-cake season, the bakery places newspaper advertisements seeking people who will work for a specified number of days. Most of these day-workers are recently arrived rural immigrants.

Temporary employment is not just about flexibility, though. The unequal terms under which urbanites and rural residents, locals and non-locals, people with *guanxi* and those without are employed has the effect of dividing workers. And that, in turn, facilitates managers' control of the labour process. The direct connection between differentiation of the work force and managements' capacity to intensify productivity pressures on some sections of the work force are highlighted by a young immigrant carpenter's description of the working conditions in a collectively owned chemical factory in which he had been employed:

> They were regulars. They had contracts, the locals. We were just temporaries, so they thought that when we outsiders came here to work, we had to do it all. It was all on our backs. And if something went wrong then we just got told to go. Any slack work, a disagreement, drop in demand, that was the end for us. It wasn't the same for them, the regulars. If they didn't work hard then, well, they looked at who it was. They could use *guanxi* to get off lightly. They might get punished. But then there wasn't really any need to make them work or punish them if they didn't, because of us temporaries. We really *had* to work. (Tape, 17 January 1993)

Just as security of employment is influenced more by *guanxi* than by the existence of a contract or education, so too the treatment given temporary workers who are dismissed in the event of a market downturn is determined by *guanxi* and local residence. When one of the workshops in the Laolian company ran out of orders and decided to reduce their work force, Che told me that three temporary workers were dismissed:

> One of them was a local who had already found another job with better pay through a friend, so she was leaving anyway. It was just a coincidence that they didn't have to look after her. Then another, she wasn't a local, and because they were all temporary they didn't have to give them any notice ... So in the afternoon as she was leaving she just got told not to come back the next day. The third, she has pretty good *guanxi*. She's a local who knows the general manager so she got treated much better than the others. She got told in advance that they wouldn't need her any

longer and she was given a retirement payment, though as a temporary she wasn't eligible for that. (Fieldnotes, 27 February 1993)

Profiting from Training

Each of the case study enterprises carries out some program of informal, on-the-job training. These schemes have multiple objectives. In Jinshagang factory the main aim of training recruits is, quite simply, low cost skill acquisition. All employees are given one month of on-the-job instruction. During this period they are paid a set amount of 120 yuan. After being shown a few times how to perform the task to which they are allotted they are given materials and samples with which to work. They sit beside an experienced worker who advises them, and group leaders check their progress frequently and give further practical demonstrations. Although all the tasks are simple and repetitive, they require very dextrous movements. New recruits' hands are said to be 'stupid'. For most tasks, it takes workers four to six months to be able to produce articles which meet quality standards at sufficient speed to be able to earn an average worker's wage on the piece rates which they are paid after their single month of training.

Laolian and Sanxian bakery also recruit trainees. But not all employees are given training. Moreover, the aim in employing trainees is not necessarily to coach them in production routines and facilitate skill acquisition, but rather to provide reliable, inexpensive labour during the busy season. Trainees are even cheaper to employ and, because they are hopeful of gaining a trade and job security, tend to be more obedient and productive than temporaries. During their traineeship, workers are paid a basic wage of between 150 and 168 yuan without bonuses. This is slightly more than half the amount paid to an unskilled day labourer. Laolian cautions trainees that the company might not be able to hire them at the end of their traineeship. At Sanxian bakery, trainees are told that at the end of the three-month training period, the most capable amongst them will be offered contracts. They are not told, as I was, that the bakery is under no obligation to offer jobs to any of them.

The in-house training of Sanxian's bakers contributes to gendered divisions in the work force. While patriarchal, macho ideologies and patterns of gender socialisation undoubtedly underlie discrimination in training, it is informal social practice which immediately determines unequal skill acquisition. There is no structured training programme at Sanxian. Each morning, trainees undertake the routine preparation and baking of bread. When this is finished, while the trainees pack products and carry ingredients, they are called upon individually to aid skilled bakers. This is a critical part of trainees' learning experience. But female trainees are almost never called upon to help. Their exclusion stems from the different ways in which males and females interact socially. Females are unwilling or unable to participate in the activities through which the skilled bakers become familiar with particular trainees, and from which spring cooperative liaisons and knowledge transfers. At lunch time, the female trainees sit and chat together. They do not join in the lunch time poker game, which is the high point of the bakers' day. When the bakers are resting between bursts of activity, the female trainees do not offer them cigarettes and sit to smoke with them, as do the male trainees. Yet these two types of interaction, involving play and exchange, are precisely the means by which the males come to know one another. Thus, when a baker who is elbow deep in cake mixture needs urgent help, he calls out the first trainee's name which springs to mind: frequently, that of the fellow with whom he has just smoked a cigarette.

The gendered pattern of enskilling usually makes the bakery management's shedding of 'incompetent' female trainees politically acceptable to the tradesmen. Yet even gender prejudice is not always sufficient to naturalise trainees' exploitation. After working as a day labourer making moon cakes through the sweltering month from August until September, Aihua was invited to become a trainee. She regretted that because she had been paid at a daily rate, the time she had already spent in the bakery would not be counted as part of her traineeship. Nevertheless, she was pleased that this provided an opportunity to gain trade skills with which she might earn up to 300 yuan each month. The foreman of the bakery was also pleased. He thought she was a conscientious, intelligent worker, and he was impressed by the way she personally initiated cooperative actions in order to learn as much as she could. However, along with all other female trainees, Aihua was dismissed at the end of the third month. The foreman was angry about what he said was simply a short-sighted cost-cutting decision: 'As soon as they have to start paying people a proper wage, they sack them! It's disgusting!' Workers' fragmentation is no more permanent than are their moments of solidarity.

Hangzhou's labour market is illustrative of trends which much of the scholarly literature on wage work, workers' identities and class consciousness would dismiss as contradictory. It is, on the one hand, one of the primary sites in which relations between the buyers and sellers of labour power are formed. Non-tenured workers are aware that the conditions under which they enter factories and participate in wage work are dictated by the principal objective of the owners and managers of capital: that is, to produce goods which can be sold to realise profit. From that angle, it might be possible to describe the relationship between Chinese workers and employers in class terms.

However, the preceding analysis also indicates that workers' experiences in the labour market and their relations with employers cannot simply be assumed from their gross structural context. At the same time that workers understand that the terms of their recruitment are framed by the pursuit of productivity and profit, they also are aware that recruitment is mediated by, and gives force to, a panoply of social notations and particularistic ties. The most important of these are residential registration, localism, and *guanxi*. These are not just cultural carry-overs, legacies from an earlier, more organic social form which are in conflict with the rational operation of a market economy; rather, they have become central to the operation of labour markets.

Moreover, as subsequent chapters demonstrate, the capitalist environment within which China's proletariat produces goods does not eventually override the operation of these non-class identities and relations and produce a convergence in experience, sense of identity and consciousness among China's proletariat. Certainly, when workers enter factories, they confront a productivist, profit-oriented ethos, oppositional interests, and hierarchical chains of command. Yet even the labour processes and wage systems which operate in these factories are impelled, in part, by residential registration, localism, and *guanxi*. Workers continue to understand work relations, identify themselves and others, and organise along the lines of these complex factors.

5 Productive Architecture

The enterprises I observed in Hangzhou were all established, and have been organised, with a view to the making of profit for appropriation by enterprise owners and managers. That is the prior meaning inscribed on the work place by management initiatives, a meaning which impacts upon all the people within. Marxist theorists suggest that the overriding logic of relations of production and appropriation in capitalist enterprises are sufficient to render workers' previous identities, interests, and consciousness irrelevant to the ways they interpret work, and relate to their employers and one another (see, e.g. Burawoy, 1979, pp. 135–52, 212–14). On the shop floor, confronted daily with the fact of their common exploitation, workers' dissimilarities are effaced (Livingstone and Mangan, 1996, pp. 131–8).

That analytical generalisation glosses complex epistemological problems. How do we find out what workers think about themselves and others, and their participation in wage work? Christine Helliwell (1996) has suggested that social scientists' emphasis upon the facticity of bounded social groups derives, in part, from their reliance upon visual information and their tendency to represent social interaction in graphic forms. In work places, such an approach is more likely to depict groups behaving in structurally consistent ways than would an analysis attuned to communication and events.

This chapter uses data compiled through observation of the case study enterprises to produce a detailed description of the regimes and conditions under which members of China's proletariat labour. And, just as Helliwell predicts, that visual data suggests that in practical as well as symbolic ways, the organisation of spaces and objects in the work place contributes to the creation of a social order structured by capitalist production. Spatial arrangements tend to oppose capital and labour, underpin hierarchical chains of management, and facilitate the exploitation, subjugation, and individualisation of workers. However, work spaces also emerge as interactive sites in which the meanings of capitalist production and class are contested and transformed through appropriation of the same significatory codes as are used by management to control workers' bodies and the labour process.

A second, closely related problem concerns the Marxist assumption that relations of wage work and exploitation will be generalised among, and similarly experienced by, all workers. This assumption rests upon conceptualisations of capitalists and workers as unitary subjects, whose ideas and actions are wholly consistent with objectively identifiable sets of interests established by their participation in a generic mode of capitalist production. If that was indeed the case, it might provide the foundations for a common identity and collective forms of organisation. Yet it is clear from the previous chapter that when Chinese workers enter factories, they are already differentiated as the bearers of distinctive, potentially antagonistic non-class identities and relations. The description of work places presented here shows that within enterprises, workers are subjected to spatial and organisational disciplines that further individualise and oppose them. Moreover, as I demonstrate in following chapters, workers' isolation, group differentiation and competition are compounded by being articulated to labour processes and wage payment systems.

The aim of this chapter is to analyse the ways spatial significations affect the development of worker-subjectivities and workers' understandings of wage work and appropriation. The chapter provides a detailed account of the architecture of managerial control, and the economic values and patterns of extraction which are expressed and normalised in the physical lay-out of two of the case study enterprises. Managers' utilisation of space as a tool with which to control labour and production elicits complex responses from workers. Certainly, they are made passive and productive. But they also challenge productivist values and organisational hierarchies, managers' control of their bodies and time, and relations of exploitation by transgressing the spatial order of enterprises' productive regimes.

SPATIAL SIGNIFICATION, SUBJECTIVITY, AND THE MAKING OF MEANINGS IN CHINESE WORK PLACES

Peoples' relations are consciously and unconsciously represented in, and influenced by their material constructions. Urban plans and buildings provide summary models of ideas about cosmological power, socio-political principles, economic values, kinship and community. Our occupation of certain buildings, or locations within buildings, induces particular behavioural responses from those around us. The built environment can exert a hegemonic effect (Bourdieu, 1984; Sundstrom and Sundstrom, 1986; Turner, 1991). On the other hand, as Mommaas (1996) has shown in his study of urban fragmentation in the Netherlands, disjuncture between the cultural values and economic promises encapsulated in the design of a place and peoples' actual lived experiences can be psychologically disturbing and socially destabilising.

Purpose-built work places are designed to support hierarchical, disciplinary, and productive regimes. But even in those work places which are not purpose built, physical adaptations and the behavioural norms which are attributed to locations and job statuses can produce similar results. Such simple things as the arrangement of screens, signs, and furniture can enable surveillance, restrict movement and communication, assert asymmetrical relations of authority and privilege, and emphasise efficiency norms. Forms of address and behaviour which are acceptable on the shop floor may not be acceptable in the boss's office. Clothing which is worn by management staff may be considered inappropriate if worn by cleaners.

In China, architectural forms and modes of speech, dress, and deportment have for many centuries acted as universally recognised markers of status and entitlement which inform public conduct and interaction between superiors and subordinates (Yates, 1994). Indeed, it is the ubiquitous orthodoxy of these signifiers which makes inversions or alternative utilisations of location, appearance, and vocabulary not just unorthodox, but clear statements of dissent. In a penetrating analysis of the politics of spatial symbolism in a Chinese factory, Lisa Rofel (1992) suggests that during the Cultural Revolution, Chinese workers' frequent departures from the factory floor and their performance of domestic chores at work served as 'a peripatetic statement of political rights to challenge managerial authority'. Rofel argues that contemporary state enterprise employees' desertion of their posts similarly expresses a rejection of reformist managers' productivist goals.

In the profit driven factories I observed in Xihu, workers would have been sacked for conspicuous dereliction of duty. Yet even in those enterprises, competing assertions of a multiplicity of identities, relationships, and values were also being made through signifiers such as spatial organisation and disorganisation. In particular, as I demonstrate below, workers privatised parts of their work places and transformed them from productive into social-recreational locations. In speech, they played with spatial concepts of hierarchy to assert their moral/ethical superiority over the owners and managers of firms.

The role of work in shaping workers' subjectivity deserves close attention. For many employees, even as participation in wage work is principally a means of earning a livelihood, it is also more than just a livelihood. In China as elsewhere, people have long considered their place and mode of occupation as a means of demonstrating their social worth. Amongst contemporary workers, the status of work places partly hinges upon criteria such as modern architectural design, the use of advanced technology in production, and the provision to workers of comfortable, clean surroundings.

Wages from work also provide a means of affirming close human relationships. The expectation that one might gain personal wealth or satisfaction from working may be of less importance than the need to give expression to social and emotional ties by demonstrating one's ability to labour for the material benefit of others (Wolf, 1968, pp. 36–44; Potter and Potter, 1990, pp. 189–94, 320).

Occupational status competition and the emotional and relational aspects of earning wages and participating in social production are clearly consonant with the interests of the state in promoting national economic growth, and the needs of the owners and managers of firms to motivate workers to produce goods for profit. Indeed, the gains to be won from hard labour, efficiency, skill, and productivity form prominent themes both in the public media and in management hype in work places. Managers and workers alike told me that many employees participate in management-sponsored production competitions in order to boost their self-esteem and earn public honour, rather than simply to win certificates or token monetary awards.

Nevertheless, even the government's and managements' representation of industry as a virtue is a double-edged sword. Workers' use their own publicly acknowledged hard work as a moral platform from which to criticise those who are not hard working. Most frequently, the targets of this criticism are officials, wealthy entrepreneurs, and enterprise managers. Sometimes, however, groups of workers subjected to intense productivity pressures will also point accusingly at other workers who, by virtue of their membership of the local community or their *guanxi*, are not suffering the same pressures. Thus, it is apparent that although aspects of workers' subjectivity such as pride in production resonate with the productivist ethos of the reform era, they are not simply a consequence of workers' functions, and their constitution and domination by capital.

Workers' subjectivity is also shaped by what Michael Jackson (1996, p. 32) refers to as their 'bodily being-in-the-world'. Thinking about one's self and its relations with others is affected by auditory, tactile, visual, and kinetic stimuli (Douglas, 1983, p. 38; Lang, 1992). In a typically folksy phrase, Geertz further points out that thinking is prompted by, and situated in specific environments: 'thinking is a public activity – its natural habitat is the houseyard, the marketplace, the town square' (1973, p. 360). From a phenomenological perspective, then, workers' physical occupation of the work space is crucial to their development of an imaginative capacity, cognitive categories, and their interpretations of identities and relationships (Harré, 1978, p. 49).

In Xihu, environmental sensitivity is particularly high amongst immigrant workers. Those who have come from villages where they worked in agriculture are unused to spending long periods indoors under close supervision. However, as I noted in the previous chapter, outsiders tend to be highly mobile. So whilst recruits who lack a sense of place and familiarity with spatial symbols are unsure of their roles and of how to respond to newly encountered architectural and communicative codes, they are nevertheless able to synthesise the knowledges, practical strategies and values they have acquired in a multiplicity of sites, and selectively apply these in the new work place. Such syncretism can produce a highly contextual and fluid form of subjective agency which cannot be accommodated in theoretical approaches which are founded upon a preconceived taxonomy of structural relations, objectively given identities, interests and political activities (Canter, 1977, pp. 118–22; Giddens, 1987, pp. 214–17).

Another all-too-frequently neglected dimension of workers' subjectivity is their relationship to material objects and the products of their labour. Things signify aspirations and encapsulate memories. They are used to express individual creativity. Such 'object fetishism' is sometimes pointed to as evidence of workers' lack of consciousness, or susceptibility to consumerism (Taussig, 1980). Certainly, workers' pride in artisanal excellence tallies with the quality aims of enterprise owners and managers, and consumerism accords with capitalists' need to promote consumption. Yet the desire to labour creatively and produce or purchase well-made, beautiful, or useful objects or services may also be presented by workers as a significant feature of their personality. Wang, an ambitious young baker employed at Sanxian, proudly told all his colleagues that he had paid the equivalent of two whole weeks' wages for the purchase of a French recipe book. Why? 'So I can make even more beautiful pastries!'

All this points to a simple, if often overlooked, truth. The material environment and the emotional and somatic dimensions of workers' existence impinges on their understandings of wage work. People who spend sixty hours each week sitting under close supervision silently assembling components for export form different opinions about themselves and their relations with their boss from those who spend the same amount of time at work talking, listening to music and moving as they please, or those who are able to leave the work place as soon as they have produced a set number of complete artefacts. The implications of this for researchers are equally simple. We need to investigate how divergent work settings affect workers' senses of identity, and their attitudes, relationships and behaviour. The following analysis of the work places and production routines I observed in Xihu weaves together these insights into spatial signification and constructions of worker-subjectivity to illuminate the corporeal experiences of, and reactions to, work places amongst members of China's proletariat.

FACTORY WORLDS

None of the work places I visited in Hangzhou in any way resembled the cruel sweat-shops which have been depicted in other Chinese cities.[1] Nevertheless, the relationships of power and exploitation which obtain between employers and employees were spatially prescribed in all the work places I observed: each was tangibly constructed as 'a piece of turf where the boss rules' (Sayer and Walker, 1992, p. 120). While the lay-out of the new purpose-built Jinshagang factory most explicitly revealed how space can be utilised as a technique of power, the employees of the Laolian company and Sanxian bakery were also confronted daily with visible signs of their differential subjugation to, and exploitation by, the owners and managers of the enterprise. However, the architectural arrangement of the latter companies inspired and accommodated symbolic acts of resistance which were unthinkable at Jinshagang.

An Ordered Tyranny

Jinshagang factory relocated to new premises alongside Shuguang Road in 1991. The new factory did not shelter behind one of those high grey walls which segregate the ordered social and economic microcosm of state owned work units from the untidy world outside (Jenner, 1992, pp. 83–96). Rather, in keeping with the ethos of reform and opening up, the demarcation between cubist factory and surrounding suburb was sketched by an iron railing. Beyond that railing, a self-disciplined, productive regime was validated by constant reference to merit, efficiency, productivity, and profit. It was expressed in the ever present gaze of management and manifest symbols of hierarchical authority. It was enforced by divisions within the work force, and an elaborate system of regulations from which flowed rewards and punishments.

Enter the factory as I did, as an 'observer'. The concrete driveway curved up to the entrance of the building between the workers' bicycle racks and the gatekeeper's room. Note that the location of the bicycle racks was not coincidental. Whenever workers arrived or departed, they were visible to the old gatekeeper whose duty it was to punch their time cards. Inside the foyer of the factory was another punch card machine at which, with the exception of the managing director and manager, all administrative and supervisory staff were trusted to punch their own time cards. The punch card machines not only marked the managers off from other employees of the collective, but they also bifurcated the work force into staff and production workers. The two machines symbolised the divide between mental and manual labour, between those who gave directions and those who received directions, and between those who earned salaries and those who were paid by the piece. At the same time, they denoted greater and lesser degrees of autonomy.

When office staff notched their arrival on their time cards, they went through a door at the left of the factory foyer into the administrative office. The office was distinguished from other working areas in the factory by several features. There was a less formal arrangement and use of space than in the workshops. Desks, littered with computers and paperwork, faced windows overlooking the driveway rather than a supervisor's station. Instead of posters enjoining silence, efficiency, and diligence, there were colourful calendars on the walls. A tall wooden display cabinet housed samples of greeting cards which the manager brought back from Japan, and the office staff's enamel lunch bowls, chopsticks, and tea cups. There was a higher level of personal expression, conversation, and casual movement in the office than in other parts of the factory. The office staff rarely donned the factory's white cotton jackets, and none of them slipped on the plastic scuffs or padded shoes worn by production workers. Communications in the office were casual, even politely flirtatious. People talked and joked (though this was subdued when manager Mao was in residence), read newspapers and books, had friends visit them at work, moved chairs about, and strolled in and out as they visited the workshops and storerooms. In fact, office staff frequently left the premises on work-related duties which were combined with shopping, lunching, or just 'skiving'.

Tasks in the office were varied, and could be paced, done cooperatively, and swapped about, in stark contrast to the repetitive, individual tasks which production workers performed. A sample of staff members' job descriptions gives an indication of this diversity and the potential for sociability. The office manager received and handled orders for greeting cards, oversaw administrative and personnel matters, delegated work to the forewomen, and ensured observance of factory regulations. In addition to his position as recruitment officer, Su was responsible for receiving and handling all orders for electronic components. The pay clerk was also responsible for overseeing the factory dormitories. A customs clerk liaised between the office manager, Su, and customs and other government departments to facilitate exports.

Manager Mao's office opened off the administrative office. Here, spatial arrangements both signified and enforced power. The manager's frequent physical absence because of meetings with entrepreneurs and officials was one of the means by which his control over the factory and its profits were ensured. But it also symbolised the effectiveness of his control. His capacity to oversee employees despite his absence was evoked by the spare mobile phone lying on his desk. When present, his authority was underpinned by a panopticonic arrangement which granted privacy to the manager while maximising the visibility of office staff: a smoked glass partition allowed him to survey the administrative office. His pre-eminence in the factory was denoted by traditional status markers such as spacious-ness, an imposing wooden desk which stood between the manager and anyone who entered his office, and a bank of telephones and correspon-dence trays.

A broad stairway led from the foyer to the second floor on which were located director Mao's office, a conference room, and a workshop. The director's office was carpeted, and furnished with a desk, leather arm-chairs, and bookshelves. These, like the factory manager's furniture, were also placed so that on the rare occasions director Mao was seated at his desk, he faced the door and anyone who entered. The office also boasted a Japanese airconditioning system. The airconditioner was of symbolic rather than practical significance. With the exception of the storeroom and printery, the whole factory was airconditioned. Indeed, on several occa-sions workers and I remarked that this made the factory considerably more comfortable than our homes. But the director's airconditioning unit was set at a lower, more stable temperature than that of the rest of the factory. When I sat shivering in a thin dress in his office one sweltering summer day, he explained to me that he installed the air conditioning unit so he could wear western suits throughout the year. In China, never to be encumbered by long underwear or to have to roll up one's shirt sleeves is not only indicative of control over one's physical environment, it also is suggestive of social controls; the ability to direct others' labour, and allocate the fruits of that labour.

Next door was the meeting ground for foreign capital and the managers of Jinshagang collective. The conference room was a ceremonial space: chandelier lighting, big oval conference table, arm chairs and coffee tables around the walls, prints of landscapes and flowers, and floor length cur-tains all betokened formal reception rather than bargaining or industry. The conference room was used only to entertain special clients, and to hold the factory management committee meetings at which the director and factory manager – empowered and insulated from the trivial problems of production by that space – instructed the office manager and forewomen on their future production schedules. Regular weekly meetings between the forewomen and dozens of group leaders were held in the cluttered storeroom downstairs, whilst meetings to address workers were always held in the workshops.

Indeed, none of the workers employed in the workshop adjoining the conference room had ever seen inside that sanctum. After asking the old gatekeeper to punch their time cards on arrival, they hurried straight up the stairs to their desks to begin bundling together wires to be plaited as greeting card decorations. Along two walls of the workshop high windows let in natural light, which was further augmented by neon strip lighting. The workers' small wooden desks were arranged in long, parallel rows of two and three, facing the doorway and the front wall against which the forewoman's and group leaders' tables were placed at right angles. As in all the workshops, thermoses of hot drinking water stood in the front corners of the room. On the front wall charts showed individual workers' attendance, overtime, amounts of leave taken and output, 1992 output and product quality compared to that of 1991, and samples of standard and substandard articles. Small gold stars next to workers' numbers denoted those who had exceeded production norms, reported for work every day, and regularly done overtime. Above the group leaders' tables, there was a large round clock. This attracted much more attention from the workers than did the charts.

There were approximately one hundred young female workers in this workshop. They all wore the factory's white cotton jacket and scuffs. A large sign, on which 'Silence!' was painted in red, hung from the ceiling. Talking was prohibited, and offenders had money deducted from their monthly bonus. There was almost no movement or sound from the workers, who were only allowed to leave their desks to go to the toilet, have a drink, or collect new materials from the group leaders or the storeroom.

Even if there had been no prohibition on movement, the workers here would still have been fastened to their desks by the demands of production. The first four rows of workers taped together bundles of fine bi-coloured wires: red/white, black/white, yellow/white, and gold/silver. The batches of wire were piled in plastic cartons sitting on the floor at their feet, along with a batch-tag which recorded the number and signature of the worker who performed each part of the production process on the carton of materials. The workers picked up the batches of 980 wires, flapped them against the table to separate them, then wedged them between two bricks to hold them in place. With their heads bent down so they could see sufficiently well to count the strands of wire, they gathered together seven strands then bound them around in the middle, where the colours met, with silver tape which came from a dispenser at their side. It took between 5 and 6 minutes to separate and tape up the 140 bundles in each batch. Some types of wire were less pliable or stickier than others, and some plaits required 6 or 8 strands rather than 7. This was the only task these workers performed all day, every working day, for the duration of their two year contract.

Behind these women sat another nine rows of workers. They made plaits from the cartons of taped wire which they collected from the front, after getting the batch-tag countersigned by the group leader. The first step in plaiting was to bend the wires around a metal plate the same width as the cards over which the plaits slip. This was done a few at a time, taking care that the silver tape sat in the exact centre of the plate. When the 140 bundles had been bent and put back into the carton, the workers took a few dozen at a time and put them to one side or in their drawer, rubbed their fingers with talcum powder to prevent chafing, and began to twist the plaits. An experienced plaiter took more than an hour to plait all the 140 bundles. Plaiters could stretch their necks and stand up to relieve their backs and legs while they continued working, while the girls taping the bundles had to remain seated with their heads bent. But the plaiters also performed just this one task as long as they were employed in the factory. I asked two workers what they thought about while they made plaits all day:

> Zhang: I don't think of anything. I'm still not very good at this. I've only been here a couple of months, so I have to really concentrate on what I'm doing to get them right. What about you, Lou? You are experienced.
> Lou: No-one here *thinks*! All I can do is look at my hands, try to get it right, do it as fast as possible ... how I can get on to the next one as quickly as I can. In fact I try not to think at all. If I think I'll feel miserable. Besides, they don't want us thinking. (Fieldnotes, 23 November 1992)

Lou was correct. Manager Mao did not encourage workers to make suggestions about production routines or design because 'they would just ruin the patterns'.

On one of my early visits to the upstairs workshop, I said to the forewoman that I found it eerie to be among so many silent people. She responded:

> Yes, it's always as quiet as this. They are very obedient. Especially when they first come in, they hardly say a word. Just hang their heads and agree with everything. You see how it is now, they are like a class of

good little schoolchildren, really quiet and hardworking. They certainly know how to work hard, these peasants. Not like city people who work in factories, who will just do a few minutes work then wander off to chat with a friend. These young girls toe the line. When they first arrive they seem quite stupid, like cattle. They get a bit more lively after they have spent a few years in the city. (Fieldnotes, 18 August 1992)

The forewoman's infantilisation of her subordinates was not delivered in hushed tones. On the contrary, as usual, she spoke loudly. In fact, when giving instructions or summoning workers by number, supervisors shouted. Nor did supervisors have to remain fixed to their stations. On an average day, group leaders spent more than half their time walking about the workshop inspecting products, asking and answering questions, and chatting amongst themselves. Moreover, they frequently left the workshop, both for work-related and social reasons. Just as spatial arrangements and levels of sound, movement, and sociability distinguished administrative staff from production employees, so too did they demarcate supervisors from workers.

Cartons of completed plaits were collected from the upstairs workshop by workers from the card finishing section on the ground floor. These workers' tasks were more varied than those upstairs. Depending upon what type of card was being produced, workers folded together the pieces of coloured, printed, and embossed paper which comprised the card, placed an envelope at the back and slipped the plait over card and envelope, then snipped the ends of the plait to make them exactly level with the top of the paper or coiled them into elaborate spirals. The card was finished by pasting an origami decoration on to the top right corner. Bundles of completed cards were then slid into cellophane envelopes, and sealed.

Although this job was less repetitive than those of other workers, in each of these assembly steps there existed the danger of producing a sub-standard article. Signs detailing the rigorous standards which finished cards had to meet, as well as samples of the many faults that could be made through carelessness or inattention, were pasted all along the walls of the workshop: 'Red paper half a millimetre out of line with white', 'Plait fitted too loosely', 'Cellophane envelope sealed crookedly'. Other posters reminded workers that they had to be fast, efficient, and quiet.

Like their colleagues upstairs, the forty to fifty women in the card finishing workshop were literally embedded in their work. They were confined by furniture, the materials with which they laboured and the articles they manufactured. The workers sat in parallel rows at desks with high wooden surrounds, which prevented them from seeing anyone to their front or back. Their desks were always littered with scissors, lids containing glue, and bundles of cards in various stages of completion. Their drawers were pulled out to catch offcuts from the plaits. On the shelf jutting out from the desk front were stacked packets of finished cards ready to be collected by the male packers. And at their feet were plastic cartons containing more plaits, paper, and envelopes. Because of the kind of tasks they performed, they had no opportunity to stand up unless they were collecting extra materials from the group leaders' desks at the front of the room, or braving forewoman Ren's basilisk glare to go to the toilet.

Forewoman Ren's desk was the focal centre of power in the ground floor workshops. It was positioned so that Ren could overlook two of the five workshops in which she had jurisdiction, as well as the exits through to the storeroom, toilets, and factory canteen. Above her desk on the wall were huge charts showing monthly productivity, percentage of products meeting quality requirements, and orders for the following months for different sections of the factory.

Ren believed that spatial order, discipline and silence were essential to the achievement of her main objective: the maintenance of high rates of productivity and profitability. These workers were outsiders, not given to self-restraint. Using the same logic that I first heard from manager Mao, Ren stated that if workers were allowed to move, it would increase the surveillance work required of shop floor supervisors, and that in turn might necessitate an increase in the numbers of supervisory staff and reduce profits. If workers chatted, they would be distracted from their simple, repetitive, but exacting tasks, and spread gossip and start arguments. If they did not sit neatly at their desks, they would develop a casual, disrespectful attitude. Ren chastised me on a number of occasions for sitting on the edge of desks or, worse, kneeling on the floor next to people's chairs, because it gave the workshop an untidy appearance. To the workers' amusement, she insisted that whenever groups of clients came to tour the factory, I squeeze my bulky western body into one of the tiny factory jackets to hide my presence:

Ren: You look just like a worker now.
SS: What about my hair and eyes?
Ren: They don't look at worker's faces, these Japanese businessmen. They are only interested in what their hands can produce, and in order. Having everyone sitting in rows working quietly. The floor being clean. They won't notice your face. (Fieldnotes, 3 December 1992)

Ordered rows of faceless, productive workers: the factory tour could end on this Kafka-esque note. Spatial organisation of the work place has been revealed as an instrument and expression of power, and a method for organising an excruciatingly labour intensive production process.

The Interstices of Tyranny

Yet to leave off there would be to imply that the productive, individualising, disciplinary effects of the spatial organisation of Jinshagang factory were unmitigated. That was not the case.

At the back of the ground floor, partitioned off from the plugs workshop and on the opposite side of a small, glassed-in courtyard to Ren's desk, were the clamping and wire cutting workshops. Although the workers there wore identical white factory jackets, were involved in assembling the same sorts of products, and were surrounded by the same posters enjoining them to be quiet, work fast, and pay attention to quality as other workers at Jinshagang, their situation was markedly different. These workshops were small and relatively self-contained. Because of the open L-shape of the room they occupied, and the location of large clamping, cutting and fusing machines, workers' desks were also arranged in an irregular pattern. Their separation from the main body of the building, the privacy afforded by the placement and noise of machinery, and the presence in this workshop – alone in the entire factory – of two group leaders who were not Jinshagang residents, allowed talk. Talk facilitated friendship and unity. In contrast to workers in other sections of the factory, all these employees knew each other's name, place of origin, and home situation. They chatted about work, family, friends, their likes and dislikes, and the weather that they, almost alone amongst all the production workers in the factory, could see in the little glassed-in courtyard. Weather formed a regular subject of conversation between them, and a tenuous link with time and lives outside work. So, too, did the young male technicians who came, blushing, to service their machines.

Of course, many of the workers in other sections of Jinshagang factory also tried to resist the spatial arrangements which subjugated and depersonalised them. Tokens of their personal identities were secreted away in their desk drawers and clothes, the only places not observed. After checking that administrative and supervisory staff were not nearby, they furtively drew out letters, photos, or objects to be shown to friends. Whenever possible, they escaped to places which were outside the factory's dominion. At meal times, they preferred to stand in groups alongside Shuguang Road and buy food from tricycle vendors, rather than eat subsidised meals in the canteen. And whenever Ren was not guarding the path to the toilets, they retreated to this smelly but free sanctuary to hold long, loud conversations. The dormitory was another uncontrolled space within which workers gave voice to their feelings about work, and, sometimes, coordinated strategies to negotiate or resist particular management initiatives. Yet even those acts implied a tacit acceptance of managements' control of the work place and their worker-selves.

To varying degrees, workers at Jinshagang factory were bodily, mentally, and socially constrained by the material and semiotic organisation of the work place. All that was non-work, any communication or movement which was not economically productive, was prohibited. At the small wooden desks which circumscribed their worlds at work, they had little opportunity to engage in any forms of creativity, decision making, or sociability. They were rendered visible and quiet so as to maximise their productivity. In contrast, the factory's managers, the office staff, and shop-floor supervisors were all distinguished to some extent by the absence of those very constraints. They were able to escape the work place, were not constantly surveyed by their superiors, could move and talk, decide the order in which to perform tasks, and choose how to present themselves to their peers and their subordinates. Their productivity was not quantified.

The management of work spaces and workers' subjectivities was an integral aspect of Jinshagang factory's production regime, and it appeared as a significant factor in the factory workers' understandings of relations of production. Spatial organisation was felt as a tool with which the Maos and their agent, forewoman Ren, enforced control of the factory. It was, in all respects, their space. But that very fact suggests that a symbolic power could accrue either from workers' territorial transgression and their utilisation of these spaces in non-productive ways, or from workers' affirmation of their non-worker subjectivities as females, outsiders, or lovers; in short, as people from other places with more complex identities and functions than those which were acknowledged in the factory. The narratives which conclude this and the following chapter describe some of the occasions on which workers broke free of the factory tyranny.

FRACTURING THE HEGEMONIC WORK SPACE

The Sanxian bakery and Laolian company also utilised space both as mode and manifestation of managements' control. But there, the observer encountered new sorts of spatial discourses. In these firms, administrative work and productive work occurred at separate sites. In neither enterprise was the separation of locations simply a consequence of inadequate space or facilities. Indeed, in both there was space to spare. At Laolian, some surplus office space was converted into a street front retail outlet, but this was an ill-conceived afterthought as virtually all sales were made through travelling representatives, trade fairs and mail orders. At Sanxian, the separation of administrative and productive locations actually caused considerable practical inconvenience. From the location of the company office and shop in front of the main entrance to the University, workers had to travel through the gates of the University and half a kilometre up a steep hill to reach the bakery. The route was travelled several times daily by the bakers, office clerks, quality controller, and the three tricycle delivery men. But rather than combine the administrative and baking sites, the bakery manager converted superfluous space adjoining their retail outlet into a restaurant.

Administrative and production sites at Laolian and Sanxian were separate for two reasons. The first reflected enterprise managers' attitudes towards their own position in society and in the firm: they wanted to distance themselves spatially and socially from workers and industry, and to occupy attractive, private environments which conveyed images of hierarchy, power, and mental enterprise. Their comfortable, spacious work sites were not just perquisites. They were, in addition, symbols of power and prestige, and functional tools of office. Workshops were, similarly, manifest symbols of the physical drudgery and unimportance of workers' positions, and vehicles for their exploitation. Before escorting me from his airy modern office to the company's cavernous, dirty concrete workshops located above the local produce markets, the manager of Laolian had to ask his office staff to show him the 300 metre long path that they had etched into the bare earth as they trekked back and forth. *En route*, he said he could not understand why I would want to visit the workshops: 'They just do this all day [waving his hand back and forth as though picking up an object and putting it down again]. There isn't anything worth looking at' (Fieldnotes, 16 June 1992).

The second reason for retaining separate administrative and production sites at Laolian and Sanxian was informed by managers' perceptions of the type of production in which their companies were engaged, the types of workers employed in their industry, and management techniques appropriate to the handling of these workers. Both managers emphasised that their companies were involved in highly specialised, flexible production routines. Detached offices and workshops were designed to provide a core of supervisory, skilled, mostly male employees with token autonomy in the labour process, and command over a contingent force of workers on the shop floor. They were also expected to instil office-oriented ambitions in this core work force.

Yet this spatial separation simultaneously gave rise to forms of critical consciousness, and allowed a far greater degree of independence, interaction, and unity than was possible in the Jinshagang factory. The Laolian and Sanxian employees' conversations and actions showed a strong sensitivity to the symbolism of hierarchy and forms of subjectivity implied by their companies' spatial organisation. Their speech played upon structural inversions of space, status, and morality. They had, for instance, retrieved Maoist categories of productive and unproductive labour in which 'real' work was represented as a physically demanding, materially productive activity, whilst office work was said to be unproductive and to consume the fruits of 'real' labour. Sanxian bakers constantly remarked that their labour produced all the goods which, when sold, provided wages for the administrative staff and profits for the company's owners. People who mistakenly came up to the bakery looking for management, administrative, or purchasing staff were sent away by a grinning baker with such cryptic directions as 'The higher-ups are down below', or 'Those who eat our labour are down below'. On setting off for the company office, Laolian technicians echoed that ironic inversion by remarking to their colleagues that they were lowering themselves to get directions from the 'higher ups'.

The oppositions drawn by the Sanxian bakers between themselves and the managerial and administrative staff also reverberated with gendered definitions of male (public production) and female (private servicing and consumption) work.[2] Bakers were mostly male, while females predominated among office staff. The bakers regularly criticised manager Rong because, as a woman, she was presumed to be inept in the 'outside' world of business, and to waste much of her time either sitting in her office 'doing nothing' or going 'window shopping'. The company's administrative staff were similarly said to spend their time at work loafing in chairs, answering the phone ('if they can be bothered'), reading newspapers, drinking tea with their friends, and networking. At lunch time, they had siestas. At night when the bakers were working overtime, they were watching television or sleeping in their beds. So far as the bakers were concerned, the comfortable conditions enjoyed by the manager and office staff were underwritten by the sale of products created by the bakers' hard labour.

Even if one rejects the bakers' appropriation of elements of Maoist and gender ideologies to assert their greater economic, social, and moral worth, it is still worthwhile considering their charge that they were subjected to more intense productivity pressures than other employees of Sanxian. A brief conversation I had with the female quantity clerk during a week long period she spent in the bakery suggested that the bakers' complaints about the different intensity of work expected of the bakers and office staff might not have been prompted solely by leftist propaganda, jealousy or gender prejudice:

> Sun: They work hard up here, don't they? It's really heavy work. Noisy. They haven't enough room. They really need more space and equipment.
>
> SS: What's it like down in the office? You spend most of your time there, don't you?
>
> Sun: Yes. It's much easier in the office than here. Quieter, more relaxed. Actually, it's pretty good down there. I like it. (Fieldnotes, 16 November 1992)

However, when I first began visiting the bakery workshops in June, I found that there too, social differentiation between supervisors and workers was spatially expressed. The bakery occupied rather dilapidated rooms along opposite sides of a U-shaped courtyard. At that time, the northern wing of the bakery comprised the foreman's office, hygiene-testing laboratory, and storeroom for finished products. This was the immediate locus of authority and status, and the site from which orders were relayed, and rewards and penalties dispensed. The food technician, a young college educated woman, clearly held the bakers in contempt. I never saw her in the bakery, and in fact she was rarely in her laboratory as she preferred to spend as much time as possible down at the office. Foreman Jiang would leave his cool office only if it was absolutely necessary. He spent most of his time rehearsing the behaviour he thought appropriate to administrative and supervisory staff. He lounged in a chair in front of a fan with his feet on his desk, playing electronic games, flicking through girlie magazines, smoking, and joking with the storeman and the group leaders who filtered in and out of the office to escape the heat of the ovens for a few minutes. He occasionally asked the workers if it was hot 'over there' when they came in for instructions and paused to have a cigarette. It was invariably four or five degrees hotter! To the bakers, Jiang and his cohorts on the northern wing behaved like unproductive 'higher-ups': 'That Jiang! He and that other young group leader are slack. They just order people about and sit in the office smoking and talking. Scheming about ways to get up in the world. He thinks other people should do all the work while he sits and watches them' (Fieldnotes, 12 September 1992).

All the bakery's products were made on the southern side of the court-yard. The pastry roller and gas burners for melting and caramelising ingre-dients were kept in a narrow entrance hall. This opened onto the dry and cold stores, and a small kitchen where lunches were cooked and utensils washed. In a pantry adjacent to the kitchen, bread was sliced in an electric slicer and bagged by hand. All preparation, baking, cutting and decoration was done in one long room which ran almost the entire length of the courtyard. This room was always very noisy, littered with equipment and ingredients, crowded, and full of seemingly uncoordinated activity as individ-uals and small groups of workers grappled with the outdated equipment, and competed for limited table and oven space. An entry from my field-notes describes a typical few minutes in the work place:

> The ventilator fan has broken and it's starting to get very smoky and hot. Deng calls out to the tall man to come and help him by tipping the flour into the sponge mixture while he mixes. The tall man says he can't: 'I'm busy. I have to finish rolling the mille feuille pastry now because Tong needs the table space for the coconut triangles.' Deng is exasperated: 'Fuck!' Instead, Zheng comes over to help, holding his arms outstretched so as not to get flour on his new jeans. Wang is trying to shut an oven door that won't close properly. He kicks it, but it still won't shut. He grabs a sheet of greaseproof paper from the table and stuffs it in the corner so that he can slam the door shut, grumbling to me, 'Damned Chinese rubbish! Look at this equipment! Why can't they get us decent ovens.' The tall man has his mille feuille pastry ready for the oven now, but Bo's walnut biscuits are ready to go in too. Bo is lis-tening to a walkman. He said it's better than the noise of the convection oven and mixers, but it adds to the noise the rest of us put up with because everyone has to shout at him to make themselves understood. The tall man and Bo have a *huaquan* game to see who will get their product baked first. The tall man loses. He wheels his trays of pastry aside laughing and shaking his head at Bo, who dances his trays of walnut biscuits into the oven. (Fieldnotes, 24 November 1992)

However, in late September it was discovered that for some time, foreman Jiang had been stealing 10 per cent of the contents of each of the delivery men's monthly pay packets. The bakers compared this embezzlement of workers' wages by their lazy foreman to the appropriation of their labour power by the owners and managers of the company, and said it confirmed their earlier claims that he was 'just like the higher ups'. Jiang was sacked and the bakery premises were rearranged.

This spatial reorganisation facilitated a political realignment within the work force. The foreman's office was relocated to the entrance hall in the south wing so that the new foreman could be close to the phone, but would join in productive work, thus addressing one of the bakers' grievances. To accommodate the foreman's office furniture, the pastry roller was moved into the already overcrowded workshop and the area vacated was partitioned off. Initially, the bakers feared that this arrangement might prove to be worse than the previous one: they were not only losing some work space but were also losing their freedom from the foreman's gaze. However, the new foreman, Tong, was chosen from their midst. Tong avoided his new office. In fact he was never seen to sit at the desk. Personally committed to forging some basis of worker unity, and mindful of his colleagues' attitudes towards 'higher ups' and their consumption of the bakers' labour, he preferred to retain his identification with the bakers and deal with his paper work amongst a jumble of utensils and ingredients on benches in the workshop.

The bakers' struggles against management appropriated many of the same spatial elements that management used to belittle and exploit them. The winter after Jiang's sacking and the rearrangement of the bakery, the bakers staged a go-slow which was intended to pressure manager Rong to improve their pay and conditions. They reoccupied Jiang's dusty room on the northern 'unproductive' side of the courtyard, furnished it with chairs from Tong's new office, and spent hours there playing poker on that quintessential symbol of exploitation, the old foreman's desk. One game, begun about midday, was interrupted at 3.30 p.m. by the old storeman, who called foreman Tong to come to the phone: 'It's Rong! She wants to speak with you.' Tong, squinting at his cards through the smoke from his cigarette, shouted that he was busy and would ring her back. Twenty minutes passed, and again the storeman called Tong to the phone to speak to the manager. Tong finished the hand he was playing before sauntering over to his rarely-used office.

The spatial expression taken by the bakers' protest involved a neat symbolic inversion. From the vantage point of the old foreman's office, they parodied the leisure and consumption activities which characterised the behaviour of 'higher ups'. And from there, they deferred receipt of the orders which now came from the southern 'productive' location they had deserted.

This examination of the lay-out of the case study enterprises has illustrated how spatial arrangements clarified status, functional roles and chains of command, and encouraged productivity and disallowed unprofitable activities. The enterprise managers drew upon almost identical principles of architectural design to convey their authority and support the supervisory role their deputies played in the work place. Yet they utilised divergent technologies of space either to coerce or gain collaboration from workers and so impose managerial control over the labour process (Burawoy and Wright, 1990).

The architecture of production at Jinshagang factory was overtly despotic and coercive. A primary method for establishing control was to fix and silence employees, and expose them to the gaze and direct regulation of supervisory staff. That was enhanced by an extensive system of rewards for obedience and high productivity, and punishments for infringement of the rules and slack work. This particular mix of methods was considered by Jinshagang's manager to be appropriate both to the type of low skilled, labour intensive production the factory undertook, and to the management of an immigrant female work force. Jinshagang workers' saw themselves as the depersonalised, productive, individualised occupants of a managed space. In that space, they resentfully acknowledged their managers' and supervisors' authority, and control over workers' bodies, time and labour.

At Laolian and Sanxian, the strategy was hegemonic. The symbolic distancing of management/mental labour from production/manual labour was intended to inspire ambition, and a desire on the part of workers to emulate the behaviour of the 'higher ups'. Lower level employees were offered some degree of invisibility and responsibility, and an opportunity to exercise authority over *their* subordinates. This was thought to be apposite for tradesmen involved in skilled work. However, the strategy was not wholly effective in eliciting employees' cooperation with management. Rather, by encouraging workers' pride in their skill and productivity, it also fostered critical evaluations of management's apparent lack of productivity, and an ethos of independence.

In short, the organisation of space in these enterprises was part of the apparatus of capitalist production, and a symbolic expression of social relations of production and appropriation. Yet it is clear that workers were sensitive to management's intent in fashioning their work places. Their experiences of spatial hierarchies and architectural technologies of control and exploitation informed their perceptions of their worker-selves and their bosses, and the substance of relations between them. They also energised workers' responses to wage work for, in trying to secure some autonomy, and in attempting to improve their terms of employment, workers made use of similar spatial metaphors and techniques to subvert managerial controls.

The visual portrait of work spaces presented in this chapter situates the workers who appear throughout this book in built locations which have purposefully been designed to support specific production relations. And just as Helliwell predicts, this optic suggests the existence of groups within enterprises which are demarcated by relations of ownership, employment, control and exploitation. Those groups are, of course, owners and management staff on the one hand, and production workers on the other. The following chapters demonstrate, however, that this line of demarcation is not always evident to workers. The factory environment in which China's proletariat labours is not clearly bisected by ownership and control, a one-way gaze, physical confinement and exploitation. Affiliations and antagonisms based upon place and *guanxi* heavily influence organisation of the production process and wage payments for workers, and fracture workers' experiences, communications, consciousnesses, and identities.

6 Labour Processes

Visual analysis makes it difficult to disentangle the organisation of relationships and activities on the shop floor from the structured environment within which they occur. In this chapter, I examine the organisation of production and workers' experience and attitudes towards wage work by attending to patterns of communication and interaction in the case study enterprises. For it is modes of command, the distribution of tasks amongst workers, and the supervision and checking of their work, as well as remuneration, which really sharpen workers' sensitivity to the extension of managerial control over production and the appropriation of profit in the work place. These are central to workers' consciousnesses of class relations (Friedman, 1990, p. 193).

The macro-logic of capitalist production in contemporary China is inseparable from the identities and relationships which precede, and have become articulated to, this mode of production. These identities and relationships affect the allocation of capital and resources among populations. They determine success in the labour market, and they influence the functions recruits perform and the treatment they receive in the work place. Thus, those who are urban residents and locals are promoted more rapidly and are not expected to work as hard as those who are rural registered and outsiders. Those with *guanxi* are favoured in the distribution of tasks, and are not evaluated as critically as those who have no *guanxi*. These criteria assume added political dimensions in the labour process. Urban residents, locals or those who have *guanxi* with managers oversee the work of rural residents, outsiders, and employees without *guanxi*, discipline unproductive or unruly workers, and act as conduits of information from shop floor to office. These divisions are further cross-hatched by sex and skill. Women usually are not given the same training or tasks as men, and rarely occupy positions of power.

By attending to the ways in which non-class identities and relations have been articulated to the labour process, this chapter attempts to explain some of the reasons why workers do not perceive capitalist production to be a relationship between classes, even though exploitation is of central importance to their interpretation of employment relations and the capital-wage labour divide is sometimes contested by workers acting in concert. It examines the communication of commands, task allocation, and quality control systems in enterprises. The chapter concludes with a description of one worker's rejection of urbanites' definition of her as a 'peasant'.

Definitions such as that are, I argue, integral to managerial strategies to simultaneously promote local employees' loyalty towards the firm, and control outsiders' labour.

COMMANDING PRODUCTION

Ma, a young lecturer in business and management studies at Zhejiang University, often came to my home to chat. On one occasion, I recounted to him some complaints made to me by two Laolian technicians. They had grumbled that one of the reasons their pay was low was that production routines were being poorly organised. They were concerned that unless the factory manager found more effective means of coordinating production, the company would fail to fulfil its orders and could be forced to close. However, when they tried to offer constructive suggestions to the manager, he had treated them in an imperious manner and refused to listen to their advice. Ma laughed when I mentioned that the workers had attempted to counsel their manager:

> They weren't business graduates, these people! If workers could tell managers what to do, what power would managers have? How would they manage the enterprise, the work force? It's always been a contradiction in socialist enterprises, an impossible ideal, this formula that workers are masters … democratic management! It's nonsense. If workers were masters they would be unmanageable, the enterprises wouldn't make a profit. We always make it absolutely clear to our business students: forget the propaganda! We can't allow them to go out into an enterprise with some confused notion about who is in control. Enterprises are run by their managers, not by the employees! (Fieldnotes, 13 November 1992)

Commanding Communications in the Labour Process

None of the managers of the case study enterprises was a graduate of Ma's business course, yet they all maintained the sort of strict control over communication and the organisation of production which Ma insisted was essential to successful market performance. In none of the three enterprises did production workers participate in any way in management decision making or the planning of production. Commands flowed from the managers down through lower level supervisors to workers. The contrary flow of suggestions was minute, and most of that which did occur was couched in obtuse subtleties of speech, facial expressions, or anonymous letters which would not cause superiors to lose face.

Neither the Laolian company nor Sanxian bakery held regular meetings at which all levels of management were represented. Meetings were called on an *ad hoc* basis by managers only when they needed to discuss specific problems with staff members. At other times, instructions from managers to individual workshop foremen and production orders were communicated by phone or notes. Shop floor supervisors' and workers' suggestions were not sought, or welcomed, by management.

At Jinshagang, there was a factory management committee which, as I mentioned, met once a month in the conference room. Office manager Qin told me that the date and agenda of committee meetings were decided by the factory manager, and that they were mostly called to discuss the manager's proposals for coordinating activities and improving productivity. When I asked if the forewomen could reject or negotiate any of his proposals, she said that they could suggest amendments, but that this was 'usually unnecessary'. Recruitment officer Su had attended some of management committee meetings, but withdrew because he considered the meetings to be a waste of time. Su said that the manager's proposals were never debated, production and industrial relations issues were ignored, and the staff spent an inordinate length of time discussing trivial questions simply because they did not want to return to work.

Certainly, the meetings were not intended to resolve problems identified by production supervisors. Not all shop-floor supervisors in Jinshagang factory were aware that a management committee even existed, much less what purpose its meetings might serve:

> SS: Do you group leaders have any input into the management committee meetings?
>
> Group leader Zhang: What committee?
>
> SS: The factory management committee. They have meetings each month.
>
> Zhang (looking around with a surprised expression, as though expecting to see a meeting in progress): I don't know anything about committee meetings. We just have meetings with the forewomen, they tell us what to do. Keep the floors clean, make the workers wear their scuffs, pay more attention to quality. The orders come down to us like that. Then we tell the workers what they have to do. The forewomen must be on this committee, then, are they?
>
> Group leader Li: Yes, them and manager Mao ... maybe Qin, too. They must be on the committee. But we just get told what to do in the storeroom. (Fieldnotes, 23 November 1992)

Jinshagang factory was the only case study enterprise in which any formal feedback mechanism existed. In August 1992 a suggestion box was attached to the wall of the gatekeepers' room. The very existence of this box served to highlight a paradox. First, it indicated just how rigidly communications in the firm were structured. Second, it was evidence of management's need to institutionalise, and thus control, endemic unrest. Sudden explosions of anger, and high rates of absenteeism and attrition had alerted the factory manager to pervasive dissatisfaction amongst the work force. However, strict hierarchical communication norms, the absolute necessity of protecting leaders' face, and workers' feelings of intimidation and job insecurity meant that they could not complain directly to their superiors.[1] The suggestion box was a means of simultaneously soliciting workers' comments on their employment conditions and personnel issues, and defusing workers' anger. According to the manager, the anonymous letters he received from the suggestion box all observed etiquette and were framed within eminently acceptable discourses of economic progress and meritocracy:

> They are always polite. They say they hope the enterprise will prosper. Then they say that as it expands, they hope that workers will benefit, that the welfare system will be improved and wages will rise … I deal with all these letters myself. If I can guess who wrote it, I speak to them. Often the letters come in batches, so I write an answer to the whole work force to be stuck up in the workshops, and explain what I intend to do to try to solve the problem. (Tape, 16 February 1993)

Jinshagang workers' reluctance to speak directly to their supervisors and their deferential tone in letter writing acknowledged their insecure, subordinate position in the factory. In the same way, so too did supervisors' speech and body language signify to workers the security and authority they derived from their position in a hierarchically structured production process. But, just as mid-level supervisors bullied the workers under their command, so in turn were they bullied by higher levels of management:

> Group leader Wu: People can be so rude and abusive! They scold us for nothing. As soon as they get a little bit of power over someone else they start putting on airs as thought they are better than everyone else. Here everyone wants to be someone else's boss. It all starts at the top with the leaders' attitudes and then everyone below them starts doing it too, behaving as though everyone below them were stupid. They find something to gripe about just so they can exert their power!

SS: What sort of things do they gripe about?

Group leader Min: Everything. We are working too slowly or working too fast. It's not up to standard. We are talking. We aren't wearing regulation clothes. Our attitude is bad. They can find any excuse to pick on us workers. Every level stands over the level below them. The boss criticises the office staff, the office staff criticise the forewomen, the forewomen criticise the group leaders. It's always like that. (Fieldnotes, 22 September 1992)

Attributing Commanding Identities

That outline of formal management structures and communicative styles between supervisors and workers illuminates modes of command in the case study enterprises. However, it fails to specify the criteria on which hierarchies of command were founded, and the logic which informed design of those hierarchies. Managers all stated that they promoted employees solely on the basis of merit. In reality, however, there existed a very strong correlation between identities and relations created outside the work place and advancement to management and supervisory positions. The same factors that I found to be salient to competition in the labour market also determined preferment among enterprise employees: that is, *hukou*, local residence, and *guanxi*.

In Jinshagang factory, all but a few of the four dozen villagers employed in the factory occupied administrative, supervisory, and technical positions. The only locals who belonged to the 600 strong production work force were newly employed, or, in one instance, suffered from mental illness. Conversely, the only non-locals who were in management positions, office manager Qin and recruitment officer Su, had good *guanxi* with the factory manager. The two non-local group leaders in the clamping and wire cutting workshops had been employed in the factory since its beginning, and were married to local residents. Outside workers told me that whilst locals and people with *guanxi* received automatic promotions to positions where they could exercise authority and be relieved of production quotas, outsiders were never considered for promotion.

Local residence and *guanxi* also structured organisational hierarchies in the Laolian company and Sanxian bakery. Neighbourhood informants, administrative staff, and workers in both these companies told me that the enterprise managers had been appointed solely because of their connections. Desirable lower level management and marketing positions and the easier production jobs in the companies were distributed by those managers, in turn, to their own familiars and local residents.

The coincidence of non-class identities and relations and organisational hierarchies within these enterprises was a by-product of managers' attempt to control the labour process in order to increase productivity and profit. Locals and employees with good social connections were viewed by both managers and other workers as being loyal towards the firm rather than towards their fellow employees. Hence, they were cast as managers' eyes and ears on the shop floor, and given responsibility for evaluating production workers' output and meting out rewards and penalties.

Managements' reliance upon locals and familiars for the performance of surveillance, supervisory and disciplinary functions led to the development of exclusive circuits of communication within work forces. Outsiders and locals, and those who had and lacked *guanxi* in the firm, did not speak openly in front of each other, even on the rare occasions when they were all employed in the same capacity. An immigrant worker who was explaining to me the system of bonus distribution in Jinshagang factory stopped in mid-sentence when one of the newly arrived local production workers walked into the workshop. The following exchange between two immigrant bakers neatly illustrates the operation of a similarly exclusive system of informal communication in Sanxian bakery:

> Shi: The hierarchy! Every factory is the same. I feel as though, well, it's not fair, is it? The higher ups giving good jobs to their neighbours and their son's friends, that sort of thing.
>
> Pan: Nothing we can do about it. Anything down below, the manager deals with that. She doesn't let us know about it. So if we have a problem up there, we just have to deal with it ourselves. We don't want to let them know about our problems. Not even some of the others, her friends up there. They tell her everything we say. (Tape, 10 January 1993)

The preferential promotion of locals and people with *guanxi* inserted management agents into work forces which already had been compromised by word of mouth recruitment and the reciprocal obligations imposed by the gift of a job, and set apart by regional, status, and gender prejudices. Hence, it is hardly surprising that workers' understandings of relations in the work place did not reflect a clear-cut exercise of power by ownership and a formal management hierarchy. Rather, they believed that employment relations were structured by the way in which *hukou*, local residence and *guanxi* had been knit into management systems and practices. The following sections show how task allocation and systems of quality control encouraged competition, individualism and feelings of defensiveness among these already fragmented work forces.

TASK ALLOCATION

At certain times, staff and workers in all the case study enterprises were subjected to intense productivity pressures. Pressures were exerted upon all the participants in work places, first, by the very fact that these enterprises were producing goods for sale in competitive domestic and international markets which experienced booms and slumps. Employees in all the enterprises were particularly conscious that their work loads, and indeed their security of employment, were directly related to the receipt or cancellation of orders. A secondary source of pressure came from the inevitably imperfect organisation and distribution of production work within the enterprise. This was illustrated by the frequency of complaints voiced by staff of the Laolian company over management's failure to coordinate purchasing, production, and sales so as to ensure regular hours of work. Finally, and of greatest significance to workers' understandings of identities and relationships in the work place, production pressures were unevenly experienced by groups of workers because of discrimination between urban and rural residents, locals and outsiders, and those with *guanxi* and those without *guanxi*.

In each enterprise, production schedules were made up by the managers and office staff according to immediate demand, handed down to the workshop forepersons, thence distributed amongst group leaders who delegated tasks to groups and individual workers. The managers all said that this procedure was clearly demarcated, formalised, rational, and equitable. They also claimed that they carefully coordinated each step in the production and marketing processes, hired extra staff to cover short rushes, set quotas and piece rates after lengthy trial runs in workshops, and that workers whose tasks changed were given at least one month on their previous wage level to learn the new task.[2]

Managers' depiction of their organisation of production and allocation of tasks as being rational and well planned was strongly contested by their administrative and supervisory staff. Office staff in all case study enterprises denied that scheduling and task allocation was clear and formalised. Instead, they complained that approved procedures were not followed by managers and that managers were ignorant of production processes and set unrealisable targets. Forepersons in Jinshagang factory and Sanxian bakery said that the managers regularly accepted orders and deadlines which could not be met without imposing excessive overtime on workers. In Laolian, production supervisors said that deadlines were often missed because of incompetent planning: 'We either have nothing at all to do, or we are doing overtime every night. The manager can't think of three things at once – buying, producing, and selling.' Managers' contention that tasks and quotas were equitably allocated was also contested by workers. Favouritism in job and task allocation by managers and supervisors was endemic. And contrary to managers' claims, workers were sometimes asked to perform tasks for which they had not been trained and for which quotas and piece rate norms had not yet been established.

The pressure for completion of tasks within deadlines was passed on from office staff via workshop supervisors to the workers themselves. Although the content of tasks was not negotiable at any stage, tasks could be spread among extra workers and timetabling could sometimes be adjusted through informal resistance, as these two conversations at Jinshagang illustrate:

(Forewoman) Ren: I work out how many days it will take each section to do their part of the task, for instance, three days in the wire cutting and clamping workshops, then four days in plugs. Then I take it through to the group leaders. I oversee all their work.

SS: What happens if the group leaders say they are really busy, for example because they have some workers away sick, and they don't think they can complete the task in time?

Ren: They just have to find some way to get it done. They have to rearrange things so it will be completed on time. Maybe one of the other sections isn't busy and can take on some of their work. Or the section will have to work overtime. If they have to work overtime then they will. (Fieldnotes, 10 November 1992)

SS: What happens if the forewoman says they can't complete an order in time?

(Recruitment officer) Su: They have to accept them. If they are busy they must work at night. Sometimes they complain, but they can't say no.

SS: So don't they ever say that they can't make an order date?

Su: Sometimes they say they could make half an order in one week, then complete it the next week. If it's an urgent order then I tell them they just have to find a way to do it, they'll have to work late. (Fieldnotes, 6 November 1992)

In other enterprises, compulsion to meet deadlines was not so direct, but none the less was irresistible. One morning at Sanxian bakery, the sudden appearance of the sales manager, asking what was holding things up and counting finished products with a scowl on his face, almost halved the time it took for cakes to be decorated, sliced, and packaged.

As a result of these enterprises' market flexibility and reliance upon 'just-in-time' inventory systems and production, workers' production schedules and tasks fluctuated markedly.[3] The increasing popularity of Jinshagang's Japanese greeting cards meant that employees manufacturing card components were regularly required to do overtime. This was universally loathed, because the workers were always exhausted: 'We're still making plaits while we sleep.'[4] On the other hand, the fact that electronic orders taken by the factory tended to be 'one-offs' had a negative impact upon workers engaged in assembling electronic components. In the breaks between completing one electronics order and receiving another, plug assemblers were often transferred to other areas such as the plait workshop. In the absence of extensive training or quota-free buffer periods, this resulted in a drop in their rate of productivity and piece rate earnings, according to young Wu:

> Wu: I can't make plaits very well. I've only done it a few times, when I first came into the factory. Since then I've spent all my time making plugs. I am really slow. I would much rather do plugs, but there aren't many to make now so it can't be helped.
>
> SS: Don't you have any choice at all in what task you do?
>
> Wu: No. If there aren't any plugs we have to make plaits, or whatever jobs there are. The group leaders say they can't help it. They just have to tell us to do whatever needs to be done ... Well, they do decide who gets to stay on plugs and who gets a different task. Some of the girls are still doing plugs. I wish I was too. (Fieldnotes, 17 November 1992)

Wu's words indicate that group leaders in Jinshagang factory could indeed influence the distribution of tasks so that some workers were given tasks on which it was easier for them to earn higher piece rates, or which were less affected by task changes than others. Occasionally, even established quotas were altered by forewomen and group leaders. Invariably, those who benefited from supervisors' distribution of tasks or discretionary adjustment of quotas were either fellow villagers, relatives, or friends. Consider the following example of partiality in quota setting in the card finishing workshop. I had spent much of the day sitting opposite the group leader at her table. Earlier, she had worked out that to complete an order by the end of that day, she needed to increase the number of cards workers should finish to meet their daily quota. I watched her distribute extra materials to workers who came to report they had finished a batch, and tell them they needed to complete another 1000 cards before knock-off time. Then her husband's young cousin came to collect her next batch of materials:

Worker: How many?
Group leader (in a low voice): 500.
Worker (also lowering her voice): 500?
Group leader: Yes, I'm doing you a favour. Hurry up. Go on, I'm busy.
Worker, slapping her on the back: Thanks!
SS: Why 500? ... (no answer) ... Why did you give her 500?
Group leader (testily): Its not the task she usually does, so she isn't very fast at it. That's why I didn't give her so many to do. (Fieldnotes, 27 November 1992)

In Sanxian bakery, tasks were distributed by the foreman 'to whoever can do them best'. Bakers who were skilled at producing certain products always made those products, assisted by less skilled workers and trainees. But there too, it was not true that tasks were distributed equally and solely in accord with individual skills. Zheng, who was employed because of his *guanxi* with manager Rong's son, was not allocated production work because he was formally charged with equipment maintenance. Although he had some training as a mechanic, one of the young women employees declared in private that she had more mechanical aptitude and willingness to learn than Zheng, who 'wouldn't even change the tyre on his own bike for fear of dirtying his shirt sleeves'. In fact, all electrical repair work was done by one of the skilled bakers, Wang, and mechanical repairs were usually done by foreman Tong and Zheng together. Zheng spent most of his time smoking and chatting with anyone who had a free minute. Twice, workers wryly commented that Zheng did even less work in the bakery than I, their foreign observer.

Moreover, the ways that tasks were ranked in importance and allocated by the bakery foreman expressed and reinforced the gender discrimination which began, as I mentioned, with the training of new recruits. Males rapidly gained expertise and were gradually given tasks to undertake independently. However, because of females' reticence and the crucial significance in training of informal exchange and interaction, female bakers tended to acquire fewer skills. Consequently, they were not given tasks which required craft competence, such as piping cream to decorate cakes. Instead, each morning after the bread dough was placed in pans to rise, the women were given jobs which skilled bakers considered boring and demeaning. They sliced, bagged, and labelled bread, fetched and carried utensils and ingredients, prepared pans, and cleaned up at the end of each day.[5] In winter when the bakery often was without water, cleaning was a particularly unpleasant task which involved scraping dough, egg, sugar, cigarette butts, and dirt off the concrete floor with metal spatulas.

There were several occasions in the case study enterprises when dissatisfaction with unequal task allocation became acute. This always coincided with rush periods, when the daily quotas were too large for the numbers of active workers rostered and they became exhausted by the demands of overtime. On the one hand, this was perceived by workers to result from owners' and managers' intensification of rates of exploitation, and they railed against their employers. On the other hand, workers' anger about the excessive work load often was directed laterally towards those of their colleagues who, because of local residence or *guanxi*, appeared to have escaped from carrying a fair share of the burden. They grumbled that urban residents, locals and those who had connections in the firm were systematically given light work loads, while other workers were subjected to more intense exploitation: a charge that, to some extent, has been corroborated in media reports (Yang, 1991, pp. 42–4; *BKWZ*, 3 November 1992).

Inequity in the allocation of tasks and the differential intensification of production pressures affects workers' understandings of, and attitudes towards wage labour, their employers, and, most especially, each other. Who are their exploiters? Who are the exploited? Clearly, the answers given do not point solely to groups who fall on either side of a divide drawn by ownership and wage work. Rather, they indicate non-class identities and relations which, together, have become integral to the development and organisation of capitalist production in China, and which, as a result of having been articulated to that mode of production, are being transformed.

QUALITY CONTROL

Quality control can become an extremely volatile issue in work places, both between management and workers, and among workers themselves. Quality systems are often designed in such a way that they individualise and set workers directly in opposition to each other. Yet they also highlight the capital-wage labour divide and can become a focus of workers' resistance to management. A detailed comparison of the vastly different forms of quality control which obtain in a state-owned silk factory, Jinshagang factory, and Sanxian bakery provides an opportunity to explore how various systems of quality control shape relations in the work place, and impact on workers' experiences and understandings of work.

Dujinsheng

Contradictory interests and opposing identities can be brought into play even in the most orthodox, benign state-sponsored systems of quality control. The organisation of quality control at Dujinsheng state silk factory combined the relatively impersonal application of rational, known, and documented standards, with pressures generated through inter-workshop and intra-workshop competitions, and antagonism between local and immigrant workers.

All the workers responsible for the quality checking of woven silk cloth in Dujinsheng were tenured urban employees. They worked in a separate workshop, in numbered, curtained-off cubicles furnished with high wooden benches. The material to be checked was spread and its length and width measured with a ruler, then the number of strands in the warp and woof were calculated, and the length of silk was inspected for pulled and broken threads. If the cloth did not exceed an 80 per cent margin of error, the weaver, who was identified only by number, would not be deducted points or lose their bonus payments. According to the quality controllers, there was never any acrimony between weavers and checkers because the checking was always done in conformity with a known standard, and all faults were documented and the degree of error carefully calculated.

Dujinsheng factory's reputation rested on its production of fine silks. The necessity to maintain this reputation for quality while encouraging higher productivity through the payment of piece rates was considered by foremen in the weaving workshops to be their biggest headache. Foremen were fined if the average quality of products from their workshop declined. With a view to maintaining high quality, they organised competitions between workshops and between small groups within workshops:

> The weavers are very proud of their skills, their technical standard is very high. There is a competition … it's to see which weaver produces the highest quality work. We put their grades up on a chart for everyone to see. Each piece is examined in the quality control workshop, so at the end of each week we give them all a grade for quality. Then at the end of three months the winners are given a certificate and fifteen yuan bonus. The money isn't much, but it's the spirit of competition between them which is important. At the end of every week they all crowd around the chart to see who has done the best work, boasting and teasing each other. In this workshop in particular, they are all locals, and there are so many old weavers who have been here all their working lives, so it's very competitive. (Fieldnotes, 12 August 1992; see also *GMRB*, 2 October 1992)

As the foreman's words suggest, local tenured and contract-system weavers' employment future, material benefits, status among their peers, and personal esteem were linked to their manufacture of silks. Those employees made disparaging remarks about the simplicity and poor quality of cloth made in workshops in which there was a high ratio of immigrant contract workers: 'They only care about money. They aren't craftspeople.' Approximately half of the silk weavers in the factory were outsiders employed on 5 year contract terms. These workers were not strongly motivated by poorly remunerated competitions designed to foster pride in what was, after all, a temporary vocation, but were very responsive to the material incentives and productivity pressures exerted by the piece rate pay system ('Hangzhou shi dangqian shiyong nongmingong', 1989; Yu Zhen, 1990).

Thus, even the operation of this theoretically impartial quality control system, in the context of divergent patterns of recruitment, task allocation, and remuneration for particular *hukou* categories, established different experiences of and attitudes towards work, and highly charged relations in the work place. It effectively linked local workers' sense of identity and job satisfaction to the quality of their product, and to the reputation of the factory. But it also set quality checkers and forepersons apart from weavers, local weavers apart from outsiders, and weavers within single workshops and work groups apart from their craft rivals.

Jinshagang

Jinshagang's quality control system was designed to fulfil two functions. The first of these was self-evident. It was intended to ensure that products met strict quality requirements. Director Mao told me his Japanese clients had strongly advised him that if he wanted to retain their business, he 'must not let the factory become a garbage bin'. Motivated by the fear that the export of poor quality products would result in a loss of orders and negatively affect the factory's profits, the factory manager made quality maintenance one of the primary tasks of administrative and supervisory staff. Forewomen and group leaders, mindful of their own bonus payments, continually exhorted workers to pay attention to quality rather than to quantity. The second aim of the quality control system was no less important to the factory's director and manager, but not immediately apparent. It was intended to strengthen management's control of the labour process by individualising workers, and compounding already fragmented identities and allegiances.

Manager Mao implemented what he described as a 'Japanese model' of quality control, which combined a high degree of direct supervision, individual worker responsibility for checking, bonus payments for meeting quality standards, and stiff cash penalties for failure to meet standards.[6] The system required every worker to sign a batch tag to show which part of the production process they had undertaken. Downstream workers examined the work of those upstream and, if they found mistakes, could appropriate the upstream worker's piece rates for that part of the assembly process. If they failed to detect a mistake and it was discovered by the next downstream worker, then the piece rates of both were added to the third worker's income. Moreover, workers were fined bonus points for producing substandard products, thereby reducing their monthly bonus payment.

This system exerted contradictory and unforeseen pressures, both upon workers and supervisory staff. Workers certainly tried to avoid producing substandard articles while working as quickly as possible, and usually checked upstream workers' products so as to protect their own incomes. On the other hand, they were loath to report mistakes in the products of people with whom they shared dormitory rooms, friends, food, and, possibly, common origins or dialects. I never heard of a case in which a worker sought to benefit monetarily by detecting another's mistakes, for to do so would have exposed them to hostile gossip and social isolation. Hence, the discovery of mistakes caused workers like Xu considerable anxiety:

Xu (holding up a plait): Oh, no! Mistress Li, look at this. The white section is too short.
Group leader Li: What are the others like?
Xu (measuring the bundles of wire): Mmmm, some are okay. This one is just right ... but look at this one. It's much too short! What a mess! What will I do? They are all mixed up. It will take me ages to sort through them. Oh, what a pain!
Group leader Li: Take them back upstairs. Tell them it's their problem. They ought to sort through them.
Xu: Oh, I couldn't do that! They will deduct her wages and scold her. I couldn't!
Group leader Li: That's not your worry. Take them back.
Xu: I'll lose time checking them all. If I take them back up, they'll be cross and the girl will get into trouble ... [looking at the batch tag] I don't know her. It's even more embarrassing if I don't know her. I don't think I could go. Couldn't you do it, Mistress Li? I'd be too embarrassed.
Group leader Li: They didn't want the problem. That's why they let it through. They think maybe no one down here will notice. But we can't let it through here or the next group will find out and deduct you.

They will have to go back. Here, I'll give you a hand to sort out the mistakes and you can take them back already separated.

Xu (returning after taking the substandard plaits upstairs): They didn't believe me! They said they never made any mistakes! It's infuriating. They checked every one again! Can you believe it? They said 'How could that have happened?', as if it were my business! They didn't want to take them back. I was so embarrassed. They weren't at all cooperative!

Group leader Li: Don't worry, it's not your fault. It's their problem. They are getting slacker all the time up there. Give me a look at that batch.

Xu: Well don't look too carefully! Don't find any mistakes. I don't want any more problems.

Group leader Li: What about quality? You rotter! (Fieldnotes, 13 November 1992)

At times, Jinshagang workers even attempted to escape the individualising effects of the quality control system by covering up others' mistakes. In doing so, they were correctly seen by their supervisors to be placing a higher priority upon worker solidarity than on the observance of enterprise regulations and support for the factory managers and their profit objectives. Supervisors responded to this by refuting the logic which informed workers' actions. They represented concealment of substandard articles as an offence against the enterprise work force as a collective body: speaking on behalf of the interests of all workers, they abused offenders loudly and harshly. Yet workers were sensitive to the irony that the supposedly collective body of workers was organised precisely on the basis of divergent identities and competing interests.

Competition to ensure quality did not just affect workers. As group leader Li's anxious reaction to Xu's discovery of defective plaits indicates, supervisors themselves were also placed in opposition and pressured by the operation of this system. When workers called upon their group leaders to try to diffuse problems associated with the discovery of substandard products, they were attempting to deflect lateral, individual conflicts into contests between workshop supervisors. Similarly, when forewoman Ren was on the prowl looking for substandard articles and threatening to deduct the bonus of entire work groups, workers directed attention to divisions between levels of management. They were fully cognisant of the fact that the group leaders had to defend their face and income by ensuring that their groups' products met standards. They also knew that forewoman Ren, mindful of her even greater face and income, was in turn responsible to the factory manager. And the manager was vulnerable to client dissatisfaction.

These divisions called into question the bonds of local community and *guanxi* which underpinned the factory's organisational hierarchy and their own subjugation as immigrant workers:

> Group leader Huang (speaking to the two dozen outside workers she supervises): I've just been told that all our bonuses this month are hanging on whether or not everyone here does a good job. In a situation like this I just have to be strict with you all. Some people have been producing substandard articles and it's affecting us all. So from now on, forget speed and concentrate on quality!
>
> Gao (looking up with a mischievous grin): It doesn't make much difference to us outsiders. Our bonuses are hardly worth getting, not like yours, Mistress Huang. It's your group leaders' work they are criticising, not ours! (Fieldnotes, 1 December 1992)

Clearly, whilst the quality control system did encourage workers to try to meet the factory's high standards, it did not always fulfil the political function for which it had been intended.

Sanxian

The themes of fragmentation, competition, surveillance, and 'just desserts' which figured so strongly in the quality control systems of Dujinsheng and Jinshagang were absent in Sanxian bakery until early 1993. Management attempts to control product quality had been impeded by the separation of administrative and productive locations which allowed mistakes to pass unremarked, and by the fact that the bakers were the only people in the enterprise who fully understood their trade. It was a company regulation that workers who produced substandard products would have their bonus reduced. However, the bakers covered their mistakes in a way which left the staff in charge of quantity and quality control oblivious to their occurrence. Manager Rong was alerted to this situation by her contacts in the bakery, and she become increasingly dissatisfied about the bakers' seemingly elastic usage of ingredients. In 1993, she undertook two separate initiatives to address these problems: initiatives which attempted to replicate some aspects of the quality control systems in Dujinsheng and Jinshagang.

The first was a plan to popularise knowledge of the production process among managerial and administrative staff so they could devise enforceable standards regarding the usage of time and ingredients, and product quality. The manager ordered the new quantity clerk to spend a week in the bakery minutely examining production routines and the quantities of ingredients required in different products.

If this initiative had achieved its objective, it would have had the concurrent effect of reducing workers' autonomy and responsibility. But the bakers felt quite secure in their superior knowledge: 'A new university graduate? As if she'll understand! Don't tell her anything, will you, otherwise we will be criticised and deducted!' During her week long inspection, the quantity clerk still had to leave the bakery at times. On a couple of these occasions, burnt and misshapen products were whisked from ovens straight out the window or into a bin. The quantity clerk also had to rely upon the bakers' answers to her questions about their use of ingredients. And these answers were liberally interspersed with qualifying statements about the variable effect upon sponge mixtures of the cold weather, the problems they had encountered using the new bag of yeast, and the excessive amount of shells to be found in Shandong walnuts. After she returned to the administrative office with her findings, I asked several of the skilled bakers whether they thought stricter standards would be applied as a consequence of her inspection. They remained confident: 'She didn't understand anything.' 'She won't tell them anything down below. It won't change.' 'We just do the work. They don't know what goes on.' Of course, manager Rong did have quite a good idea of what was going on, but in the absence of reliable information was unable to devise the desired system of standards.

The second of Rong's strategies to raise and stabilise product quality in the bakery was a plan to improve bakers' training. This plan was still being formulated when I left Hangzhou in March 1993:

> I'm not satisfied with the quality ... it's too uneven, not up to standard. I'm going to select some backbone workers from amongst them. I'll send them outside to do some training. In addition, just recently while I was in Shanghai I decided to invite a few master bakers to come and teach them. So with a combination of sending people away and inviting people here, we should be able to improve their techniques. (Fieldnotes, 25 February 1993)

Rong also expressed the hope that such a training programme would encourage the bakers' sense of loyalty towards the enterprise and herself.

When I discussed this proposed system of training, honours, and rewards with the bakers, they were concerned that it might indeed have the effect of increasing some employees' loyalty to Rong. Many suspected that workers who had *guanxi* with the manager would be chosen to go away to train, even though none of them were master bakers. None of the highly skilled bakers believed they would be selected to go away to study. Even the perfectionist Wang, who was so adept that everyone crowded around to watch his finishing flourishes in cake decorating, said he had no chance of being selected. Indeed, Wang predicted that Rong would send the extraordinarily lazy and incompetent mechanic, Zheng, and her own son: 'They will just get a free holiday in Shenzhen!' If these people suddenly acquired artisanal status, it was feared they would impose the control of those 'down below' to a degree which previously had proved impossible even with the manager's agents amongst them. The bakers also saw the scheme as an affront to regional pride and their self-esteem as master craftsmen: 'Petty upstart Shanghai bakers lording it over us here? Treating us as though we are all ignorant peasants? That would be terrible! I'd rather leave!' Rong's plan was also condemned as a threat to informally established lines of skill-based authority within the bakery. The bakers' conversations made it clear that anyone who participated in the training programme risked being stigmatised and isolated.

Although the quality control systems in Dujinsheng, Jinshagang, and Sanxian all operated according to similar principles, they differed in important respects in the way they influenced relations in the work place. In the state-owned Dujinsheng factory, the 'impartial' measurement of cloth quality by privileged local employees set local weavers in competition to establish their craft credentials. These credentials proved their membership of a highly accomplished, socially responsible urban collective, in contradistinction to poorly skilled outsiders who were said to be motivated simply by greed.

The links between individual skill, collective enterprise, and urban sophistication and altruism evident in Dujinsheng were reversed in Sanxian. There, craft pride motivated a defence by the bakers of their collective independence against attempts by manager Rong to utilise self-interest and regional status competition as a basis for controlling not only product quality, but also the work force. In Jinshagang, the quality control system was designed to further individualise and pressure an unskilled immigrant female work force which was already segregated by place of origin and *guanxi*. But the system sometimes heightened workers' sensitivity to the factory's appropriation of their outsider identities as a tool for dividing, disempowering, and exploiting them, and generated contention not only between individuals and work groups, but also between management and supervisory staff on the one hand and production workers on the other.

Thus far, this analysis of the labour process has centred on the divisive manipulation of workers' identities by management. But, as is illustrated by the bakers' representation of themselves as productive in contrast to their unproductive managers, and Jinshagang workers' definition of local and outsider identities as an axis of exploitation and conflict, it is apparent that workers also deployed a rhetoric of identity in their attempts to resist management's control of the labour process.

'STRATEGIC SOCIAL POSITIONING' IN THE WORKPLACE

Fran Elejabarrieta's concept of 'strategic social positioning' illuminates the dialectical process by which identity simultaneously can be performative and transformative: 'the concept refers not only to the symbolic occupation of a space of identity and action which needs to be defended, but also to the dynamic through which positioning expresses identity and allows individuals to build the space of reality in which their identity can be expressed' (1994, p. 248). This suggests that aspects of status and identity that figure in the subordination of workers, such as *hukou* and outsiderness, might also inspire workers' self-expression and activism. Workers' understandings about their bosses and themselves are all constituted both outside and within the work place through reference to a multiplicity of experiences and discourses. Their subjective responses to wage work are similarly complex.

The story I tell here suggests that outsiders try to compensate for their individuation and degradation in the labour process partly by maintaining and referring to positive aspects of those same indices of identity that have been made critical to their subordination in contemporary China's political economy and their exploitation in capitalist firms. Especially in moments of confrontation, they reject the rational-economic ethos which has naturalised their subjugation, and assert their moral superiority as outsiders.

The train of events which was set in motion on 25 November at Jinshagang factory was propelled by the mobility of Japanese capital and pressures of global competition. The factory's clients had complained about product quality. In a meeting that morning, manager Mao admonished the forewomen that if rising costs were not offset by improved product quality, future orders would be sent to firms in Vietnam. To underscore his concern, he brandished a stick: he was thinking of introducing productivity quotas and a productivity-linked pay scheme for supervisory staff. Later that day, these messages were duly transmitted from forewomen to group leaders. The group leaders felt insecure and angry.

In the card finishing workshop that wintry afternoon, the bent heads of the outside workers were only just visible amongst piles of cards and boxes. The local group leader, resplendent in the gold jewellery received at her recent marriage, approached a young woman from Anhui whom she had scolded a few times during the day for producing substandard work. She stood over the worker and looked down at the card in her trembling hands, then leafed through the completed cards which were stacked on her desk. 'What are these?' She picked up a few cards and held them up high for public censure. 'Look at this! Really! What an idiot! I've told you so many times and you still can't get it right. How can you be so stupid? Stop work immediately before you ruin any more materials. Come with me!' The group leader stalked back towards her desk, followed only by forty pairs of eyes. The worker swore. Grabbing her few tools, she broke them against the edge of her desk, scattering paper, paste and boxes. Then she jumped up, ran past the rows of white-coated, gaping figures sitting at their desks, and escaped through the back door of the factory.

Two local office staff, a male and a female, were sent to the factory dormitory to tell the worker that she was fired, had forfeited her 200 yuan bond, and had to pay for the materials and tools she had damaged. They were also instructed to make sure she had not vandalised the dormitory or other workers' possessions. On their return, they reported that she was quiet and not intent on mischief. Together, the staff laughed about what they thought was the worker's overreaction to the group leader's criticism. They were amused at the fact that the woman and her two elder sisters who also worked in the factory were all sleeping together in one bunk because of lack of space in the dormitory. After a few general remarks about uncivilised outsiders, 'Especially the ones from Anhui!', the office staff set off home.

The following morning, the worker's eldest sister came to the factory office. She complained to manager Mao that the male staff member who had gone to the dormitory the previous afternoon to speak with her sister had stolen 400 yuan that had been hidden inside her quilt. She insisted that as he was a Jinshagang villager, the manager must reimburse her. The manager responded that the theft should be reported at the nearby police station, and offered to delegate someone to accompany her there. The woman refused to go, and repeated her demand that he take responsibility for the alleged actions of his fellow villager. Mao frowned: 'If you won't go to the police station, you should return to work. Otherwise you will be fined for shirking.'

While they were arguing, the man whom she had accused of theft arrived, forewarned and self-righteous: 'How dare you say I stole your money!' He slapped the woman hard on the side of her face. She started screaming and lunged towards him, but the factory manager and other office staff interceded. The worker's hands were held tight, she was pushed out of the office, and the door was locked behind her. The shocked manager rebuked the staff member for the assault, while the woman stood outside the door screaming out her moral advantage, 'You hit me! You've hurt me! You've stolen my money and now you have injured me! You have to give me back my money and take me to a hospital. I won't work here any more. You have to give me the money you took, and my bond money, and pay me my wages!' The shouting continued until the manager opened the door to apologise for what had happened. He instructed one of the local female clerks to accompany the worker to hospital, because she moaned that her head was aching from the blow.

They went to two hospitals in the city: places in which neither felt comfortable. The worker was dissatisfied with the first doctor's diagnosis that there was nothing wrong with her. The second doctor gave her aspirin, and said she would feel better if she lay down for an hour. At both hospitals, the worker made a point of telling all the staff and patients she met that she was employed at the Jinshagang factory, had been robbed by a villager, and the factory manager had ordered the thief to beat her because she was an outsider who dared to demand justice. She asked the clerk to take her to the main provincial hospital for a third examination, but the clerk, embarrassed by the worker's slandering of her fellow villagers to city people, refused.

The two returned, and the worker's protest incorporated spatial transgressions. She threw her aspirin on the floor and occupied a chair in the office. She insisted that in addition to her original claims, the manager should also give her the fare back to her village so she could see a 'proper doctor in Anhui'. Her complaints repeatedly drew analogies between the factory's employment of its immigrant work force, and her own experience of robbery, assault, and humiliation. The employment relation was represented not as a contractual exchange between owners/managers and wage-workers, but rather as the robbery of outsiders by a territorially defined population: 'You people from Hangzhou all plot against us outsiders, stealing our strength and our money, stealing our labour! Because I demand justice, you beat me and then take me to a hospital where a Hangzhou doctor gives me poison to put me to sleep! You are all robbers! I don't want to stay here any longer. I want to go back home to live amongst honest people. Give me back my money.' Eventually she performed the greatest possible infringement of the factory's disciplinary code: she lay down on an office desk and went to sleep. At 4.30 p.m. her second sister came in from the workshop to provide moral support.

Mindful that he might bear some responsibility for her assault, manager Mao agreed to pay any medical costs the woman incurred in Hangzhou. But he refused to give her the 400 yuan she claimed had been stolen, travel expenses to Anhui, or her bond money. His offer was rejected. At a loss, he asked the local police to send someone to the factory to help resolve the issue. The policeman listened to both sides of the story and told the sisters that the alleged theft of the money was not the manager's responsibility, and that for the police to take any action they must be able to prove that 400 yuan really was stolen. The elder sister interpreted his advice as further evidence of the perfidy of Hangzhou people, and shouted, 'You are a Hangzhou person too! You local police are only going to help *them*. Why would I listen to you?' The policeman departed, muttering about the stupidity of 'peasants'. At 8.30 p.m. manager Mao also left, telling the women they could sleep in the office if they wished. After he had gone, they returned to sleep in the dormitory.

On the morning of the third day, three men who shared the sisters' place of origin were called in as mediators. The manager was out, but the men listened to the office staff's account of what had happened, then went to the dormitory to confer with the sisters. In the afternoon, the worker who had originally fled the card workshop came to the factory and reached an agreement with the manager. The three workers had their pledges returned and were paid wages owing since the last pay day. From this money, a small sum was deducted to cover the costs of the materials and tools that had been damaged. Then the sisters left Jinshagang.

Participants' re-telling of these events yielded markedly different interpretations, and the contradictions between their interpretations shed light on the ways in which syncretic socio-spatial identities were strategically deployed in the work place, and different conceptualisations of work were being made and contested. In telling their versions of events, the characters in the story all struggled to gain some measure of control over their situation, and defend or advance their interests through discursively defining themselves, each other, and the relationships which obtained between social groups.

The group leader who had originally scolded the worker acknowledged she had played a role which was shaped by global competition and foreign and local business interests. She was resentful of these forces which, eventually, might cast in doubt the significance of her identity as a local employee of the village collective and her consequent native status, ownership rights, and income security. Yet she said her anxiety had been fed principally by the belief that the incompetence of the workshop's employees would obstruct her from achieving the improvement in product quality demanded by the manager. She represented herself as a hard-working, enlightened, modern middle-level manager, struggling to fulfil her proper duties with only unreasoning primitives under her command: 'She wasn't able to learn to do the job. She kept making mistakes and being rude

They are peasants, these people, not workers. Everyone knows Anhui people are wild. Not like us' (Fieldnotes, 27 November 1992).

The workers' protest was, of course, a refutation of precisely that view. The first sister's response to the group leaders' criticism of her work demonstrated a rejection of the identification and evaluation of her as a peasant trying to be a worker. Her rush for the door was similarly an escape from the factory's control over her body, identity and labour. The elder sister's accusation that the staff member who had gone to their dormitory stole her money repeated the motifs of regional identity, spatial violation, physical persecution, and theft which figured so prominently in her interpretation of the territorial basis of capital/wage-labour relations. Together, the sisters denied the rights of the enterprise owners and managers to turn outsider-ness to their own ends, instead constructing their Anhui origins as a source of ethical superiority and social strength. Moreover, their moral claims and bargaining methods were vindicated. As a consequence of their irrational, 'wild' style of negotiation with that archetypal economic rationalist, manager Mao, they extracted a much more favourable exit package than would otherwise have been available. Their protest was a public celebration of an autonomy granted by their different perceptions, values, and practices.

To manager Mao, annoyed at the hours he had wasted trying to negotiate with the three sisters and the face he had lost in the process, repayment of their pledge and back wages was a small price to pay to restore order in the factory office. More importantly, however, Mao interpreted these events as evidence of deep-seated problems in the factory's work force. The criterion of local residence upon which the factory's organisational hierarchy and patterns of control were based had become anachronistic and counterproductive. The firm had come to rely on the employment of outsiders rather than locals, but their 'enthusiasm for production' was being affected by their exclusion from promotion opportunities and local supervisors' arrogance. Manager Mao's plans for dealing with what he perceived to be poor relations within the work force accorded with his understandings of international 'best practice'. He decided to introduce a comprehensive, purely meritocratic system of promotion and remuneration. He also proposed to buy a 'muzak' system, to be played in the workshops at lunchtime to soothe tensions. By eliminating localist discrimination and creating a bland sameness of environment, he would reduce antagonism between supervisors and workers and encourage outsiders' feelings of identification with the enterprise and its globalised future.

Local employees expressed quite different interpretations of these events, and in doing so revealed conflicting interests and identities. Jinshagang villagers employed as office staff and workshop supervisors were crestfallen that manager Mao had yielded to such crude tactics. They believed the sisters should have been sacked without recompense. Return of their pledge and back wages would be perceived by the rest of the factory's immigrant work force as an invitation to slack work and insubordination. Huddling together at their lunch tables and in corners of the workshops, the local group leaders all agreed that, at least in the short term, they would have to be vigilant: 'Otherwise, they will think they can get away with anything and still get their money back.' In their stories, they mounted an emotional defence of the economic and ethical advantages to be gained from continuing the localist bias in promotion, as against the meritocratic system advocated by the manager and outsiders. On the other hand, the factory's two urban employees, office manager Qin and Su, the recruitment officer, tried to dissuade local staff from responding by increasing surveillance and sanctions against outsiders. They did not interpret the sisters' actions as rebellion, but rather as evidence of 'peasants' natural inability to comprehend the law. They advocated a rational-bureaucratic response: circulating a document which clarified all employees' contractual obligations.

Many of the immigrants employed at Jinshagang did indeed decode the story of the Anhui workers' protest as a triumphant rejection of Hangzhou employers' control over their bodies, labour and identities. They said the women could not tolerate their denigration and exploitation by locals, and had engineered their exit in such a way as to make a political statement and win economic advantage. By recouping their money, they had disproved locals' assumption that outsiders were stupid and powerless. And finally, they claimed that the sisters' actions had encouraged the manager to begin to dismantle the system of localism which exacerbated divisions in the work force and rendered them all vulnerable to exploitation.

However, let us not fall into the trap of imagining all outsiders as a collectivity, possessed of similar attributes, attitudes, and interests. Several workers from villages in northern Zhejiang who considered themselves to be urban sophisticates concurred with the Jinshagang group leaders that the behaviour of the Anhui sisters was indeed 'wild'. They did not believe any money was stolen, and thought that the eldest sister's denunciation of Hangzhou people as thieves who stole outsiders' strength was ridiculous and rude. It had merely demonstrated her superstitiousness and 'backwardness'. In their remarks, they laid claim to membership of the modern, rational, economically productive community reified by contemporary neo-liberal ideologues and urban media and represented by Jinshagang.

Although production in Jinshagang was founded upon managements' control of the shop floor and the labour process and its ability to extract surplus value from contingent workers, discrepancies in the telling of these events cast doubt on theorisations which invoke dichotomous, structured oppositions revolving around proletarian/capitalist experiences, proletarian/capitalist identities, and proletarian/capitalist consciousnesses. Instead of exposing an homogeneous proletariat, these stories reveal a polysemous proletariat whose members had radically different experiences and understandings of work. Non-locals and those who lacked *guanxi* were subjected to greater productivity pressures than those who were locals or were well-connected. Their identities were not as closely bound up with their occupations, and they defended those identities as a source of autonomy from wage work and alternative values to those propagated by their employers and their local, better connected colleagues. Their divergent understandings of work were expressed in resistant practices which drew on regional histories, territorial displacement and spatial subjugation, as well as their more immediate experiences of discriminatory employment.

In short, even whilst workers acknowledged the fact of their exploitation, they were aware that this was facilitated by, and calibrated to their differentiation by *hukou*, membership or non-membership of local communities, and *guanxi*. Whatever sameness was given workers by their structural position *vis-à-vis* capital was simultaneously fractured by the identities and relations which set them apart, for these had been made central to the labour process. The following chapter on workers' perceptions of wage systems further explicates their experiences and consciousnesses of wage labour as an exploitative relationship between groups who identify (and are identified by) non-class criteria.

7 A Cipher of Class: The Wage-Labour Bargain

Ownership of capital, control over production processes, and the payment of wages are at the heart of capitalist class relations. The workers I spoke with in Hangzhou all laboured in firms they did not own in return for wages. In keeping with Marx's ideas on class, they described the conditions under which they sold their labour as exploitative. They believed their exploitation had been made possible – in fact, inevitable – by state-sanctioned territorial and socio-economic inequalities, asymmetrical access to opportunities, and the lawful and *de facto* privatisation of resources and firms. One might expect that this belief would encourage a sense of common purpose and identity among workers.

However, many workers were convinced that the organisation of capitalist production, employment of wage labour and appropriation of workers' surplus product were facilitated by factors which are not addressed by classic expositions of class. In the context of economic reforms, *hukou*, localism, and particularistic social networks, together with the controls exercised by local officials, established the conditions under which some people became bosses who hired workers, profited from their labour, and reinvested to further their accumulation of capital, some employees enjoyed relative autonomy in production and a share in profits, whilst the majority of workers laboured for little more than their subsistence requirements.

This chapter examines patterns of remuneration and workers' evaluations of the wage bargain. It begins by surveying media debates about wages, for the rhetoric of these debates has established parameters and standards by which workers assess their situation. The following section argues that workers' opinions that wage payments were inequitable and exploitative were consequent, first, upon the fact that although state and business spokespeople recommended that payments should reflect productivity, in practice they did not. Second, and more importantly, their judgement was informed by their own experiences of the way localism and particularism had granted ownership and control of firms to exclusive social groups, whilst denying them an opportunity to own businesses. The chapter concludes with an analysis of workers' protests against a practice which they considered to be at the root of their fragmentation, disempowerment, and consequent exploitation: partiality in wage payments.

THE DISCURSIVE FIELD

Money: in 1992 and 1993, China's media was full of it! In the avalanche of reports on who had money, how they earned it, and whether or not they deserved it, one could detect a concerted effort to redefine the principles which underpinned relations of production, distribution, and accumulation, and concepts of equity.[1] However, these attempts at redefinition did not proceed without debate.

The dominant, party-state sanctioned line of reasoning in the press and on television applauded individual competitiveness, the operation of market-determined meritocratic principles, and a consequent increase in income disparity as a practicable and just means for spurring economic growth and governing income distribution. In ceding the central party-state's authority to adjudicate issues of distributive justice to the market, spokespeople for the new orthodoxy concurrently represented the market as a rational, impartial arbiter of the national interest and individual worth.

Sceptics, whose criticisms frequently appeared in the labour newspapers *Gongren ribao* and *Zhongguo laodong bao*, questioned whether the market was either an efficient or fair mechanism for distributing income. They countered the logic of market meritocracy by dwelling upon the potentially negative economic and social implications of increasing the gap between rich and poor and creating labour markets in which people competed on unequal terms. They also posed the politically and morally contentious question of why the party-state was encouraging private enrichment through the exploitation of labour, and was dismantling public redistributive systems.

Most media debates over income and wage payments revolved around a few common themes. Three of these themes surfaced regularly in the conversations of workers in Hangzhou. The first concerned the macro-distribution of wealth and income in society. One side of this argument, following Deng's slogan that 'to get rich is glorious', commended business people for having invested their capital, hard work and acumen in economic growth (Yabuki, 1995, pp. 289–94). The new rich were portrayed as industrious, creative risk-takers, employers of the jobless, conscientious tax-payers, and benefactors of worthy causes (*FBIS*, 16 February 1990, 10 September 1991; *HZRB*, 29 May 1992, 30 June 1992; *ZGGSB*, 18 May 1992). It was said that through the operation of market forces, attempts at emulation, trickle-down effect and expansion of job opportunities, the enrichment of these people would eventually benefit society at large (*HZRB*, 21 May 1992).

An opposing view was presented by maverick journalists who argued that the total income gap in society was already excessive, and that too much money accrued to the rich (*RMRB*, 12 July 1991; *GRRB*, 26 May 1992; *GMRB*, 21 May 1992; 12 May 1992, 4 August 1992; Hangzhou shi dianshitai, hereafter *HZSDST*, 13 February 1993, 14 February 1993). That claim was substantiated by the publication of information on the source of bank savings deposits, which revealed that the combined savings deposits of China's wealthiest 36 million people exceeded the deposits of the poorest 800 million (*XWHB*, 10 August 1992; *YCWB*, 11 March 1993; Prybla, 1997, p. 18). Other contributors to this argument focused on the undeservedly high incomes of two specific groups: private business people and the heads of large public and joint venture firms (Guo, 1997, pp. 81–2). Their conspicuous wealth was said to have generated dissatisfaction over corruption and inequalities of opportunity. It was also held to be antithetical to national developmental objectives because their money was dissipated in unproductive consumption, and, in the absence of effective institutions for monitoring business activities, too little tax was collected by the state for infrastructural development and the expansion of education and welfare. These critics of the new orthodoxy implicitly condemned the party-state's failure to observe fundamental principles of equality of opportunity and social redistribution.

Increasing income disparities between geographical areas and ownership sectors were a related subject of concern. Government surveys have predicted that the gap between urban and rural incomes will triple by the year 2005 (Guo, 1997; *CND*, 11 February 1998). Employees of the foreign and joint venture firms which have proliferated in coastal cities earn many times more than employees of the state-owned firms that still predominate in China's old industrial centres in the north and west (*ZGLDTJNJ 1996*, p. 209). Moreover, wages in the private sector of the economy are increasing at a much faster rate than in the public sector. In 1994, wages in foreign and joint venture firms had increased 79.7 per cent over 1993 whilst, in the state sector, wages increased only 35 per cent during the same period (*SWB*, 27 June 1995). On one side of the debate, employees of urban, foreign funded and private enterprises were celebrated for having braved the market place in order to realise their true worth. On the other side, increasing income differentials were condemned for inspiring materialism and envy, and reducing farmers' and public sector employees' 'enthusiasm for production'.

Linked to arguments over the range of, and rationale for, income disparity was a micro-justice debate about the ways in which various types of jobs should be valued by the market and positioned on a taken-for-granted, hierarchical status continuum. Many contributors to this discussion advocated a new deal for those engaged in administrative, managerial, and research work. Mao's privileging of manual, productive labour was attacked as an irrational and anachronistic denial of the objective value-adding effects of white-collar work (*GMRB*, 13 May 1992, 27 May 1992, 7 September 1992; *HZRB*, 6 May 1992). Those whose work could not be assessed simply in terms of material output argued that information and intelligence would be essential to the development of China's socialist civilisation and economy. It was held to be an outrageous inversion of international norms that some research scientists earned less than market traders, and some managers earned less than the labourers they directed (*GRRB*, 26 May 1992; *GMRB*, 27 May 1992).

That reasoning, too, was strongly contested. Journalists pointed out that the administrators, managers, and academics who were demanding that the government reassess their worth to the market economy were not showing confidence in the principle of market pricing for their own labour. Besides, most of these people already enjoyed high cash incomes. They also had significant non-wage benefits from their jobs: opportunities for free travel and hospitality, income from bribery and corruption, and access to a vast array of publicly subsidised services. These advantages were not accessible to the majority of workers and generally could not be accounted for in wage packages (*GMRB*, 21 May 1992, 2 October 1992, 7 November 1992).

The third controversial theme which surfaced both in the media and in my informants' conversations concerned the attempt by the central party-state to popularise the idea that wage levels should be adjusted by market forces, enterprise profitability, and individual productivity. Individuals' output and their corresponding income would, naturally, be affected by the fact that 'some people are physically of a high quality and have advanced technical skills, while others have a poor physique and few technical skills' (*GRRB*, 26 May 1992). The wage systems that characterised foreign invested and rural enterprises, purportedly based upon supply and demand for special skills and labour, 'scientifically' established methods of evaluation, and workers' essentially 'rational' economic nature, were held up as exemplary models of efficiency and fairness (*GRRB*, 7 July 1992; *HZRB*, 5 April 1992; *ZGLDB*, 12 May 1992; *GMRB*, 26 March 1993). There were a multitude of wage schemes (piece rates, payment according to post requirements, individual contracting of quotas, bonus payments for over-quota production, retail sales-linked bonuses, employee share-holding) which were espoused as ways of directly linking workers' output and enterprise profitability to individual incomes. The payment of piece rates was especially recommended as an efficient, easily quantifiable, and just form of 'distribution according to work' (*an lao fenpei: GRRB*, 9 July 1992; *ZGLDB*, 18 June 1992).

In response, ACFTU officials, writers for the labour press, and workers have protested that the introduction of these pay schemes encourage employers to view labour power as a commodity which should be utilised to the utmost (*RMRB*, 12 July 1991; *GMRB*, 13 May 1992; *ZGGSB*, 18 May 1992; *ZGLDB*, 12 May 1992, 27 August 1992; *GRRB*, 26 February 1993). They objected that 'the aim of reform is to give economic results, not to adopt a strategy of exhausting workers in going all out for production' (*GRRB*, 11 June 1992).

Moreover, reports disputed the claim that markets had the capacity to set an equilibrium price for labour. Critics pointed out that labour markets were political creations which were rendered imperfect by remnant practices from the era of central planning, such as *hukou*, and by self-interested intervention by local governments. Hence, labour markets could not be expected to regulate wage rates in an economically rational and efficient manner:

> The price structure of the labour market is extremely distorted. There are serious discrepancies between the status of workers from urban and rural areas, between different types of ownership and industrial sectors, and between workers and administrators. Labourers do not enjoy a free choice of jobs, and do not engage in equal competition in the labour market. (*ZGLDB*, 27 October 1992)

And sceptics also questioned the party-state's wisdom in assuming that the introduction of productivity based wage systems would indeed make payments rational and fair. Although there was widespread support for the principle 'distribution according to work', researchers and journalists maintained that many firms simply pretended to adhere to this slogan whilst actually utilising different criteria for determining remuneration (*Dangdai gongren, DDGR*, no. 5, 1991, p. 17, no. 9, 1991, p. 23; *ZGLDB*, 18 August 1992, 1 December 1992). In a number of enterprises in all ownership sectors it was shown that strict productivity norms were applied only to outsiders, or to those who were without *guanxi* in the workplace (*BKWZ*, 3 November 1992; *GRRB*, 8 June 1992, 11 June 1992). Journalists cited these cases as evidence that wage differentials had increased between regionally and relationally defined groups, rather than between the physically adept and inept, the skilled and unskilled, and the productive and unproductive. And they maintained that workers' dissatisfaction over distribution which did not accord with the slogan 'more work, more pay' (*duo lao, duo de*) had given rise to a pervasive wage-labour mentality which manifested in apathy, cynical materialism, and an increasing incidence of go-slows and wild-cat strikes (*BKWZ*, 3 November 1992; *GRRB*, 3 June 1992; *SHKXB*, 9 July 1992; *ZGLDB*, 19 May 1992, 5 November 1992). My own observations of wage systems and workers' responses to partiality in remuneration in the case study enterprises lends support to that argument.

In summary, the party-state's attempt to popularise the notion that the objective, invisible hand of the market should reward business people and workers alike has generated numerous points of contention. There has been controversy over the desirability of increasing income inequalities within society and between geographical regions and ownership sectors, the relative value of different income earning activities, and the kinds of wage system which are, or are not, economically optimal and politically and socially appropriate. On the one hand, powerful voices in the media have attempted to persuade people that there are economic advantages to be gained from allowing market forces to reward business people for their initiative and investment, and workers for their skill and productivity. On the other hand, this view has been contested by researchers who have drawn attention to the theoretical and practical problems raised by the party-state's abrogation of principles of social reciprocity, approval of private employment and exploitation of wage workers, the imperfection of contemporary markets, and enterprises' reluctance to implement meritocratic principles.

These debates established standards which were drawn upon by workers in the case study enterprises when evaluating their own experiences of employment and receipt of wages. Indeed, money was the stuff of which most conversations were made. Measured in working time, output, wages, and costs of living, money was talked about in corner shops, hospital clinics, hairdressers, public baths, government offices, bus stops, factories, *qi gong* meetings, and at meal tables. In each of these everyday situations, the issues, discursive styles, theoretical perspectives, and 'proofs' which figured in media debates were subjected to scrutiny. In short, the media polemic politicised workers' experiences of wage labour, encouraged expectations of equality of opportunity and productivity-linked remuneration, and established standards by which workers evaluated their wages and purchasing capacities and found them wanting.

WAGES

What you see being paid in the light and what actually gets paid in the dark are completely different things! (Fieldnotes, 2 February 1993)

If one was to believe enterprise managers, by 1992 China had become a market meritocracy. The slogans 'distribution according to work' and 'more work, more pay' were the shorthand answers I received to all my initial questions about wage setting. Wages were said to be structured so as to provide workers with productivity incentives, and distributed solely on the basis of individual merit.

Further probing was necessary to elicit the means by which merit was assessed. How was the output from different tasks compared? Did time rates comprise a proportion of the wage? How were bonuses decided? Did all employees receive the same benefits, welfare provisions, and holidays, or on what basis were these differentially allocated? These questions met with qualified answers, many of which suggested that distribution might not always be 'according to work', and that formal, publicly stated criteria for determining wages were regularly overridden by informal, concealed practices which valorised urban *hukou*, membership of local communities, and *guanxi*.

Time and Overtime: Measuring a Day's Work

the wage was a cipher with more than one author. It embodied codes inscribed by many different authors, whose premises were not entirely the same. It was a cryptic summary of many different assessments of the significance of the passage of time. (Senenscher, 1989, p. 174)

To varying extents, people in both urban and rural China have long been accustomed to measure the time it takes to complete tasks in money terms. Now, most Chinese workers' wages are supposed to be calculated according to a combination of clock time spent working, and task time. This synthesis allows owners and managers to exert much more direct control over the labour process than does payment simply by either time or task (Thompson, 1991, pp. 352–403).

In non-state enterprises in particular, the importance of costing production to ensure profit has prompted managers to ensure that workers' time on the job is actually spent working. In all the firms I visited, workers' punctuality was punched by a machine, or noted in a book by forepersons. Clocks were clearly visible to all employees. In Jinshagang factory, wall posters specified the many uses to which workers' time could *not* be put, and the amounts which would be deducted from workers' wages if they were found 'wasting' time. I have described how the manager of Sanxian bakery tried to survey production routines so she could calculate the time necessary to produce particular products and 'make full use of the workers'

8 hours'. When this proved unsuccessful, she instructed administrative staff to make random visits to the bakery to check whether the bakers were working. Workers were highly sensitive both to the specific ways in which their time at work was regulated, and to the profit motive which inspired that regulation.

In China, as elsewhere, different groups of employees must toil for varying lengths of time and produce different quantities of goods to earn comparable livelihoods. This results not only from ongoing transformations in productive technologies and markets, but also from the fact that powerful elites influence public evaluation of different jobs and amplify the value of those skills they possess (Moore, 1978; Young, 1990). It is almost universal for males to earn more than females, and for technicians to earn more than manual labourers. Among people of the same sex undertaking identical jobs, wage variations sometimes result from differences in individual capacity and productivity. Yet in addition to differentials established by the operation of these common factors, in China wage payments are also strongly affected by *hukou*, membership and non-membership of local communities, and *guanxi*.

The standard working week in China in 1992–93 was 5½ days, comprising a total of 44 hours. There were no national regulations specifying a minimum wage.[2] Many people in the state sector in Hangzhou candidly admitted that they actually spent less than 30 hours working each week, and some said they really worked only a few hours each day. In 1992, the monthly wage range of these people ranged between 230 and 400 yuan. Many state employees were oblivious to the amount of time spent on the job by workers in capitalist enterprises. One of my neighbours who was dissatisfied with her position as a college teacher limped in to see me after having spent a day job-hunting in her best high-heeled shoes. As she slumped on a stool rubbing her tired feet and sipping tea, she told me she was appalled at the conditions imposed upon contract workers in the factories she had visited:

> I went to one electronics factory, they said it was a good unit, a joint venture. But when I went in it was dreadful ... I just never imagined it could be like that! They have to sit in one place all day doing the same thing, just taking things off a production line and putting them back again. They aren't allowed to move, even to answer a phone call. And their wages are really low, lower than the staff's. They have to work overtime, too, most nights. My friend who works there said they work until midnight sometimes. I couldn't do it! ... I had never realised how well off we are. We grumble about our wages, but we get more than

they do, as well as all sorts of welfare and benefits and distributed goods. And we work less than half the amount of time – if that! (Fieldnotes, 1 December 1992)

Managers of the case study enterprises said that each week they spent between 35 and 55 hours overseeing business. Between half and one-third of this time was spent away from their desks, entertaining customers, suppliers, and the government officials with whom they had to deal. In return, they earned between 400 yuan and 1000 yuan in wages. Although most managers complained to me that they thought their monthly salaries incommensurate with their position and contributions towards enterprise profits, only the bakery manager ever remarked that she actually spent too much time on the job:

It's completely unreasonable. There's no connection between the amount of effort and worry I put in and my income. It's time, I have absolutely no time to rest … because of the moon cake orders everyone needs to be told what to do, so I can't take time off even though I am sick. I am always busy and always worried! I used to play sports and go dancing and have holidays, but at present I don't even get one day to rest. (Fieldnotes, 20 June 1992)

Most contract and temporary employees worked longer hours than manager Rong. Office staff and technicians tended to work between 40 and 50 hours. But immigrant seamstresses in Party Secretary Zhao's leather factory tacked and sewed up to 100 hours each week during the latter half of the year when export orders were being filled. As a consequence, they were often so exhausted by the end of the day they were unable to return to their dormitory, and fell asleep next to their machines. Aihua worked approximately 75 hours per week. Each morning she cleaned, washed, and shopped for three households, while during the day she also worked as a street sweeper, tea-picker, baker, factory worker, or canteen cook. Despite their long working hours, the wage range for contract and temporary workers was only between 160 and 350 yuan. And because they were required to spend almost all their time labouring rather than loafing, they received much lower real wages per unit of work time than the state employees and enterprise managers mentioned above. Indeed, the amount of time they devoted to earning a living was determined by the fact that their daily rates were so low they had to maximise their working time in order to meet their needs and satisfy minimal wants.

Rates of pay for contract and temporary employees' time were consistently modified by management's need for skilled workers and pervasive gender discrimination. As Knight and Song (1993) note, the effect of gender bias on wage payments is weaker among skilled than unskilled workers. But irrespective of the content of tasks, women's work is often categorised as unskilled. And because they generally receive less education and training than men, women do predominate in less demanding occupations. In 1992 highly qualified workers paid on a monthly basis, such as Laolian's male engineers and Qi, the saleswoman for Xerox, earned between 300 and 400 yuan each month. Unskilled women in Hangzhou generally received between 100 and 200 yuan per month as labourers, production line workers, cleaners, and waitresses, while unskilled men received between 150 and 250 yuan as labourers, production line workers, and carters. Daily wage rates were somewhat higher. Skilled male workers such as electricians were paid up to 16 yuan per day, while seamstresses earned 12 yuan. Unskilled day labourers in non-state firms received between 8 and 10 yuan. Those employed by government departments, such as street sweepers, sometimes received as little as 4 or 5 yuan per day.

Time rates among contract and temporary employees in Hangzhou were also mediated by localism, just as Minchuan Yang (1994, p. 168) discovered in Shenquan village in Sichuan. Whilst pay for local residents was roughly equivalent to the amount earned by their peers in other eastern provincial capitals, immigrant workers' pay tended to be pegged to the lower wage rates received in rural areas. Owing to entrenched stereotypes about the character, quality, and standard of living of people from particular regions, payment even fluctuated in response to people's place of origin. For example, in 1992 cleaners were usually paid between 0.8 and 1.5 yuan per hour. In a conversation with a seamstress working opposite my home, I learned that this variation was partly conditioned by the cleaner's roots:

Seamstress: How much does your cleaner cost?
SS: 40 yuan per month.
Seamstress: For one hour each day?
SS (thinking of all the extra things Aihua did for us): Mmmm, usually more than that. An hour and a half, sometimes more.
Seamstress: Where is she from?
SS: From Shangyu.
Seamstress: Shangyu! Then you are paying her too much! It should only be about 25. (Fieldnotes, 25 June 1992)

Similarly, in Jinshagang factory local and non-local residence dictated whether workers were paid by time or by piece. That, in itself, generated a sizeable income gap. Local unskilled employees were paid a fixed monthly wage of between 250 yuan and 400 yuan, while outsiders earned a basic daily rate of 2.47 yuan and piece rates which, together, resulted in monthly wages of between 180 and 260 yuan.

Localism also influenced the length of time people worked. At Jinshagang, supervisory and administrative staff, almost all of whom were villagers, did not have to fulfil quotas. Hence, they found it easier than outsiders to be excused from overtime. Overtime was compulsory for outside employees unless they were exempted on medical grounds. Forewoman Ren explained that if workers 'shirked their responsibilities' by refusing to perform overtime, their monthly bonus would be reduced and, if this occurred frequently, piece payments would also be docked. Jinshagang's manager and forewomen insisted that this rule actually benefited production workers. Outsiders were keen to maximise their earnings by doing overtime: if they worked an extra 6 hours until 10 p.m., another 3 yuan was added to their daily rate, and they earned additional piece payments. 'Besides', said manager Mao, 'as most workers come from the countryside and live in the dormitory, they have nothing better to do at night'.

Yet local and outside workers alike groaned about the fact that extension of their working hours, whether voluntary or compulsory, resulted in higher profits for the company, but did not significantly increase their income, much less compensate for their poorer quality of life. Locals complained that overtime prevented them from improving their occupational skills. Three group leaders who had been taking night classes in Japanese and accounting abandoned their studies because of lack of time. Outsiders' constant lack of sleep made them physically clumsy, and bad-tempered with each other. They had almost no time to spend with their families or friends, or in maintaining the social intercourse and exchange relations which are critical aspects of individual personhood and group sociability in China. Even bodily hygiene was sacrificed in the pursuit of higher outputs:

SS: What are you planning to do over the Spring Festival holiday?

Chao: Wash! We've done so much overtime I haven't washed for two weeks. Look at me, I must stink! I haven't even had time to change my clothes. It's disgusting. [laughing] Hey, Li, if we keep working like this we will start smelling so bad they will have to let us out early so we can get to the bathhouse!... All I do is sleep and work. I've only seen my baby a couple of times in the past month. She's always asleep when I get home. And I have to go to see my father. He's been sick in hospital for a few weeks and I haven't been able to get to see him either. (Fieldnotes, 19 January 1993)

The imposition of overtime was even resented in enterprises in which workers were paid what appeared to be relatively generous compensatory rates. In the bakery, workers were paid a flat rate of an extra 10 yuan to work overtime. Although this amount was equivalent to a day worker's full wage, bakers said they were reluctant to do overtime because the amount of work required of the few who were told to stay back after hours was always too great. The same set of bakers, comprising skilled outsiders, was always instructed to work overtime. The obligation to provide these bakers with assistance compelled junior employees to stay back for a few hours without pay. As I explain below, the resultant inequalities in payment and work load produced tensions which the bakers perceived as undermining their own attempts to forge some sense of unity in the work place.

The necessity for members of China's proletariat to toil long hours and the relatively low wages they receive is, of course, closely connected to the fact that there is a massive pool of semi- and unskilled unemployed people willing to replace anyone not prepared to work the hours nominated by their boss. Workers invariably referred to the labour surplus when discussing their miserable working conditions and their inability to pressure for pay increases:

> Shi: Labour is so cheap! They won't pay us any more while there are 10 people willing to do the job for the same amount, or even less.
> SS: Is it easy to change jobs?
> Shi: Even if we change jobs it might not be any better. For people like us there isn't much choice. The wages are always low and the conditions are always bad. We're really pathetic ... we must be stupid! Why do we put up with it?
> Tong: We aren't stupid. Its the labour surplus. That's why workers have no power to change anything. (Fieldnotes, 15 September 1992)

Piece Rates

Many contract and temporary workers, including some technical and supervisory staff, said they would prefer to be paid by the piece rather than according to work time. They believed that unlike time rates, piece payments directly link time spent working and productive output to individual remuneration. Citing media reports, they claimed piece payment would obviate partiality in wage distribution and provide workers with material incentives. In the Laolian workshop one searing summer day, I watched engineer Gui, foreman Zhen, and a skilled worker, Feng, soldering circuit boards while they addressed that most popular of all conversational topics, dissatisfaction over their wages:

> Gui: I read that people in Wenzhou ride motorbikes to work. They finish their work in 4 or 5 hours, and then leave, go to a second job. On their motorbike! It's because they work for piece rates, so while they are working they don't sit around chatting. They do their quota then leave.
> Zhen: Yes, that's the best way to get what you deserve for your work.
> Feng: Mmmm. It's good if the amount paid for each piece is fair, and business is okay.
> Zhen: Now, here … we've got a real problem. We have to stay on good terms with the higher ups and watch our backs. It would be better to have a straight piece rate system. Then we would know exactly how much everyone should get. No one would feel as though they had been unfairly treated or worry about being reported for slacking off. We wouldn't have to worry about all the complications of *guanxi* then. (Fieldnotes, 29 July 1992)

In reality, although piece systems are becoming one of the most common forms of payment in enterprises keen to boost output and profits,[3] they may be considerably less beneficial for workers than Gui, Zhen, and Feng envisage. Piece rates offer no wage security. There is no allowance for the unforeseen, such as task changes, hiccups in material supplies to workers, or mechanical breakdowns. And as piece payment is often associated with the decomposition of production into simple tasks, it increases the likelihood that workers will spend extended periods of time doing highly repetitive, simple, but exacting jobs under intense psychological strain. The pressures a piece rate regime exerts on workers to maximise output in order to boost their earnings, and the factors which might prevent them from making even a subsistence living, were made explicit when I asked Pan how much she and her colleagues earned at a local collective factory:

> Pan: We earn between 50 yuan and 200 yuan each month.
> SS: 50? How could it be so little?
> Pan: We just assemble tiny electronic parts. Some of the workers don't have very good eyesight. It all depends on how much you produce, so if you can't see well you will only get 50 or 60 yuan … It makes everyone really tense. We have to keep watching how long it takes us to do things, that we aren't too slow, knowing we have to produce enough in one day to earn a day's wage. It's just the rate, 1 yuan per 300 pieces. That's what pressures us. (Tape, 11 January 1993)

As piece workers have to monitor their own rate of productivity, Hangzhou factories which paid by the piece and incorporated bonuses for meeting quality standards employed a much lower proportion of administrative and supervisory staff to workers than did those paying time rates.[4] In Pan's factory and at Jinshagang, the average ratio of all managerial and supervisory staff to production workers was 1:20. At Laolian and Sanxian, the average ratio of managerial and supervisory staff to production workers on time rates was approximately 1:4. The preponderance of productive workers compared to administrative and supervisory staff was critical in the higher profits made by the former two factories.

In order to set piece norms at a level which ensured enterprise profitability, management had to calculate the average length of time it took an experienced, hard-working employee to produce a given quantity of high quality goods. That allowed managers to vary the size of the quota attached to different tasks. In Jinshagang, to complete one task worth 2.5 yuan, workers had to clamp 9000 terminals on to electric wires, tape 6000 coloured wires into bundles for plaits, make 400 plaits, or decorate and pack 600 greeting cards. Whenever the factory received an order for a new product, the workers allocated this task were placed beside forewoman Ren's desk so that their rate of output could be monitored closely over weeks, or even months. A quota norm for the task was set according to the length of time it took them to produce the article once Ren was confident that they had become highly proficient. Workers like Chen, who had been given the task of assembling a new plug, were acutely aware of the role that quota setting had in determining the owner-managers' profits and workers' wages:

> SS: Are you being paid by the piece yet?
> Chen: No, they are *still* deciding on the rate! At the moment, we are getting a set 4.2 yuan per day. If we work overtime, and we always do, we get another 3 yuan, and 6 mao for dinner ... nearly 8 yuan. As a daily wage for an unskilled person like me that's okay. It's just that the hours are so long. Nearly thirteen hours ... Ah, there is no point in getting depressed, is there? Girls coming from the countryside usually think it's good to begin with. Us older workers don't like it, though.
> SS: Why not?
> Chen: There isn't any opportunity to improve. *They* get richer, but we don't! Even after a couple of years working here, we are really fast, but we can't earn any more. Around 200 yuan each month. We can't get more because we are already doing overtime all the time. It isn't fair, is it? What do you think about it, compared to the wages in the

other enterprises you go to? Is this piece system fair? (Fieldnotes, 11 January 1993)

I responded to Chen's question by describing the pay systems and wage ranges which obtained in other enterprises I visited, then asked: 'What do *you* think about this system?' For a moment, she lifted her head and gazed around her at the rows of white figures hunched over their desks, then turning back to the plug and tiny screws in her hand, she muttered, 'Of course its unfair! It's blatant exploitation.'

In contrast to claims that piece payments provide positive incentives to workers to maximise their output, it is clear that most piece workers actually felt coerced by these wage regimes. At Jinshagang, workers had few means of increasing their earning capacity other than by arguing for a lowering of the quota required for each task. Management agreed to lower quotas in 1991 and 1992 in response to workers' complaints about their incomes declining relative to the cost of living. Still, to maintain their earnings the factory's outside workers were obliged to arrive early, work through most of their half-hour lunch break, and, if they were not ordered to do overtime in the workshop, take wires back to their dormitory to plait at night. Because of the simple, repetitive nature of all the factory's assembly routines, there was no possibility for workers to store time by working in bursts at easy tasks.[5] Although, theoretically, there was no upper limit to the amount they could earn, not even the most skilful, industrious piece workers could make more than a low-to-average wage.

Bonuses

Monthly and annual bonus payments have long been one of the most important components of income in China, sometimes comprising more than basic wages (Walder, 1990, pp. 140–5; *DDGR*, no. 9, 1991, pp. 23–4; *ZGLDB*, 11 August 1992). Bonuses are almost always paid to contract employees working for time rates, and are sometimes also paid to employees working for piece rates. Workers employed on a daily or hourly basis do not receive bonus payments. At Jinshagang, Sanxian and Laolian, monthly bonuses were between 10 and 100 yuan, with production workers receiving less than technical and supervisory staff. Production workers' annual bonus payments ranged from 20 to 300 yuan. Technicians, supervisors and sales staff received up to 1000 yuan as annual bonuses.

Enterprise managers claimed that bonus payments directly reflected individual employees' contributions towards enterprise profitability. And in keeping with the media's advocacy that wage systems be efficiency-maximising, transparent and just, they said employees' contributions were strictly calculated according to the effectiveness with which they performed managerial and sales functions, their quantifiable output, achievement of known, measurable quality standards, and punctuality.

Workers disagreed. They charged that in many instances, bonus payments were actually determined by local residence and *guanxi*. As I noted, these attributes were also instrumental in promotion. However, so far as workers were concerned, the main reason local residents and familiars were differentially rewarded was not because of their seniority, but because they acted as agents for management on the shop floor. Consider the coincidence of local residence, surveillance, and bonus payment which Han, the young woman from Ningbo, described in the joint venture factory in which she worked:

> A lot of the time the locals aren't even required to do much work. They just stand around watching us. They count the things that we outsiders produce, calculate how much money we are making for the company that they can put in their pockets as monthly bonuses, and into their end of year envelopes. We get lower wages, less bonuses, and less than half of what they do in distributed goods. If a local who has been working in the same workshop for the same length of time I have gets 1000 yuan at the end of the year, the most I could expect is 500 yuan. (Fieldnotes, 5 February 1993)

A similar system operated at Jinshagang. As administrators and supervisors, villagers were entitled to higher bonus payments than outside production workers. And among village employees, kinship, rank, and *biaoxian* – the image of loyalty and politeness that subordinates manage to project to superiors – figured as the most important determinants of annual bonuses.[6] At the end of 1992, director Mao awarded himself 470 000 yuan, about 150 times more than the average annual income of urban workers in China. His two sons, manager Mao and his younger brother who occasionally served as an office assistant, both received more than 20 000 yuan.[7] The forewomen and office manager each received between 9000 and 11 000 yuan. Group leaders and local workers received between 2500 and 5000 yuan, and a thick eiderdown. Canteen gossip held that group leaders who were friends of the Maos had received the larger amounts. In contrast to the hierarchical and particularistic criteria which determined locals' annual bonuses, the bonuses paid to Jinshagang's outside employees reflected their ability to meet quality requirements and their length of service. They received monthly bonuses of between 10 and 40 yuan, and quilts of varying thickness as annual bonuses.

In Laolian and Sanxian, bonus payments were supposed to be kept secret 'so as to encourage the hard workers and do away with egalitarianism and jealousy'. Workers claimed that this was not the rationale behind managers' injunction to secrecy. Instead, they said that it was because the size of the bonus fund was unrelated to their companies' market performance, and the distribution of bonuses did not reflect individual contributions. Sanxian's bakers frequently complained about the small quantity of money which, seemingly irrespective of output and sales, was available for incentive payments. The bonus fund simply comprised whatever was left over after payment of running costs and the two investors' pre-determined profit share. But according to the bakers, running costs were inflated to 'eat up' money which rightfully should have been theirs:

> The two heads, they fly back and forth from America to China a couple of times every year. Then when they are here they eat and drink well, entertain all their relatives and friends at company expense. That's all calculated as running costs, all their flying around and living it up. It's never seen, that money. That should be our bonuses! You know what we got as a bonus at the end of last year? 50 yuan! That's all. Less than it costs one of the bosses to pay his departure tax at Hangzhou airport! On what we are getting after they have had their fling, we are lucky if we have a few yuan over at the end of every month. If we do, the old lady and I go to the market to buy some fresh meat. Otherwise, we have to make do by taking our son to the park with a lunchbox of cold *baozi*. (Fieldnotes, 20 February 1993)

Employees of Laolian and Sanxian also believed that the amounts which were distributed as bonuses were determined by particularistic criteria, and payments were kept secret so as to conceal the fact that they were not related to work that was visible or output that was quantifiable. Instead, they were related to *guanxi* and the performance for management of internal espionage. Pay receipts confirmed the bakers' allegations that the mother of one of their colleagues who was employed to wash their uniforms earned higher bonuses than did the master bakers:

> She is friends with Rong. Always giving her little presents, doing things for her, telling her everything that son of hers says we did at work. Rong relies on her gossip to find out what's happening. So Rong thinks she is wonderful. That's why she earns more. Because she gets along with the manager. It's not a 'more work, more pay' system. It's 'more *guanxi*, more pay'. (Fieldnotes, 14 November 1992)

Some workers argued that discriminatory bonus distribution was not universal. In keeping with the economic rationale propagated in the media, they reasoned that because joint venture and private firms depended upon their own profitability in order to survive, they were more consistent in calculating bonuses solely according to individual productivity and quality requirements than state firms. Hence, they gave clear incentives to workers to increase output.

The logic of that argument is false on two counts. First, it assumes that discriminatory payments are economically irrational. Yet many employees in the non-state sector were aware that wage discrimination formed an integral, and rational, component in managerial strategies to control the production process and govern labour. Individual output was a minor consideration in deciding the amounts of bonus to be paid to local residents and acquaintances because these people helped managers achieve other profit-related objectives: increased productivity, reduced wastage of time and materials, countering workers' subversions, and the dismissal of troublemakers. The second error of logic is the idea that bonuses will motivate workers to boost product quantity and quality. However, for workers who were the subjects, rather than the agents of management systems of surveillance and control, the decoupling of output and remuneration rendered bonuses ineffective as inducements to industry.

'Benefits' and Leave

The growth of markets over a decade and a half of economic reform, together with wage increases which have almost kept pace with inflation, have reduced workers' reliance upon enterprises for the provision of goods and services. Nevertheless, in 1992 this still formed a significant component of remuneration. The availability of leave was another vital issue in workers' evaluation of the wage labour bargain. Despite the fact that the party-state proposed that enterprises' provision of non-wage benefits be discontinued and leave entitlements be standardised among all employees, an examination of the allotment of 'benefits' and leave illustrates that similar distributive criteria were applied in their allotment as in monetary payments.

Managers tended to represent their provision of material goods to workers as a form of benevolent profit-sharing, rather than a wage component. Each time I asked manager Mao about Jinshagang's distribution of profits, he mentioned that these had been used to supply 'free' meals to workers. Jinshagang's production workers were aware that if the canteen meals had not been subsidised, they would have to pay several times more than their current expenditure to feed themselves. Nevertheless, they did not consider meal subsidies either as philanthropy or an unearned 'benefit'. Instead, they argued that provision of subsidised meals was actually a component of their wages. It was also a means of ensuring that their time and energy would be expended within the factory: that in the morning they would be at work by 7.30 a.m., and in the evening, they would still be at work. Besides, everyone agreed that the canteen food was awful and the servings meagre: steamed buns and gritty, thin rice gruel for breakfast, rice and watery winter melon or cabbage for lunch and dinner. On important festival days, shreds of meat were mixed with the vegetable that was ladled into workers' enamel bowls. Workers said that those who tried to survive on the canteen food became ill.

The same attitudes were expressed by all workers whose employers provided them with meals. One winter day as we sat in a square of pale sunlight in the bakery courtyard, I commented that the lunch the bakers were eating was much better than that provided by other enterprises. It was cooked in smaller quantities and included fish as well as vegetables:

SS: For free food, it's good!

Little Deng sharply corrected me: We earn this food. It isn't free at all! The money for our lunches, the manager just takes that out of our wages. They think we don't understand that, but we do. You should be able to see that! Anyway, count it up. It's not worth much. 8 to 10 yuan for a day's wages, and 1 extra yuan's worth of food. It's still lousy. (Fieldnotes, 17 January 1993)

In addition to cooked meals, workers in the case study enterprises also received fruit, spiced sausages, tea eggs, biscuits, candy, cool drinks, movie tickets, and even annual day trips to scenic spots as non-monetary wage payments. However, in the distribution of all these goods, outsiders and those without *guanxi* were not eligible for the same range or amount of distributed goods as their local and better connected fellow workers. A conversation between two rather inebriated young friends about their previous work place maps the distributional patterns delineated by *hukou*, localism and *guanxi*. Concurrently, it illuminates managers' use of these identities and relations in recruiting loyal agents into the work force:

Wu: The factory was profitable.

Cui (interrupting): It was profitable allright, but it wasn't any good to us outsiders.

Wu: No, not to us down below.

Cui (interrupting): Especially outsiders.

SS: In what way weren't they good to you?

Wu: For instance, whenever they were organising welfare or distributing things we just didn't get anything, or much less than the locals.

Cui (interrupting): Some arse lickers... If they really crawled to the leaders, flattered them, showed them how loyal they were by telling them what was going on behind their backs so they'd think, 'Hmmm he's a good fellow', then maybe they would be better off... but in fact that sort of person is despicable! The very worst, aren't they? But the ones like that always got more than us. (Tape, 17 January 1993)

Unlike state enterprise employees, very few of the locals and none of the outside workers in Hangzhou's capitalist enterprises got paid holidays, and there were limited circumstances under which they were eligible for paid sick leave. If they had one rest day each week, they missed one day's pay. When factories closed at Spring Festival and in mid-summer, workers had to take unpaid holidays ranging from a few days to two weeks. In enterprises which did not close, local workers were rostered to work. In some firms, however, only those immigrants who had won the approval of management were allowed to go home to celebrate the festival with their families. Most of these enterprises did not observe public holidays such as National Day or Women's Day. Instead, employees were some-times compensated in lieu of time off. For example, Jinshagang's predom-inantly female labour force worked on Women's Day in 1993. In fact, in Chen's section they worked until 10.30 p.m. The following day, local women were given envelopes containing 38 yuan to signify the date, March eighth. Outsiders' envelopes contained only 15 yuan. As Chen tucked her envelope into the pocket of her white coat she grimaced and muttered, 'March eighth! It's more like 3 yuan for us and 8 for them! Even as women we aren't equal.'

Hangzhou labour regulations stipulated that contract and temporary workers employed in firms and institutions in urban areas were eligible for paid sick leave.[8] The regulations gave little indication of what actually happened in practice. Contract workers at Laolian were paid a basic daily wage for up to two weeks if they could show proof of illness. However, their temporary co-workers did not receive any pay at all if they were ill. In Sanxian bakery, workers did not receive any sick pay unless, Lin said, they happened to be on good terms with the office manager:

SS: What would happen if you got sick or were injured? Would you be paid? Would you stay here or go home?

Bo: Of course I'd go! I'd have no choice. People like us, we are just relying upon our physical strength. If we get sick or injured then we are of no value to them. If we are useless, we can't make any profit for them. Everyone knows they won't spend any money on medical care for us. That's our fate, see?

SS: And you?

Lin: I've had two arguments with the office manager, and to my way of thinking it's time I switched to another unit, because he will definitely make life difficult for me next time I have a problem. If I have to see a doctor, for instance, he'll refuse me. Not approve time off to go to the hospital. He will say work is too busy and if I go I will be shirking, so I would lose my whole day's pay. And he'll say the unit hasn't any money to pay for the medical examination. So its time I left. I've got no option really. (Tape, 20 January 1993)

The same regulations did not apply to the employees of rural enterprises, though these people were eligible for paid leave and compensation for their medical expenses if they suffered industrial injury or illness. At Jinshagang factory, manager Mao told me that he voluntarily paid a minimum daily rate of 2.47 yuan per day for up to six days to sick workers, which he described as yet further proof of the firm's commitment to profit-sharing amongst employees. After six days workers received nothing, and 'malingerers' were fired. However, workers in the factory disputed the availability of sick pay: 'If we don't work, we don't get paid, that's the rule. We can't afford to get sick.'

National regulations which granted all female contract workers paid maternity leave and guaranteed that they could return to their jobs after parturition were also ignored with impunity in all the case study enterprises. At Jinshagang, where all but a handful of employees were women of child-bearing age, only one month's unpaid maternity leave was granted to employees. Local workers who took more than one month's maternity leave were criticised and missed out on their usual high annual bonuses, but were allowed to return to their previous positions. Outsiders who took more than one month's leave were considered to have resigned and had no guarantee of being re-employed. If the factory did allow them to return, Wang discovered they had to start again as new recruits:

I took nine months off. After she was born I went home to my mother's in Jinhua to feed her. Then when she was 8 months old I came back because I thought I would be welcome here. After all, I knew the work and the people. I'd worked here for three years. But they said I had to start from the beginning again. It was really unfair. I didn't need to train again. It upset me, having to pay another pledge and be on beginner's wages for one month. (Fieldnotes, 8 January 1993)

This review of wage structuring and distribution demonstrates that actual patterns of wage payment were inconsistent with the formal criteria for remuneration based upon individual contribution which was advocated by the government, promoted in the media, and enunciated by enterprise managers. Co-workers undertaking the same tasks did not always receive the same pay and benefits. While some workers were paid solely according to their output, others were differentially rewarded because they were local residents and friends of managers who monitored and reported upon their colleagues' behaviour. Dissatisfied over the failure of enterprises to link pay to productivity, workers complained that the wage labour bargain was unfair and exploitative. What did they mean by these terms?

INEQUITY AND EXPLOITATION IN THE WAGE-LABOUR BARGAIN

The very mention of rich people touched a raw nerve with many workers. Time after time I heard the comment: 'It's too unequal, too unfair. The people with power get rich. Workers are the only "dry office" left'. If I inquired how it was that power was transformed into money, they would sometimes answer, 'They get rich because they control everything… licences, factories, big construction contracts. Everything!' But at other times, the same people would say, 'They own things, and their profits come from our work.' When I pointed out that rent seeking from office involved quite different people from those who owned firms and employed wage labour, my informants frowned: 'There's no difference! These people are all friends! They come from the same place and have *guanxi*. If you have one, you have the other… power, property, *guanxi*, money.'

Clearly, in the course of analysing how money was made and distributed in their society, workers had come to the conclusion that control and ownership were monopolised by groups constituted through the local state apparatus, place and networking. This notion not only informed their identification of groups in society, but also their evaluation of the wage-labour bargain.

Structuring Inequality

None of the workers I met was a believer in egalitarianism, if that is taken to mean equal returns irrespective of effort and actual input (Turner, 1986).

However, they did firmly support the ideal of equality of opportunity. And they believed equality of opportunity was denied them by the allocation of resources, credit, capital, licences and management positions through the nexus of officialdom, and place-based *guanxi* networks. This process concurrently enriched and empowered officials and local business people, whilst rendering the displaced and those who lacked *guanxi* vulnerable to exploitation.

It was the talk of old Ma, as we sat around a steaming hot-pot at Aihua's one winter's night, which best articulated the notion that the convergence of local officialdom and business underpinned the contemporary creation of exploitative production relations. Old Ma's personal history provided him with a wealth of experience with which to make sense of present trends. He had been born to the concubine of a wealthy business man. His father was shot in the street on the first day the Japanese entered Hangzhou, and the family property and business were confiscated by the occupying army. After 1949, what remained of the family's business was returned to Ma and his brother. However, within 5 years it had been nationalised and Ma had been branded a member of the bourgeoisie:

> It didn't seem to matter which campaign (was being waged), I was always the target! I was a capitalist rightist for 20 years. Had to wear a cap, learn from the peasants, and lost my wife to an old red cadre. But then when Deng came to power, the village I had been sent to *wanted* capitalists. Instead of being in charge of a hoe and a couple of *mu* of paddy, they put me in charge of a little light fittings factory. I've been making money for these damned communists ever since. (Fieldnotes, 24 February 1993)

Although he was persecuted during the Maoist period, Ma said that the combined force of political campaigns and public opinion had kept officials fairly honest then:

> There were some bad ones, but most of them had some pride. They had their position, and that gave them face and power. That was enough. After all, it was more than anyone else had! The bad ones, they would squeeze people, but it wasn't just money they were after. (Fieldnotes, 24 February 1993)

But now, grumbled Ma, wealth interests officials above all else. Thus, their ambitions coincide with those of business people. After describing to me occasions when he had witnessed officials extracting rent from their positions and colluding to capture or establish companies with business people, Ma turned theatrically to the other people around the table and asked them to verify what he had said. They duly embroidered his argument with personal anecdotes. Then Ma continued his incisive analysis:

Nowadays officials use their power to make money for themselves, and their business associates use their money to get power. They are all becoming friends. This generation of big entrepreneurs will marry their kids off to the children of high officials. They will form a big clan of powerful, rich people. They will start donating universities, hospitals, dams to the people in their villages and neighbourhoods, and make them *their* communities. Their kids will become mayors, directors of the hospitals, and the chairpersons of family companies that monopolise things like electric power and foreign trade. It has already happened in some places. And together, they will extort whatever they like. They will be able to exploit ordinary people as much as they want. Just like in the old days, eh? (Fieldnotes, 24 February 1993)

Coincidentally, only a few days after dining with Ma, the managing director of Jinshagang factory furnished an example of precisely the sorts of trends the old man described. The *guanxi* relationship forged between director Mao and the head of Jinshagang village government, together with Mao's patronage of community projects, smoothed the way for him not only to increase his property rights in the factory, but also to accumulate further property. Above, I mentioned that in 1993 Mao awarded himself a whopping 470 000 yuan annual bonus. Local gossip condemned the amount as excessive. Acknowledging that his receipt of such a large sum 'doesn't look good', Mao donated 400 000 yuan to the local primary school. However, later that year the village head rewarded Mao for his generous gift by presenting him with a new building comprising a ground floor restaurant, second floor karaoke bar, and luxuriously appointed third floor apartment. Mao leased the lower two floors of the building. The 400 000 yuan donation to the school would be recouped in rent within two years, and Mao would remain owner of a valuable property.

Most employees of the case study enterprises were young first-generation workers who had grown up during the reform era, and they lacked old Ma's breadth of experience. Nevertheless, their conversations echoed his conclusion that a synthesis of power and money forged through connections between local officials and business people was giving rise to a group which was alienating public property and exploiting the labour of those who lacked political, economic and social capital. Like Ma, they also described this group as comprising *guanxi* networks, clans, or, in the usage of outsiders, urbanites and locals. But although they eschewed the term class, they did not hesitate to draw analogies between patterns of accumulation in China's market socialism and western capitalism: 'It's not so different from the west. Although there, capitalists start off with money and build up commercial and industrial empires, whereas here, people start off with power and contacts then do the same thing' (Fieldnotes, 17 August 1992).

Contract and temporary workers' ideas about the social structural basis of inequality extended to the conviction that they themselves were being dispossessed and forced to labour in capitalist firms by the modes of operation of officials and territorially constituted networks. They complained that they had no choice but to become wage workers. If, in the midst of their complaints about low and discriminatory pay, I inquired why they themselves did not set up a business, they said they were rendered impotent by place and lack of connections, and their consequent poverty:

> That's impossible. I don't have the *guanxi* or the capital. (Fieldnotes, 26 February 1993)

> Outsiders haven't a hope. We haven't any capital or property, we can't get loans, we can't get licenses. We have to work for wages to survive. (Fieldnotes, 2 February 1993)

Inequity and Exploitation at Work

Cross-national research into the ways people assess remuneration indicates that people expect to be paid for their effort in keeping with a range of socially approved norms and stated criteria (Turner, 1986, p. 96; Reis, 1987, pp. 132–42; Hermkens and van Kreveld, 1991, p. 120). In Hangzhou, in keeping with the thrust of contemporary media discourses on wages, it was widely held that individuals' ability and industry should be rewarded. A corollary to this was the notion that rich peoples' wealth should derive from their own talent and hard work. Unequal outcomes were considered to be acceptable and, indeed, desirable, if they were consequent upon the play of intelligence, skill, effort and risk in a competitive arena.

Norms which stress the impartial evaluation of merit in wage setting can also engender the expectation that employees should be objectively assessed, and be rewarded equally and adequately for comparable work. A sense of inequity may derive from a cognition of discrepancy between what one should reap according to publicly agreed standards, and what one actually gets (Ajzen, 1982, p. 162; Deutsch, 1985, p. 226;

Turner, 1986, p.122). And in Hangzhou, it was apparent that workers' negative evaluations of their lot were grounded in the knowledge that social structural relationships denied them equality of opportunity, and biased distributive practices within enterprises denied them a just wage. My informants were engaged in an almost constant critique of the dissonance they detected between contemporary ideologies of impartial meritocratic distribution and what they perceived to be the localistic and particularistic practices that characterised pay systems in their work places. This, in turn, fed their belief that society was unfair and irrational:

> Lots of things here don't make sense. People doing the hardest jobs get the lowest wages, and people doing the least amount of work often have a high income. Things that are rational are often illegal. And things that are legal are often completely unfair and irrational. No wonder people steal things, is it? (Fieldnotes, 28 July 1992)

In like manner, the phrases with which they gave voice to their moral outrage over unfair patterns of remuneration drew upon the state's and media's rallying cries for wage reform. These were modified to become parodies of particularistic practice: 'That "distribution according to work" stuff, it's all empty propaganda, showcases they put on the news. It's actually "distribution according to *guanxi*".' The widely circulated slogan 'more work, more pay' was modified to express workers' belief that they were being cheated of their just rewards: ' "More work, more pay", crap! It's more like "more work, less pay".' Another informant coined a version of this same slogan which exposed what they believed to be the social-structural dynamic underpinning inequality: 'more work, add more bosses; more bosses, add more officials!'

However, in addition to their anger over blatant discrepancies between rhetoric and practice, the workers' sense of inequity was clearly informed by their experiences of partiality in wage distribution, and their belief that this was one of the mechanisms which underpinned managers' control of the shop floor and production processes. In short, unfairness facilitated exploitation.

The term 'exploitation' was used almost as frequently by workers as was 'unfair'. Moreover, it was used by informants, irrespective of occupation and background, to refer to a specific type of relationship. Their talk explicitly characterised exploitation as employers' purchase of labour power for an amount less than the value of goods that labour would produce, their organisation of production processes and intensification of productivity pressures so as to maximise output, and their realisation of surplus value as profit. At Laolian and Sanxian, workers repeatedly defined managers' attempts to control activities on the shop floor, extension of their hours of work, and setting of wages relative to the quotas of goods they were required to produce as exploitative. In the export-oriented Jinshagang factory, workers' concept of exploitation also expressed an appreciation of the connection between the party-state's reform of property rights and labour markets, global disparities of wealth, and capital's on-going search for cheap labour and higher profits:

> What they are actually exporting from this company is cheap labour, isn't it? People in Japan and Australia, you all have reasonable conditions and high wages there, don't you? So processing is done here in factories like this where we outsiders work all day and all night and earn almost nothing. The local bosses get rich from exporting our labour, don't they? Boxes and boxes of it. Cheap labour. It's cheaper to work us to death in their factories here than if they were just labour contractors who sent us workers over to you, because then they would have to buy our plane tickets and feed us there. Isn't that so? (Fieldnotes, 30 January 1993)

To this extent, workers' notion of exploitation is consonant with Marx's conceptualisation of surplus appropriation. Yet many members of China's proletariat considered other employees – officials, managerial staff, urbanites, members of local communities, and workers with *guanxi* – to be the architects, agents, and part beneficiaries of their exploitation. In other words, exploitation was not seen to be a relationship between binary social classes, but rather a relationship which obtained to varying degrees between groups which were defined by their position in government, place and network.

These issues were all foregrounded in talk at Sanxian bakery during the autumn. Consumers had responded to the onset of cool weather by rapidly increasing their intake of bread, cakes, and pastries. Manager Rong instructed a group of bakers to work overtime to meet the stepped-up demand. After several late shifts, the bakers told Rong that they would need more hands if they were to fulfil the orders within the 6 extra hours they thought their overtime pay covered. But the following day, the same number of people were told to stay back to produce an even larger quota of products. The bakers who had been delegated to do overtime were indignant that the 'higher ups', locals and friends of the manager would disproportionately benefit from this extension of their working hours:

> Deng: We should have stopped. We told her there should be more people on but she wouldn't listen. Her friends, they don't care. Their bonuses

will be high this month and they haven't had to work harder for it. All that money comes from what we make up here! But we won't be getting any benefit from it.

Bo: That's so, it all comes from us working till midnight, doesn't it? If it weren't for us there wouldn't be any money for them! They get too much compared to us, down there. They are exploiting us outsiders.

SS: Don't the locals get exploited too?

Bo: Of course, but it isn't as bad for them.

Deng: The factories reckon it's better to use outsiders because they make more profit out of us. We work harder, and cost less, and if we kick up a fuss they can sack us. So they earn more money from us. (Fieldnotes, 6 December 1992)

Resentment over unfair payments to locals and well connected employees sometimes seemed to outweigh dissatisfaction over the fact that all workers were exploited to a greater or lesser extent. The bakers said they would prefer to be subject to what they imagined to be the objective and impersonal operation of a genuinely capitalist market economy based upon clearly defined contractual obligations, even though that would also involve exploitation: 'At least in capitalist enterprises you get paid for hours worked or items produced, don't you? Here, we get exploited in the same way as capitalists' employees, but we don't get paid in the same way' (Fieldnotes, 15 September 1992).

This prioritising of the issue of unfair pay over that of exploitation deserves close attention. In fact, perceptions of inequity actually sharpened workers' sensitivity towards the conditions which underpinned their exploitation. Without discounting the sincerity of the bakers' belief that market-determined merit is the most just foundation for income distribution, it is nevertheless clear that there was a political agenda to their enthusiastic support for meritocratic pay systems. They realised that so long as partiality in wage payments continued, they would not be able to overcome their fragmentation and contest owners' and managers' exactions:

If Rong gives you a bit more than me, then you wouldn't want to complain, would you? It's like this. She is friends with some of the workers – her son's old school friends, and the washing lady. So the ones with *guanxi*, they get high bonuses. And if everyone is standing around complaining about their pay, they won't say anything. Or they will say it *is* fair! So not everyone feels the same way. We aren't united. That's why Rong can do whatever she likes, tell us to work harder or stay back at night. We can't resist because her friends are among us. (Fieldnotes, 10 January 1993)

The bakers perceived the inequitable payment of wages to be integral to the creation and recreation of divisions among them, and thought that those divisions, in turn, were one of the mechanisms facilitating managerial control of the labour process and their common exploitation. Their support for impartial, meritocratic payment was, in part, founded upon the expectation that a fair wage system might provide a basis for overcoming their fragmentation.

CONTESTING INEQUITY, RESISTING EXPLOITATION

In the case study enterprises, managements' control of production hinged upon rewarding locals and familiars for their performance of surveillance tasks, and coercing immigrant employees and those who lacked *guanxi* into producing surplus value. In an article analysing the relative effectiveness of coercion and consent as mechanisms for extracting effort from workers, Burawoy and Wright (1990) remark that consent is generally a more effective method for eliciting effort than coercion. And, argue Burawoy and Wright, as workers are rational economic actors who share with management an interest in the sustainability of enterprises, so long as they believe the wage labour bargain is fair, they will be willing to discourage the free-riding of individuals and collectively produce sufficient surplus to ensure enterprise profitability. Capitalist hegemony, underpinned by ideas about autonomy, merit and fairness, obviates the necessity for surveillance and threats.

In seeking to explain workers' compliance as the outcome of systemically structured, rational economic interests, this theorisation fails to take into account the political motives that might encourage workers to participate in the construction of just such a system. In the case study enterprises, workers' agitation against discriminatory payment and the fragmentation it sustains is pressuring employers to adopt wage systems which are founded upon less divisive, more universal criteria. Workers are forcing bosses to play, and pay, according to state-sanctioned rules such as 'distribution according to work'. In doing so, workers themselves are devising a new consensual bargain, one in which their effort is traded in return not only for a productivity-linked wage but also, and more importantly, for the construction of a common condition which would allow them to organise collectively to contest their exploitation.

This can be deduced from the substance of workers' demands. At both Jinshagang and Sanxian, workers' requests that managers ensure wages were linked to individual productivity were not intended to narrow the total range of wage payments or reduce the incomes of owners and managers.

Rather, they were meant to selectively reduce the income of the top wage earners who acted as management's agents, and raise the income of the most productive workers on the shop floor. The objective was to eliminate the ties of loyalty which bound some workers to management, and encourage solidarity among workers.

Let me give specific examples. Outsiders at Jinshagang signalled their dissatisfaction with the wage system through high levels of attrition, spontaneous outbreaks of abuse and flight, and letters of complaint deposited in the opinion box. Manager Mao told me that by the end of 1992, wage inequity had become the most frequent topic addressed in workers' letters: 'The outsiders all know the locals get more than they do. They keep complaining that it is inequitable, that the income gap isn't fair because they work harder than the locals. They say that distribution really should be according to "more work, more pay"' (Tape, 16 February 1993). His perception that differential wage payments generated discontent and work place conflicts reinforced his own feelings of dissatisfaction over local employees' low level of productivity compared to that of outsiders. Mao decided that the factory's automatic employment, promotion, and preferential payment of members of the local community was becoming an obstacle to increasing profits. He negotiated an agreement with the village government that, henceforth, villagers' employment and promotion would no longer be guaranteed. Moreover, in order to appease outsiders and boost the productivity of those locals already employed, he began to implement a pay system in which output and quality were the twin standards by which all employees, irrespective of their place of origin, were evaluated and paid:

> As a business, I have to think about what sort of contribution workers will make in the future, focus more upon the workers who are really productive. We should pay both locals and outsiders what they are really worth, so that people making the same contribution towards profits earn the same amounts. All I care about is their ability, what they do for our business. Nothing else matters. (Tape 16 February 1993)

In making these changes, manager Mao simultaneously eliminated a cornerstone not only of the binary hierarchical organisation of the factory's work force, but also of the communitarian ethos of Jinshagang village. This caused great consternation among local employees. Their concerns centred, on the one hand, around the demise of values and institutions which prioritised local residence. Unless communal norms, rights, and redistributive obligations were acknowledged and given substance in the preferential recruitment, promotion and remuneration of local employees, they doubted whether their village would be able to retain its cohesive character. If this trend was to proceed unchecked, relations between fellow villagers would become cast in wholly contractual terms, thus discounting what it meant to be a villager.[9] When local staff received their first pay packet after the introduction of productivity quotas, one group leader wept and several sulked openly. Their distress was less a consequence of the reduced amount of money they had received than of the fact that they had been treated as mere wage-workers, rather than as locals. They had lost their identity, face, and authority by being evaluated according to the same standards as 'dirty kids from Anhui'.

On the other hand, they expressed doubt that the new wage system would be any more reflective of individual contributions than the old. Instead, they said that the criteria for positive discrimination in wage payment had narrowed to kinship and *guanxi*. In the future, only manager Mao's family and favourites would enjoy job security and be exempt from productivity pressures. One evening shortly after the introduction of these changes Huang, a local group leader, was seeing me out of the factory when Mao appeared in the doorway. The usually exuberant Huang silently shrank into the shadows of the foyer and backed through the double doors leading to the workshops. The following day I asked her what had precipitated her uncharacteristic behaviour. She answered: 'Didn't you see manager Mao in the doorway? We're not supposed to wander around unless we're doing our job. *Everyone* is terrified of him now! If he gets a poor impression of you, you're finished! [snapping her fingers] That's it! From now on, his word is everything' (Fieldnotes, 10 March 1993).

Although locals felt that a gulf had opened between the manager and themselves, and they had begun to compare their situation to that of outsiders, they did not immediately express any more sympathy or affection for their immigrant colleagues. Nevertheless, over the long term, experience of similar processes of production and extraction might magnify the gulf between owner-managers and local employees and erase the divisive effects of localism among the work force. This would open the way for workers to collectively organise and negotiate with management.

In contrast to the relative success enjoyed by Jinshagang's unskilled, immigrant female workers in pressuring Mao to link pay to productivity, the appeals by Sanxian's male artisans for manager Rong to implement 'more work, more pay' fell on deaf ears. Throughout the autumn of 1992, as their monthly wages failed to fluctuate in response to total output and individual productivity, the bakers became ever more discontent. They refused to fulfil orders during the day, thus making it necessary for ever more bakers to stay behind to do overtime: 'Why work harder if we aren't paid more? It doesn't make any difference to our wages because we don't get much anyway. But it hurts the higher ups and their friends. They get less if we don't work!' (Fieldnotes, 14 November 1992).

When I left Hangzhou in March 1993, the bakers were spending almost as much time playing poker as they were working, and were not receiving any monthly bonuses. However, they said that their go-slow was also having the effect of lowering the income of Rong's friends to a level almost the same as their own. They joked that eventually, this could either result in their mass sacking, or the voluntary resignation of the managers' allies.

Manager Rong denied that the bakery failed to follow the principle of 'more work, more pay'. That, she said, certainly was not the reason why the bakers' incomes did not keep pace with increased output. Other factors had to be taken into account. The first and foremost of these was, as I have mentioned, that there was insufficient money left in the welfare fund for distribution. Second, although the foreman said he always gave particular assignments to the same skilled bakers and I had actually seen them making those products day after day, Rong denied that there was a clear system of allocating specific tasks to individuals. Therefore, she said it was difficult to reward individual productivity and she had to rely upon workers' *biaoxian*. The third factor Rong said prevented her from paying more to highly productive workers was that overtime was becoming increasingly necessary not just because demand was growing, but also because the bakers refused to work a full 8 hours during the day. When I asked Rong whether it was possible that their refusal to work was an expression of dissatisfaction with partiality in wage distribution, she disagreed and said it simply showed that the bakers suffered from the same sort of 'iron rice bowl' mentality that afflicted permanent state employees.

Rong's remarks about workers' 'iron rice bowl' mentality echo criticisms made by government spokespeople and the media of workers' old-fashioned egalitarianism: criticisms which, I have argued, are part and parcel of attempts to rework members of the proletariat as competitive, individualised producers. While Rong's utilisation of this discourse illuminates her own motives and attitudes, it fundamentally misrepresents the bakers' actions. Although their tactics to pressure her to implement merit-based wage payment contributed in the short term towards a process of wage levelling, that was not their intention. Instead, the bakers aimed to reduce the rewards paid to Rong's agents for their surveillance activities. They anticipated that this would encourage more inclusive patterns of association among workers, and so pave the way for concerted action to improve their common lot.

Of course, the workers' actions are open to multiple interpretations. Orthodox Marxists might argue that their espousal of the virtues of meritocratic wage systems is an expression of workers' 'false consciousness'. From a Gramscian perspective, it might be considered an example of consent 'given by the great masses of the population to the general direction imposed on social life by the dominant fundamental group' (Gramsci, 1971, p. 12). If we were to proffer a Weberian analysis, it could be that workers were adopting a more modern, rational, and legalistic attitude toward the wage-labour bargain. But whilst all these explanations encapsulate a grain of truth, they neglect the subversive political intent of workers' appropriation of the discourse of meritocratic payment. The unskilled workers at Jinshagang and the skilled employees of Sanxian were both laying claim to publicly recognised norms of economic efficiency and wage equity, and using these to critique their employers and try to unify workers hitherto divided by *hukou*, place and network. The irony is inescapable: if their tactic succeeds, it will be at the cost of rendering entire work forces susceptible to intensified productivity pressures.

The recruiting, architectural, production, and wage systems examined here have illuminated the sources and consequences of differentiation among China's proletariat. Employment in capitalist work places generates a multiplicity of experiences, consciousnesses, and identities. With few exceptions, workers believe that the conditions which necessitate their waged employment and facilitate their exploitation are established outside the work place, by regional disparities, place and *guanxi* networks, the power of officials, and the unequal distribution of wealth and opportunities. On the basis of identities defined outside the work place, members of China's proletariat are constituted, managed, disciplined, and remunerated as distinct categories of workers. Locals and people with useful connections are subject to quite different technologies of control, perform quite different roles, and suffer different rates of exploitation, from outsiders and those who lack *guanxi*. This fact then feeds into new identity constructs, and new types of social relations: the meanings attached to being a local employee in an enterprise powered by outsiders' labour incorporate concepts of part-ownership, the exercise of authority, and rights to profit sharing. Conversely, being an outsider in that same enterprise evokes dispossession, displacement, disempowerment, and exploitation.

The importance accorded to *hukou*, place and network in recruitment, the organisation of production, and remuneration should not be interpreted as evidence that traditional patterns of association remain unaltered in contemporary China, and neither should it be assumed that these simply mask cleavages between emergent classes. Rather, as shown in this examination of workers' employment experiences, these non-class identities and relations have actually been made fundamental to the creation of capitalist relations of production, processes of surplus appropriation, and the further accumulation of capital.

Clearly, these shifts have consequences for the identities, consciousnesses and behaviour of China's reworked proletariat. In the immediate realm of the work place, groups of urban workers, locals, and the well connected are emphasising those features which distinguish and advantage them as against other members of the labour force. These are being eroded, as their disadvantaged colleagues strive to find a basis to resist their differentiation and exploitation. Localism and particularism are being refashioned as workers dispute whether the rights and obligations entailed by urban and local residence and familiarity should take precedence over productivity, skill, or other criteria for recruitment and remuneration. These contests over identities, social values, and systemic relations are also played out beyond the confines of the work place. I turn, now, to examine workers' understandings of the connections between localism and particularism, and wealth, power, and consumption in the neighbourhoods in which they live.

Part III
Labours of Representation

The most resolutely objectivist theory must take account of agents' representation of the social world and, more precisely, of the contribution they make to the construction of the vision of this world, via the *labour of representation* (in all senses) that they continually perform in order to impose their own vision of the world or the vision of their own position in this world, that is, their social identity. (Bourdieu, 1991, p. 234)

8 Neighbourhood Identities, Neighbourhood Dispositions

How do workers' experiences of waged work colour their perceptions and depictions of the people who inhabit their social world? Do workers who stand alongside one another on the factory floor share identities, and what Ira Katznelson (1986, p. 18) refers to as dispositions: interpretations of the social system, and values and morals that are formed in the course of interaction and provide a cultural frame for action? These questions invite an investigation of connections between participation in capitalist production, and workers' representations of their own and others' identities, their attitudes towards various groups in their community, and their patterns of social behaviour; connections which, too often, are assumed, rather than empirically investigated.

The analytical foci of this chapter are place, power and wealth, and consumption as forces which are creative of collective identities and central to workers' representations of social structuration and social formations. The analysis is undertaken through an examination of neighbourhood interactions, the material culture of housing, and competing values and claims to moral superiority. My objective is to demonstrate how and why workers' understandings of place, power and wealth, and consumption reflect their experiences of changes in relations of production, and figure prominently in their strategies for dealing with their position in those relations.

THE PLACE OF IDENTITY: LOCALS AND OUTSIDERS

In Hangzhou, I was told that the reason place-based identities separated locals and outsiders in enterprises was, simply, that place structured most aspects of social life. Workers asserted that their life chances were partly determined by their places of origin and the ways in which they were integrated into networks in those localities. When explaining this belief, they mentioned factors such as the uneven geographical distribution of resource endowments and state and foreign investment, the labour market effects of the residential registration system, corporate community ownership of the means of production, and marked inequalities of wealth and power within communities. So, too, were their social identities and their evaluation of, and interaction with others heavily influenced by place.

185

Place as a Structuring Mechanism

The single most important fact distinguishing Hangzhou residents from non-locals was their occupation of a municipality which boasted rapidly expanding financial and communications facilities, industry, and commerce. The city attracted investment largely because of the advantages it already had over other cities and towns; advantages which themselves were the outcome of previous investments. Ordinary Hangzhou workers acknowledged that they benefited in innumerable ways from the city's infrastructural, transportation, and communications developments, the growth of employment opportunities, and the provision of education, welfare and health care. Suburban village residents similarly agreed that the local governments' establishment of collective enterprises, and their use of enterprise profits to improve infrastructure and provide jobs, education, pensions and medical services had made their lives relatively easy. The prerogatives of place were integral to Hangzhou residents' identities.

Contrast these benefits derived from residence in Hangzhou with conditions in some rural communities. Time after time, outsiders from poor areas told me that their villages had no industries and only small, owner-operated commercial enterprises. There were few credit providers, and rudimentary transportation and communications. The only work available was in the already overpeopled agricultural sector. Hence, they felt they had little option but to move to the city to look for work. But there, they were marked as aliens by their accents, dress, poor education and lack of skills, and, above all, by the poverty which drove them outside to work in return for a meagre wage.

The effects of place on identity were compounded by *guanxi* networks which radiated out from local governments, enterprises and institutions. These determined the distribution within communities of resources, credit, profits, job opportunities, and welfare benefits. For example, more than a dozen workers who came from townships near Shaoxing and Ningbo said that the blessings brought to those places by industrialisation were enjoyed only by a limited number of well-connected people. Because their families were not associated with officials or enterprise managers, they had been excluded from becoming shareholders in collective enterprises and could only get the worst paid, most menial jobs in those firms. There was no possibility of becoming self-employed or operating a private business because, lacking *guanxi*, they could not get loans and would have had to pay excessive amounts for operating licences. Thus, they too felt they had few options but to go to Hangzhou to seek work.

So it is that in the reform era, place is seen both by locals and by outsiders to have a structuring effect. It is a vehicle of class relations:

> The biggest difference between us locals and the outsiders is not just that we don't do as much work as they do, or that we get paid more. It's power. Locals control the factories. All the managers, forepersons, and group leaders are locals. So they make decisions which always favour us, like who gets the first pick of the distributed goods, who works late at night, how big outsiders' quotas should be, how to distribute bonuses between staff and workers ... And if the outsiders question their decisions, they will increase their workloads, cut their bonuses, or fire them. What the locals say goes! (Fieldnotes, 5 February 1993)

However, to point to the structural underpinnings of the relationship between locals and outsiders is simply to state what is obvious to all who are familiar with Chinese society. Of greater interest is the way in which popular perceptions of locals and outsiders as structurally opposed groups have been expressed and reinforced in a multiplicity of social interactions, institutional arrangements, and discourses about morality which resonate with the objectives of state and capital, and endorse relations of exploitation. In the reform era, place-inflected cultures have been reinvented in tandem with place-structured class relations. The connections between place-inflected cultures and place-structured class relations are evident in distinctive patterns of housing, leisure, mediation, and competing claims of respectability and responsibility.

Interactive and Institutional Dimensions of Place-Based Identities

The localistic nature of housing ownership and occupancy exacerbates social differences between people already set apart by their divergent property rights in enterprises and their conditions of employment. As I mentioned in Chapter 3, local workers all occupied heavily subsidised, publicly owned apartments, or owned their own houses. A few local workers' families also owned buildings which were rented as shops and homes. Outsiders, in contrast, either occupied dormitory accommodation or rented rooms in houses owned by local residents.

Outsiders' accommodation was certainly no worse than the worst public housing occupied by residents of the neighbourhood: that is, they shared with several others a bare concrete room which lacked facilities, appliances, and all but the most basic furniture. However, even outsiders' privately leased rooms were rarely much better than the worst of public housing, whereas most locals lived in homes which were considerably better. Local workers' homes all had cooking facilities and piped water, whereas approximately half the outside workers I spoke with did not have access to a stove, and water had to be fetched from taps outside. Similarly, most locals' homes had some internal walls which provided privacy, whereas only a few outsiders occupied dwellings in which there were internal walls.

The differentiating effect of housing extended well beyond the issue of physical comfort, as the situations of Xu and Bo illustrate. In 1993 Xu and Bo were both in their mid-twenties. They worked at Sanxian bakery, where they earned approximately the same incomes. Both liked listening to the same rock and roll musicians, and both identified quite closely with the amoral, opportunistic characters in Wang Shuo's novels. They agreed that Zhang Yimou was China's best film director. Judging from their comments on magazine advertisements, they also liked the same sort of clothes. Yet despite these similarities of age, employment, income, and taste, they were characterised by vastly different standards of living and patterns of consumption. And those, in turn, were of central to their identities.

Bo always referred to himself as an outsider. His parents lived in a new house in a village near Shangyu, where they cultivated land. When Bo first began at the bakery, he slept on a desk in his urban cousin's office. Before long, the cousin asked him to move out because, Bo said, he was an embarrassment: his accent and clothes marked him as a peasant. The small, unfurnished room Bo rented in a village adjacent to Qiushi cost 60 yuan each month, approximately one-quarter of his average monthly wage. Each month, he also sent 80 to 100 yuan home to help pay off the money borrowed to build his parents' house.

Xu, on the other hand, was every bit a Hangzhou resident. He lived rent-free with his parents, workers who inhabited a publicly owned apartment. They leased out what used to be their two-roomed home on one of the city's busy streets as a clothing shop. Rent from the shop premises was to be used to pay for Xu's imminent marriage.

Consider, now, how their divergent accommodation situations affected the two men's ability to publicly present themselves and participate in simple, but vitally important, social exchanges. After payment of rent and remittance, Bo could only eke out an existence which was devoid of what Xu considered to be 'the bare necessities, not luxuries', such as warm water for bathing, meat or fish and beer with each evening meal, a packet of imported cigarettes to smoke with friends and colleagues each day, a leather jacket to keep out the wind, and Nike running shoes so that his feet didn't ache at work. Bo gaped when I asked him if he drank beer with his meals:

> No! I'm an outsider. I can't afford more than 1, maybe 1.5 yuan on a meal. Noodles and *mantou*, it can't be helped. No beer ... Fruit, that is a really rare occurrence, buying fruit. After rent and sending money home, I have only got around 50 to 70 yuan. It's really tough. It's hard enough to find money to eat and clothe myself – not many, maybe three or four pieces of clothing each year, socks and a shirt when the old ones wear out, not fashionable stuff, just plastic sandals and sandshoes ... That's why I said 1.5 yuan for each meal. 30 to 40 yuan just for my dinners for one month. A packet of cigarettes every few days to smoke at work. The locals ... they are so much better off than we are because they live at home, eat their parents' food. So they buy good cigarettes, and that's a problem for me, because I have to give them back good ones so we can stay on good terms. If I didn't hand out good cigarettes I would be held in contempt. But if I bought a packet every day I'd go hungry. So I can't give many. (Tape, 17 January 1993)

Patterns of social interaction and leisure activities were similarly circumscribed by workers' place of origin. Locals enjoyed many social pastimes. However, these activities generally involved other urbanites. Older natives said their social activities revolved around the local union branch, a fishing club, *taijiquan* and *qi gong* groups, networks of stamp collectors, and the retired residents' association. Many said they regularly got together with neighbours and friends to enjoy each others' caged birds or fish, and exchange flower cuttings. A few young locals said they occasionally had gone out with immigrant colleagues. But none had ever visited these work mates at their dormitories, or invited them to their homes. Youngsters sometimes attended dances organised by the union branch, but said they preferred city discos. Several, including Xu, had gone to rock concerts which had featured such luminaries as Cui Jian. Weekly entertainment consisted of playing ping pong and pool at the union's social club or video games in entertainment centres, trips to the cinema, and *mahjong* and poker games with old school friends, neighbours, and relatives. Many young workers also had hobbies which required considerable expenditure, such as photography and attending aerobics and calligraphy classes. Xu said he was paying a driving instructor to teach him to drive a car, 'Just for fun!' All local informants had a television in their homes.

In comparison, outsiders had much more limited social horizons and fewer leisure activities. None of the outsiders I spoke with said they belonged to any associations in the neighbourhood. Although the chairman of the union branch said that all contract workers in the University enterprises could attend union functions, only a few outsiders even knew of the location of the union's social club and none had been to dances there. They had not joined in the *taijiquan* or *qi gong* classes that were held at the university gate because 'that's just for locals. Besides we are usually at work then.' Only two had ever paid a social visit to the home of a Hangzhou resident. On their rare outings, they said they were usually accompanied by colleagues from their dormitory or fellow villagers who worked in the city. Despite the fact that many outsiders expressed a liking for gardening, birds, and fish, none tended pot plants or had pets. Their sense of isolation was intensified by the fact that many not only felt excluded from urban activities because of their outsider-ness, but also because when they returned to their villages, they felt they had grown away from their old friends and no longer belonged there. Their existence as outsiders had begun to supersede their identities as villagers:

> Lin: When I go home now I feel … sort of strange.
> Gao: It's like that for me too, now. I don't even feel like going home. We've been here a long time.
> Lin: When I go back, all my old friends and cousins come to see me. We used to be like sisters. They all say, 'Don't go back to Hangzhou, stay here!', but I don't really want to see them any more. We don't speak the same language. They are all still living with their parents, never going anywhere or doing anything different. We just aren't on the same wavelength. Now I'm closer to my friends here. (Fieldnotes, 15 January 1993)

Outsiders' utilisation of commercial entertainment facilities was limited by their small surplus income. In contrast to locals, they said they could not afford to go dancing or to the cinema more than a few times each year. None had ever been to a karaoke bar or a rock concert, and only a couple had ever gone to a disco. Less than half the immigrant employees in the case study enterprises had access to a television set. In order of frequency, they said they spent most of their spare time reading, chatting, playing cards, and watching television.

Having low incomes, high expenditure on basic necessities, and limited social interaction also reduced young immigrants' opportunities to find partners. When I asked the young baker, Bo, how often he went out with women, he laughed:

> How could I invite a woman out for a meal or to go dancing? Karaoke bars? … Unthinkable! The entrance fees are too high. People like us,

we have to support ourselves and send some money home, and if we spend too freely there either isn't anything to send or there isn't anything to live on. Our lives are hard. If we ever went dancing or to Karaoke bars, we couldn't get by. Even if I liked someone, I couldn't ask her out. As soon as we went somewhere, all my money would disappear. I'll just have to find a girlfriend who wants to stay at home. It won't be easy! (Tape, 17 January 1993)

These distinctive behavioural patterns among groups defined spatially and structurally have been augmented by the exclusive scope of urban institutions. Take the case of dispute mediation. In the event of civil disagreements, disputes amongst urban residents were usually settled by the neighbourhood committee or neighbours. In Jinshagang village, disputes were referred to neighbours, old relatives, or the village government for resolution. Industrial disputes involving local employees were handled either by formal organisations or through informal mediation. Urban contract employees said that if their contracts were infringed, they could appeal to the union or the labour bureau or request mediation from someone with whom they had *guanxi*. Villagers said they would complain to village leaders or someone connected both to them and the enterprise manager. All local employees agreed that the success of such an appeal would depend heavily on the enterprise manager's *guanxi* with leaders of the union and local government.

In contrast, immigrants tended to call upon fellow villagers, other outside work mates, or, in the case of building gangs, on the labour contractor, to help mediate disputes. Outsiders and members of the Qiushi neighbourhood committee told me immigrants did not have recourse to formal channels of dispute resolution in urban areas unless it involved a crime or the infringement of a registered labour contract. Yet even in those circumstances, it appeared that outsiders had good reason to turn to other arbiters. According to the leader of the neighbourhood committee, 'With theft, or if a fight occurred, outsiders would be unlikely to go to the police, because everyone knows that they are responsible for most of the crimes committed! That's why *we* all have to lock our doors and windows!' Certainly, outsiders said they dared not report offences or ask police to intercede to settle conflicts. And they thought there would be little point in appealing to the union or labour bureau in the event of a contract infringement because these organs tended to support, and be supported by, local employers. In sum, arbitration agencies were perceived by outsiders as reinforcing the controls and forms of exploitation established by place, and enacted in divergent patterns of accommodation and social interaction.

Moral Discourses on Place-Based Identities

Urbanites' and outsiders' divergent identities were also expressed in morally charged discourses about their respective economic roles. One manifestation of this was, of course, urban residents' image of peasants as dirty, fertile, irrational and pre-modern, in comparison with their imagined clean, ordered, modern community. Here, I submit that talk about geographical immobility and mobility also conveyed images of groups which, by virtue of their positions in China's political economy, were distinguished by either respectability or responsibility.

Under central planning, the spatial distinction between urban/rural was fundamental to all aspects of administration. Spatial dualism underpinned different patterns of ownership, production, and distribution in the economy. It determined the direction of surplus extraction and investment. The populace of the countryside, fixed in place, disciplined and made productive by the state, funded industrialisation of the cities (Nolan and White, 1984). Local organs ordered the social and reproductive lives of urban and rural residents. The rewards and punishments designed to elicit particular patterns of behaviour from these populations were wielded by local officials, local institutions, communes and enterprises. People who traversed the borders of administrative territory and work unit became systemically displaced, unconstrained by local disciplinary and productive systems, and, hence, potentially dangerous.

In 1992, I found that urban residents, particularly those who were (or had been) employed by the state, still tended to praise people by referring to the degree to which they were geographically settled, embedded in the state-owned urban economy, and receptive to norms which valorised the 'organised interdependence' of members of a stable, closed urban society.[1] A couple of casual comments illustrate how respectability was held to be a function of people being anchored in place and political economy: 'She's very reliable, She's worked in the rice cooperative for more than twenty years'; 'Public security isn't a problem here. Everyone has been living with their neighbours for years. We're very settled, not like private business people or outsiders!'

Many local residents expressed trepidation at the idea of moving to another city or job. If they were to move, they felt they would be lonely, and, because of their removal from their network, would be at risk and incapable of resolving difficulties. Conversely, they tended to view people who had swapped occupations or transferred between enterprises as being of dubious character. People who crossed territorial boundaries were regarded with even more suspicion. Locals often described outsiders' hooliganism as a corollary of their spatial mobility and social displacement:

> They come into the city and behave really badly. They don't know any-one here, so they don't care what anyone thinks of them. They throw rubbish on the ground, spit everywhere, wear dirty ragged clothes, steal things. This mobile population is responsible for all the bike thefts and fights on the streets! How could we locals respect them? (Fieldnotes, 14 January 1993)

This reasoning, in which the residential and occupational immobility enforced by central planning became metaphors for respectability, was countered by outsiders' claims that their mobility was a demonstration of social responsibility. Appropriating elements of the party-state's propa-ganda about traits which befitted participants in a modern market econ-omy, and invoking peasant traditions of economic self-sufficiency, they depicted themselves as independent citizens who possessed initiative and drive. Outsiders took considerable pride in pointing out that, unlike Hangzhou residents, they were not reliant upon the state for jobs, housing, subsidies, or welfare. The fact that their survival totally depended upon thrift and their own efforts at farming, labouring, and petty business was represented as a virtue. Concurrently, their representations of their identity duplicated the same individualising, liberal ideology which constructed them as 'free' wage workers and set them in opposition to other competi-tors in the labour market.

Moreover, they accused Hangzhou natives of irresponsibility precisely because they were relics of the planned economy. Urbanites were repre-sented as being lazy, dependent, a burden upon the whole society. Their living standards were underwritten by funds extracted from the agri-cultural sector, and their jobs in the loss-making state sector had been allocated by government agencies. People who inhabited suburbs like Jinshagang were also said to be indolent because their collective enter-prises were powered by outsiders' labour. In his harsh Shaoxing dialect, the old storeman at Sanxian attributed the degeneracy of locals to the fact that they did not have to assume responsibility for, or work hard to earn, their own livelihood:

> Look at the University students here! The ones that come from cities, they are a lot of spoilt children. Like bandits! They don't study. Their parents all have good jobs, plenty of money, comfortable homes, so they tell their kids to come to University to study. But they don't study at all.

They don't have to ... they'll get given jobs regardless. So they spend all their time playing, looking for lovers ... I can't stand seeing all these boys and girls groping around in each others' trousers! Disgusting! It's different if they come from the countryside, of course. Then they have to fulfil all the older generations' social aspirations and make sure they find jobs, so they work really hard. (Tape, 10 January 1993)[2]

Competing claims of respectability as against responsibility were also advanced in discussions about distinctive patterns of reciprocity among locals and outsiders, despite the fact that their gift exchange and mutual help practices did not appear to differ markedly. Local residents told me they often exchanged small gifts such as cooked food, surplus fruit and vegetables, reading material, and cigarettes with neighbours and friends. They helped relatives and friends with child minding and in situations such as house moving, marriage, and sickness. Money was only given or lent to close relatives. These actions were all represented as examples of their decency and civility, and their willingness to sustain familial, neighbourhood, and social ties. While most locals acknowledged that outsiders also seemed to exchange goods and help each other, they suggested their behaviour was qualitatively different: it betokened old-fashioned rural clannishness and narrow-minded egalitarianism. Moreover, urbanites frequently described outsiders as being essentially more materialistic and greedy than locals, and lacking socialist ethics. They attributed their venal behaviour to the fact that they had been steeped in the poverty and petty-mindedness of village life, were uneducated, and had no social stake in the development either of the city or the nation.

Outsiders disagreed. They accused locals of miserliness. This was traced, in part, to their inability to adapt to an increasingly competitive environment. Faced with job insecurity and declining incomes relative to other social groups, urbanites attempted to buttress their standards of living by parsimony. However, even greater explanatory importance was attached to the types of relationships which existed between locals and outsiders, and among local residents. Locals behaved in an ungenerous fashion towards immigrants because they perceived them solely as cheap labour which produced profit in 'their' enterprises: 'They don't treat us as though we are people, just because we are poor and have to work for them – as if that makes us less than human!' On the other hand, they argued that the forces which integrated Hangzhou residents – local governments, work units, networks and kin groups – also promoted competition for advantages, *guanxi* leverage, income and face. Therefore, locals were also stingy towards one another. Although locals voiced a rhetoric of socialist solidarity, they did not genuinely participate in community. Things were said to be different in the countryside, where people were knit together by transparency and a sense of mutual responsibility:

> In the countryside you can't *not* help people. You can't lie to people, cry poor. Everyone has a fairly clear idea of how well everyone else is doing, so if you don't help people when you can, you won't get any help from others when you need it. But here, the officials, teachers, old tenured workers, they are always pretending they haven't any money. They have, of course! They complain to everyone that they are broke and can't pay the right price. If you asked them to advance your pay, or if their neighbours needed a loan until next month, they would say no, or add interest on to the loan before they gave it to you. In the villages everyone lends and borrows, and no one adds interest. It's all the same there. You borrow from me when you need it, and in a few years' time when my son gets married you return my money and I borrow from the next person. There is never any interest paid on loans. Here, they are mean. Every situation is turned into an opportunity to get as much as they can out of other people. (Fieldnotes, 26 November 1992)

The changes set in motion by economic reform, particularly the reduction of state control of production and redistribution, emergence of new forms of ownership, development of labour markets, and creation of an ideology of market freedoms, gave new substance to the identities of, and relations between, locals and immigrants in Hangzhou. Locals relied upon the labour of outsiders to produce profits in local enterprises, but resented the intrusion of these peasants into their old worlds of work and neighbourhood. As outsiders ruptured the stability and 'organised interdependence' of urban society, they concurrently enlivened the state-promoted image of the reworked proletariat as a productive, motivated and self-sufficient contractual work force. That representation of autonomy, mobility, and responsibility as contemporary virtues was parried by locals' assertion that they were a settled, respectable, ethically superior people.

One might conclude from this that workers did not share an identity as workers or a distinctive ethos. But the effects of place in identifying and segregating workers were being mediated by workers' conviction that factors other than place were integral to the transformation of social relations. Power and wealth were critical in workers' representations of identity and their delineation of an alternative status hierarchy and social values.

POWER AND WEALTH: BIG PEOPLE AND SMALL PEOPLE

Sangren (1995) has pointed out that power requires both an agent and a subject. Among workers in Xihu, power was not seen as a force transcendent or external to society. It was, rather, a product of social interaction, and productive of the terms of interaction. Power implied the ability of some people to influence or control others. It bestowed a positive capacity to utilise opportunities, carry out projects, and direct others' activities in order to produce and appropriate wealth. Power was also described in negative terms relative to the speakers' own lack of control over their own and others' activities, and an inability to utilise opportunities and acquire wealth. Power was experienced by its subjects as domination, organisation, discipline and extraction.

Sources of Power

In the eyes of tenured and non-tenured, local and immigrant workers alike, the main agents of power were officials. Power flowed from, and through the operations of the state. But that pinpointing of the source of officials' power was blurred by workers' conviction that officials functioned not just as state representatives and administrators, but also as entrepreneurs and the friends and agents of business people. Networking allowed them to extend their power spatially and temporally into big business ventures, the stock exchanges, financial institutions and trade corporations, and the media.

The notion that officials' power came from multiple sources and types of activity indicates a significant shift in perception. At the end of the Maoist era, Lowell Dittmer (1978, pp. 29–30) distinguished between two forms of power: *quanli* and *shili*. *Quanli* denoted formal power derived from the authority of the CCP and the state, and officials' role as guardians of Communist myth and ideology and their legitimate, functional spheres of administration. *Shili*, or informal power, came from officials' individual command over resources, infrastructure, public space and licensing, and from the interaction, reciprocal exchange and intermarriage which extended their *guanxi* networks. My informants referred to officials' power as *quanli*, yet their descriptions of how officials accumulated power betokened *shili*. In the minds of workers, these two meanings of power were reconciled by the articulation of state power with production and accumulation in the market economy. Like He Xin, they thought new sources of money-power were being constructed within the confines of the state: 'This network of *guanxi* revolves around various centers of power, expressing itself through a hierarchy of profit, binding people into voluntary and involuntary relationships of dependence. It is like a massive and invisible mafialike organization enmeshing the whole of China (1992, p. 135).'[3]

The acquisition and deployment of power by individuals has always been structured culturally by gender and generational hierarchies. In China, power, like wealth, is *yang*. It exists in the public arena. As such, it has been naturalised as the rightful possession of older males. In the hands of females, unless power is expressed as nurturance, it is dangerous.[4] Among the almost all-female work force at Jinshagang, the (male) manager's exercise of power was seen to be commensurate with his position and person, whilst workers complained bitterly that the power he had delegated to the (female) office manager and forewomen had 'gone to their heads'. Similarly, the hard-working, ambitious manager of the bakery, Rong, was thought by her employees of both sexes to be excessively dictatorial. Her poor health and the difficulties facing the business were seen to be a consequence of her natural inability to exercise power. The male bakers, in particular, said women were too simple-minded, socially inept, and habituated as consumers to be successful in business:

> A general manager should be a man because they are more intelligent, stronger. To be a manager you have to know how to handle situations. You need to have *guanxi*, be able to find the right doors, socialise with officials and clients. All Rong does on her business trips is go sightseeing and shopping! (Fieldnotes, 14 November 1992)

Culturally ascribed male power intersects with, and is buttressed by, power derived from the paternalistic state. After complaining to me that because she was a female immigrant it was impossible for her to be anything other than a contract worker on a production line, one informant mused on the distribution of power among the big people, or *da ren*, in society:

> It's great to be a big person! If you can be emperor, that's the very best. The next best thing is to be leader of a province, a city, a government department, or a big successful enterprise. Then after that, it's good to be the old man of a family. If you are a big person, then no matter whether you are right or wrong, everyone under you has to listen and obey! (Fieldnotes, 4 March 1993)

Representing Power

The power of the state is authorised, Geertz suggests, by sets of symbols which 'mark the center as center and give what goes on there its aura of not being merely important but in some odd fashion connected with the way the world is built' (1983, p. 124). Geertz's statement confuses intent and effect. In China, whilst symbols of state are certainly meant to legitimate officials' exercise of power, they do not always function efficiently as ideology.[5] Workers were highly sensitive to a dissonance between the rhetoric and symbolism of just rule and the real exercise of power. And their perceptions of the gap between rhetoric and reality informed a critique not only of the activities of individual local bureaucrats, but also of the whole concept of an homogeneous nation which was central to the sanctioning of officials' power.

Officials' power was justified by, and encoded in, the aims, rituals, and myths of governance. One of the main aims of governance was, as I noted in Chapter 2, promotion of national economic growth. The rituals of governance involved seemingly endless participation in meetings, conferences, tours of inspection and official banquets. Televised and reported in the newspapers every day of the year, these gatherings of the powerful (older, male, be-suited representatives of departments, municipalities, corporations) were shown to be venues in which decisions of national import were made. The delegates were there, the audience was told, to devise plans to reform the economy and open China for trade and technological exchanges, revolutionise agriculture, improve industrial efficiency, and improve the quality, morality and standard of living of the population. These ceremonies simultaneously represented officials' power as a technology of national modernisation, and a public good. Economic progress and social harmony were predicated upon the correct performance of binary subject positions by these disinterested, knowledgeable agents of power, and the obedient masses.[6]

My neighbours and employees in the case study enterprises frequently remarked upon the contradiction between this representation of selfless labour in the service of national economic growth and what they saw and heard of officials' actual behaviour. Officials did not undertake any physically taxing labour, did not hurry, and did not encounter polluting substances or extremes of temperature whilst at work. Indeed, they did not do what my informants defined as work. Work involved productive activity in return for profit or payment, whereas officials enjoyed life-long sinecures and opportunities to extract income and bribes from others, despite the fact that they did not produce anything. A popular pastime of workers was to recount cases of official corruption which had been reported in the news. These conversations usually drifted into fantasies about the lives of officials: 'Ah, what an easy life it would be! Sitting in an office all day, smoking, reading the paper, drinking tea. Just watching the presents arrive at the door – cases of wine, food, television sets, offers to participate in joint ventures' (Fieldnotes, 20 February 1993).

In this vein, workers sometimes conceptualised officials' power as a quantifiable property. It could be measured by the amount of money, goods, and benefits received, and by the achievement of personal objectives through using the labour and services of others. This notion prompted some to speculate that because officials furthest removed from the central party-state were less strictly monitored and freer to extract rents from office, they actually had more power than their superiors in Beijing. One morning, the bakery's van was stalled on its delivery run to a small town near Jiaxing by a funeral procession for a deceased bureaucrat. As we sat in the van, waiting for the long line of vehicles to pass and vainly trying to block out the discordant sounds emanating from the brass band accompanying the procession, the driver regaled me with his interpretation of the situation:

> Look! It doesn't even cost them anything to die! Those government vehicles will take them all the way out to the grave. They will have commandeered a piece of hillside with good *fengshui*, and built a great big tomb for free with concrete and tiles from the local state-owned construction company, and the labour of the workers in the company and the peasants who used to own the land. After the funeral, they will all go off for a feast. They will eat crabs that would cost me 50 yuan a kilo in the market, but when they paid, the vendor would have considered his licence, smiled, and said 'Please be my guests. It's not necessary to pay.' Then they would put on their public hats: 'We are civil servants! We must pay for everything we use.' And they will have paid 3 yuan per kilo! They couldn't get away with this in the centre of Hangzhou. Someone would complain. Journalists would photograph the number plates and it would be in the newspaper or on the evening news, along with a demand that the private use of public vehicles be stopped. But in these little towns they are the law! The locals don't know otherwise. They think they would be thrown in prison if they reported them. They're probably right. Look at them sitting up being grand! (Fieldnotes, 20 February 1993)

Occasionally, cynicism about bureaucrats' exercise of power in pursuit of national economic growth was echoed by officials themselves. Consider this frank exchange between Gao, the owner of a small clothing shop, and a bureaucrat from the Xihu Industry and Commerce Bureau who had spent the afternoon harassing Gao's female customers:

> Official: How do you manage to preserve your looks, heh? What is your secret? Is it *qi gong*? With a body like that you would be a great

dancing partner. Do you want to come dancing? You obviously don't have as many worries as Xiao Gao here.

Gao: No, but she has more worries than you do. She has to work, doesn't she, not like you! That's why she doesn't have a big fat belly like you. That is what happens to you Party members who fatten at public expense! What are you doing here, flirting with women? You should be out implementing reform and opening up!

Official (chuckling): Oh, this is exactly how I go about implementing reform and opening up! (Fieldnotes, 9 June 1992)

Workers also drew upon media representations of officials as the agents of national modernisation to call into question the composition of the nation. As they watched or heard news readers solemnly announcing national tours of inspection or new national policies, they sourly asked why they, members of China's masses, had never been invited to travel at public expense to 'play at conferences' or discuss the future of the nation. They reminded one another of previous speeches which had prophesied improvements in the economy and the living standards of the populace, but only resulted in increased profits for business people and a rise in the cost of living for workers. During a conversation about the television coverage of National Day activities in Beijing, I asked baker Shi whether the parades and ceremonies had kindled a sense of patriotism in him. He replied: 'Officials and intellectuals can feel patriotic, go out to demonstrate their patriotism, because they get paid to have a day off! We don't. If we don't work we don't get paid. So you see, that's the limit of national pride' (Fieldnotes, 19 October 1992).

Wealth

If ideas about power were shared by workers of all ilk, ideas about wealth varied dramatically. In China in the mid-1980s, a household earning 10 000 yuan per annum was considered enviable. In 1993, only those with hundreds of thousands of yuan were considered to be rich. Then, people generally agreed that the wealthy were engaged in some form of business. Their wealth was described as comprising property, savings and cash, income, personal valuables and consumer goods. However, beyond these common determinations, my urban neighbours, especially those who were tenured state employees and intellectuals, tended to voice quite different understandings of wealth and the wealthy to those who were contract workers or were outsiders. These divergent ideas were historical products, bound up not only with stories about the genesis and characteristics of the wealthy, but also with the relative subject-positions adopted by those who, in identifying the wealthy as a group, also sought to make statements about their own social positions, relationships and values. After analysing conflicting attitudes towards the accumulation of wealth, I turn to examine workers' perception that in the socialist market economy, there has been a synthesis of power and wealth.

Adjudging Wealth

'Most business people', I was told on countless occasions by my securely employed, eminently respectable urban neighbours, 'have a shameful past. They are ex-convicts and formerly unemployed youth. No-one respects them. Their ideology [*sixiang*] is poor.' Business people, like powerful people, were usually assumed to be male: women were said to lack the shrewdness, ambition, and strength required for business, and risked their virtue if they travelled alone or bargained hard with men. Irrespective of the obvious existence of vast differentials in wealth, almost all individual labourers and private business people were said by my urban neighbours to be rich, and their wealth was thought to have had an inglorious beginning: it was acquired through illegal and unethical means such as tax evasion, bribery, speculation, profiteering, cheating, and the production of fake goods and shoddy workmanship. These imputations of immorality were sometimes extended after my neighbours had consumed a few bowls of rice wine in the evenings. Then, wealth was said to beget further immorality in the forms of sexual promiscuity, intemperance, and habitual gambling:

> Lou: These private business people no sooner get rich than they turn bad. The richer they get, the more promiscuous they become. That's what wealth brings. They behave just like the old landlords, buying up all the pretty young women!
>
> Lou's daughter (grinning mischievously at her boyfriend): No wonder all these men spend their nights dreaming up schemes for getting rich! (Fieldnotes, 12 February 1993)

Intellectuals tended to express similar opinions about business people. Entrepreneurs' participation in the market economy was sexualised. It was an attempt to compensate for inadequacy, and a source of base gratification and moral pollution. Business people were poorly educated, devoid of public spirit, and neglectful of their children. It was assumed that they suffered from low self-esteem because respect and status were consequent upon those very criteria which traditionally had distinguished intellectuals and officials: academic achievement and bureaucratic appointment. Business people squandered money on sensual pleasures and conspicuous ornamentation for fear that the government might halt private economic activities.[7] A vivid expression of the problems which intellectuals attributed to wealthy peoples' lack of education, status and security can be found in a book by Cheng Shu (1992). In a passage reminiscent of the warnings on the dangers of carnal desire in the introduction to the erotic classic *Golden Lotus*, Cheng synthesises Confucian and Marxist-Maoist puritanism to draw an analogy between the corrupting influences of money and women:

> this thing money is just like women, it both exercises a great seductiveness, and it also gives us a sense of moral danger. In the eyes of the wise gentleman who upholds social morality, it more closely resembles prostitutes and syphilis, it is a breeding ground for evil and a pitfall for morality, a poisonous viper which corrupts people's souls ... Whenever some kind of evil enticement is mentioned, money and women spring to mind. This not only reflects traditional morality, but also people's dread of uncontrollable, alien powers. (pp. 129–30)

In short, the consensus amongst informants whose personal stakes lay in the state delimited spheres of employment and possession of educational capital was that no respectable person would ever voluntarily choose to become a private business person. Such a transformation would result in a loss of prestige, or face, for their entire family.[8]

These attitudes toward business people were not always shared by members of the contingent work force. Many contract and temporary workers had themselves been engaged in petty commodity production and commerce, or had relatives and friends who were self-employed. Unlike my neighbours, they drew clear distinctions between business people according to the amount of money they had and, more importantly, the manner in which they made it. The heads of sizeable enterprises and people involved in large scale construction, catering, wholesale trade, real estate development, and stock market speculation were always held to be wealthy. It was common knowledge that they enjoyed incomes several times greater than the average workers' wage. Yet despite the fact that they too earned many times more than most workers, self-employed tradespeople, stall owners and market vendors were not considered wealthy. This distinction had less to do with the sum of money earned, than with the notion that the former group were believed to have acquired their wealth by ingratiating themselves with officials, and using hired labour to produce goods and services from which they profited: 'They don't work themselves. They never get their hands dirty. They make thousands every day because they own buildings and things, or run companies as though they own them. They hire workers, and get them to produce their wealth. That's how people get rich' (Fieldnotes, 18 October 1992).

Neither did contract and temporary workers intimate that business people suffered from a lack of self-esteem, low status or a sense of insecurity. Indeed, more often they expressed a diametrically opposed view. In contrast to the relatively narrow status hierarchy determined by official position and educational qualifications that mapped the social horizon of my tenured Qiushi neighbours, contract and temporary workers saw wealth as a primary principle of identification, a prerequisite for the attainment of status, and a fundamental source of security:

Jin: Intellectuals would rather have face than money. They think business people are pretty low.

Che: Intellectuals cry poor! They think they should be paid well and respected just for talking in front of their students and telling everyone how to live.

SS (to Jin): So what sort of standards do you use to assess people these days? You just mentioned face. Is that the most important criteria?

Jin: No … It must be money, mustn't it? With the cost of food, schooling for kids, housing reform, health care … What is the point of putting on airs and talking about your face if you can't buy food or pay your rent? It's definitely money – actually, that's what *gives* you face these days. (Fieldnotes, 28 October 1992)

An Unholy Synthesis: Money-Power

Ole Bruun (1989, pp. 19, 91, 155–7) once described bureaucracy and business in China as parallel and fundamentally conflicting social hierarchies which were articulated by exchange relations. All the workers I met would have agreed with Bruun that bureaucrats were associated with business people. However, they did not think that officials and business people manoeuvred in separate social hierarchies. They certainly were not thought to be in conflict. Nor were they seen as being connected only by exchange relations though, as in all social relations, exchange was obviously an important lubricant. Rather, workers conceived power and wealth as interrelated and overlapping spheres of operation and identity. From their vantage point by the roadside, at the factory gate, or in the market place, the well-dressed officials and business people who travelled by car to dine at expensive hotels were indistinguishable.

The vehicles for synthesising power and wealth were, of course, place and *guanxi*. It was common knowledge that local officials and business people had become friends, business partners, or affinal relatives. A second, less obvious, element in workers' representation of this syncretic identity was that officials and business people were thought to have a similar mode of livelihood. Money-power did not come from their own productive activities, for in fact both groups were thought to be inactive and unproductive. Instead, it derived from their control over the labour of others and appropriation of the produce of that labour. Workers, in contrast, were negatively defined by the necessity of having to work for a living. In short, the powerful, wealthy big people in society were identified by their unprincipled exploitation of small people:

> Rui: The people who have power have all the opportunities. They don't work. We small people all have to work for them.
> Chen: That's right. That's how they get rich, power and money. If you have one you have the other. (Fieldnotes, 11 January 1993)

Workers' association of power and wealth as characteristics which identified the big people in their society was not accepted or deployed by many of the people to whom it was attributed, even though they sometimes acknowledged that they had certain specific features in common. Instead, officials interpreted the distinction between power and wealth as one which contrasted such traditional values as moral and intellectual superiority and public service against the immoral pursuit of private commercial interest. Business people, on the other hand, tended to characterise that distinction as an anachronistic legacy of the time when private sector activities were thought to be 'irregular'. They denied the existence of a power/wealth divide by drawing attention to the economic interests of officialdom, and their own acts of public patronage and service.

As officials' power has increasingly become economic rather than purely political and administrative, and business people have become assimilated into the realm of the local state, so too has their manipulation of symbols of power and wealth altered. There has, for instance, been a marked change in the sorts of spatial configurations people identify as centres of power. Power no longer resides solely in the impenetrable, monumental brick and concrete offices which squat in the midst of every city, and betoken the authority of the central party-state. Now, power is also produced in many of the same sites as wealth. Money-power can be seen in action at the board meetings of village share-holding corporations, in the construction of executive residential complexes, and in the management of export and technology zones: urban development schemes which give material form to evolving relations between government and business in the reform era. Jinshagang's manager Mao described this synthesis of money and power in terms of a reversal of symbolic agency:

> When the factory first began exporting products, I invited the local customs officials to lunch at a big, new foreign-owned hotel. They came along looking really scruffy and not knowing what to do. They looked like peasants and didn't know how to cope with all the cutlery, dishes, polite waitresses. Now when I take them out to lunch they arrive in new Japanese cars and wear better quality suits than I do. They walk in as though they own the hotel! (Fieldnotes, 20 October 1992)

The geography and appointment of housing further illustrate reversals which have attended the synthesis of power and wealth. When economic reforms began, the location, furnishing and size of urban housing provided a clear index to position in a strictly graded hierarchy of state power. In the beautiful lakeside suburbs which were occupied by Hangzhou officials, streets were wider and better sealed than in other neighbourhoods, electricity transmission, water supply and drains worked more efficiently, and old trees shaded the pavements. The furnishings of officials' homes mirrored their assertions of political, moral and intellectual superiority. Polished wooden bookshelves contained the speeches and biographies of Communist leaders. Awards, calligraphies, and uplifting revolutionary scenes decorated walls. A conversation between Laolian employees about a serialised television drama set in the pre-reform era suggests that, given the critical shortage of housing which has plagued city residents since the 1950s, floor space may have been the clearest of all indicators of position in the state hierarchy:

> Wu: They aren't doing badly. It's an enormous house!
> Jin: Yes. He must be a high cadre.
> Che (interrupting): What, do you think he is a factory Party secretary or something like that?
> Wu: No, higher. With a house like that, at least a department chief. *High* cadre. (Fieldnotes, 28 October 1992)

By 1993, however, the size of housing was no longer a particularly effective yardstick either for identifying gradations in the state hierarchy, or for differentiating between the powerful and the rich. Many lower level officials, suburban peasants and business people inhabited large apartments in city skyscrapers, and free-standing villas in planned, well-serviced suburbs.

Their sitting rooms sported furniture carved in Song style from mahogany and teak, or fashioned from tubular steel. Paintings, karaoke machines, satellite televisions and glass fronted bars stocked with imported liquor offered an escape from the day's drudgery. In contrast to the restrained asceticism and sublimation of the individual which once characterised the homes of the powerful, money-power puts surplus on display and indulged the domestic self.

These transformations of neighbourhood and home were not simply expressions of a new, syncretic identity forged by the merger of money and power. The point is that people's ability to manipulate these symbols of money-power actually functioned as a password into the networks which generated money-power. Concurrently, they signified an array of social and economic relations which, according to the workers who defined themselves as small people, were founded upon big people's control and exploitation of labour.

Common ideas about the sources and operations of power and the emergence of money-power in the reform era did not efface differences of identity, values and morals among workers. Patently, some groups were promoting their own identity constructs and ethical standards over the competing claims of other sorts of workers, as well as those being advanced by officials and business people. So, too, did various groups of workers represent business people in different ways, depending upon their own status and functions in the political economy of reform. What did change, however, was the old notion that place and bureaucracy were the main forces structuring society. Now, business people were universally thought to be acting in concert with local officials in such a way as to reconfigure social relations, the distribution of wealth, and the shape and texture of life in urban neighbourhoods. As a consequence of this common perception, particular aspects of different workers' identities and attitudes were beginning to converge. In particular, workers had begun to share an awareness and a resentment that they were the subjects of money-power, and the producers of others' opportunities, power and wealth:

> The children of the rich and powerful are also rich and powerful. Economic reform has been good to them. It's given them many more opportunities than it has given us poor people. The children of the poor will remain poor as long as they are denied opportunities, as long as they haven't any skills, any capital. It will be hard for them all their lives. We can only dream about getting rich. It's a dream for me. I'm just a peasant who has come here to work because it's the only way I can keep my head above water. But I still fantasise that the poor, one

day, might be able to get rich. The people being born now, I fantasise that by the time they are my age, they might be able to do business, set up enterprises. It's impossible. Just a dream. They mightn't even have enough to feed and clothe their children. (Tape, 10 January 1993)

THE CONSUMPTION OF FACE: BUYING IDENTITY

Consumption publicly advanced what was considered to be one of the most significant of all identity claims. With the exception of beggars, whose livelihood depended upon manifest poverty, every person I met in Hangzhou wanted to appear well off. That objective was motivated by the desire to actually be well off, and a belief in the efficacy of consumption as a form of sympathetic magic: displays of wealth would open doors to the restrictive social circles within which power and riches were generated.

Even as it goaded workers to compete in discriminatory labour markets and to work for inequitable wages in order to fulfil their wants and desires, consumption was considered to be an open arena in which identities and relationships could be transformed. In comparison with the social closure and relations of control and exploitation established by place, power and wealth, consumption promised the possibility of expressing belonging, contesting exclusion and overturning domination. Consumption also provided a fertile repertoire of organisational principles and material symbols with which to identify and represent people, and thence decide on appropriate responses toward them (McKracken, 1990; M. Lee, 1993; Miller, 1994).

Hence, despite the fact that place, power and wealth all determined marked disparities in levels of individual expenditure, the universalising logic of consumption competition also produced remarkably similar identity orientations and values among Chinese workers. This, then, is the 'democratic social function' of consumption parodied by Baudrillard (1981, p. 58): 'confronting the hierarchy of power and social origin, there would be a democracy of leisure, of the expressway and the refrigerator'. It is, however, a democracy circumscribed both by limited buying power, and by peer pressure to conform to particular consumer-images.

Dressing Up

Dress encapsulates ideas about self and anticipated audience. It functions as a signifier of tastes, wealth, level of confidence, and as a restrictive code which can be read only by people who have been able to acquire specific types of cultural expertise. Dress is used to assert eminence, evaluate degrees of difference, and intimate shared experiences and attitudes. In exchange, dress can initiate and consolidate relationships.

People in Xihu dressed their way up in society. At Jinshagang factory, the tailored suits, Italian shoes, gold and diamond jewellery, and mobile phones affected by the factory manager were intended to be, and were correctly interpreted by his employees as, statements about his wealth, cosmopolitanism, and association with international business. Yet whenever workers commented upon his clothing, they were forced to confront their own ignorance and inferiority. Not only had they never been shopping in Tokyo where the manager purchased many of his clothes, they did not even dare to enter luxury clothing stores in Hangzhou. Hence, their remarks on their boss's attire were always accompanied by a confession that they were out of their depth: they could only guess at where they had been manufactured and how much they cost. On the other hand, they were fully cognisant of the price and status statements of clothing and jewellery stocked in the large department stores in the city. Confident assessments were made of the social standing of a supervisor's fiancée simply on the basis of an inspection of the gold jewellery she was given at her engagement. Apparently, she had married well, for his family was obviously much wealthier than her own.

Jinshagang workers' clothing was similarly utilised in their evaluations of one another, and their construction of a shared identity. When they first arrived at the factory, outsiders from poor, remote villages had few items of clothing. They wore dull, shapeless trousers made of strong material, and buttoned cotton shirts and jackets. Their attire suggested that they were still close to the soil, manual labour, and material want. Many of the factory's older employees felt this brought the whole work force into disrepute: 'It makes everyone feel embarrassed when they arrive looking like that. They look like stupid peasants.' They expressed their disapproval in unfriendliness and snide remarks. Thus, the new arrivals were pressured into adopting a style of clothing which erased their origins. In some cases, a whole year passed before the newcomers summoned sufficient courage and saved enough money to purchase the gendered, age-graded clothing and cosmetics that stamped them as feminised, acculturated, socially competent members of the urban work force. In contrast, immigrants from the wealthier villages of north-eastern Zhejiang arrived at the factory in bright, pastel dresses, or blue jeans and running shoes, carrying a suitcase full of clothing. They were immediately welcomed by the older residents of the factory dormitory, who made sure their 'sisters' were comfortably settled.

Sensitivity to the fact that clothing is a cipher of wealth and status leads people to go to great pains to manipulate their public image through the medium of dress. Old Du was employed to ride his tricycle to deliver the bakery's products to shops throughout Hangzhou: a tough job which, he said sadly, people held in contempt. In late autumn, Du discovered to his great embarrassment that he alone, amongst all his friends and fellow workers, did not possess a western-style suit. To regain face, he decided to purchase a suit immediately. His wife objected strenuously: 'Why dress up like a boss to pedal a tricycle around the city? It isn't practical. It would be uncomfortable and would wear out within a year. Besides, it isn't warm enough for winter!' Her objections were overruled, and the suit was duly bought. Although he loathed riding in the trousers ('Too tight in the crotch over my long underwear!'), and the jacket had to be concealed beneath an overcoat, old Du wore his suit proudly each day. He never missed an opportunity to flash the brand name tag which remained on the jacket sleeve, and mention that his suit had cost him 500 yuan: the equivalent of almost two months' wages! However, the style of old Du's suit was soon superseded. His bid to renovate his identity and gain prestige was impeded by the fact that to project an image of wealth, one must wear fashions which change annually.

Dress and jewellery are also important articles of exchange in the creation and maintenance of *guanxi* relations. In a situation where *guanxi* is expected to generate wealth, people agonise over calculating the amount to be spent on gifts, and ensuring that the monetary value will be apparent to the recipient. I became the unwilling purchasing agent of a gift from the manager of a trade company who wished to obtain low priced goods from a township enterprise, to the wife of the managing director of the enterprise. The 'token' gift was a 24 carat gold chain, which cost several hundred US dollars. When the gift giver described to me the sort of chain that I was to buy, they said design was unimportant. The crucial thing was to obtain a certificate of purchase which detailed the weight and purity of the chain, to be presented along with the gift.

Food

Food formed another site for people's purposive, competitive manipulation of social identity. Mary Douglas has observed that in most societies, there is a sharp distinction between the sorts of places in which food is consumed, the type of food which is consumed, and the manner in which it is consumed, by those who are powerful and rich, and those who are not: 'If food is treated as a code, the message it encodes will be found in the pattern of social relations being expressed. The message is about different degrees of hierarchy, inclusion and exclusion, boundaries and transactions across the boundaries' (1975, p. 249). In China, the consumption of food can be socially empowering or disempowering. To gain access to the restrictive *guanxi* networks of money-power, it is necessary to project an image of wealth by consuming the food of the wealthy. The consumption of plain food would be taken as an expression of need, which would limit one's social circle to others who were, to a greater or lesser extent, also needy. They would, correspondingly, be less useful in moving beyond the boundary of need.

In Hangzhou, the rich frequented expensive, fashionable restaurants, and foreign hotels which, in 1993, required payment in foreign exchange.[9] In the course of establishing and sustaining their connections, entrepreneurs said they visited several different restaurants each week. While eating out, they exuded confidence and authority by the manner in which they ordered food, recommended new dishes, and paid bills. Banquets comprised a significant item of business expenditure, and the higher the official with whom one did business or the bigger the deal involved, the greater the sum to be spent on food. On the other hand, although the rich also consumed an impressive volume of food at home and had purpose built rooms and furniture for dining, that figured as a relatively small component of their domestic budgets.

Workers' meals were usually consumed in factory canteens, dormitory corridors, and at their homes in all-purpose dining-living rooms which, sometimes, also served as bathrooms, bedrooms, and studies. Food was usually the largest single item of expenditure in workers' budgets. On the rare occasions they dined out, workers tended to eat in ordinary restaurants which served the high-calorie food with which they were familiar and that they considered to be good value. On each occasion I ate with workers in a restaurant, they expressed anxiety over the possibility that we might be cheated with substandard cooking or excessive bills, and complained about the amount of profit that would be earned by the restaurateurs from our meal.

The sorts of food consumed similarly served as an index of identification: an index which, as Bourdieu (1984, p. 177) remarked of French food, was scaled from luxury (urban wealth) to necessity (rural poverty). Meals of the wealthy were theatrical displays of scarce produce and surplus provisioning. At banquets, plates of shellfish, wild and imported animals, artistically cut and arranged meats and vegetables arrived on the table and then were replaced, often barely touched. At the homes of the rich, large quantities of meat, fish, and out-of-season vegetables and fruits were consumed (and also discarded, according to several scavengers who worked the streets of our neighbourhood). In contrast, workers' and farmers' houses produced very little food garbage. Their meals comprised much less meat and fish, and a higher proportion of cheap protein, rice, flour products such as noodles and steamed breads, and seasonal vegetables. Because of my fondness for rice, *doufu*, and vegetables, I was scolded on several occasions for expressing the tastes of a poor peasant: 'Don't you care what people think of you?'

In pursuit of a particular identity and social standing people tended to discard foods that became associated with poverty, and adopt foods they thought were indicative of wealth. Correspondingly, so too did the wealthy continually change their tastes in order to differentiate themselves from those they viewed as their social inferiors (McKracken, 1990, pp. 93–100). Food fashions radiated out from metropolitan centres of wealth, according to Song, the purchasing agent for Sanxian bakery. And they changed so rapidly, the bakery had difficulty keeping up with people's constant search for edible exotica:

The richer they get, the higher their expectations and the greater the demand for new products. They want lots of new varieties, and really good ingredients. It's hard to keep up with it. In the past we southerners ate very little bread or cakes. Now, the Chinese people who have been overseas say they have toast for breakfast! If ordinary people have guests at home, they get cakes to eat... See those mille feuille? You know, two years ago you wouldn't have been able to buy mille feuille on the streets of Shanghai. They would have been available in the big foreign hotels. But now we are selling hundreds of them every day in little shops in Hangzhou! (Fieldnotes, 4 December 1992)

Weddings

Weddings illustrate other strategies by which people manage identities, acquire face, extend their *guanxi* networks, and attempt to get ahead in society. Take the choice of spouses, for example. The fact that young workers said they would only marry someone they loved suggested a marked change from the prioritisation of familial and social considerations over personal desires in mate choice which Sulamith and Jack Potter (1990, pp. 196–203) observed in rural areas in the 1980s. Yet when I inquired further into what sorts of people my informants liked, they immediately responded not by describing character types or even physical appearance, but rather factors that could consolidate or advance their own and their families' social position. They were attracted to people who had similar, or better residential registration, place of origin, education, occupational status, connections, and incomes than themselves. Educated urbanites like recruitment officer Su, and Qi from Xerox, would only marry another highly educated Hangzhou resident or someone from a larger city. Young Che, in the Laolian company, intended to marry a Hangzhou engineer. At Jinshagang, Li and He said gloomily that it would be impossible to find an acceptable partner in their home villages, and few male immigrants were educated enough to consider marrying. Unfortunately, however, urban men looked down upon rural women. Storekeeper Ge was engaged to a man with a college education: 'His family is well connected, but he has rural *hukou* too.'

Moreover, although urban parents appeared to have relinquished control over their children's choice of partner, they still oversaw the all-important organisation of wedding ceremonies. The spiralling cost of wedding ceremonies was a popular topic amongst my informants. And, as with the north American potlatch, competition to increase the prestige of kinship corporations and gain entry into more powerful and richer networks was said to be the main factor inflating the costs of weddings. In 1993, marriages in Hangzhou generally cost between 15 000 and 50 000 yuan: more than double the average cost at my previous visit in 1989.[10] Most of this money was spent on gifts between the bride's and groom's families, purchase of new furniture, jewellery and clothes for the young couple, and a wedding feast. The groom's family was usually responsible for between half and two-thirds of the expense. Although everyone bemoaned the exorbitant expenditure associated with weddings, they also said it was unavoidable: every healthy young person was expected to marry, and every marriage had to be arranged and celebrated in a style that would indicate that the two families were at least as well off, or wealthier than, those they considered their peers. To do otherwise would be to throw away an opportunity to secure *guanxi* connections and improve the family's standing.

Since weddings involved such an large expenditure and were central to identification, representation and the formation of social links, they were also a focal point of tension within and between families. Two cases provide contrasting perspectives on the stresses and struggles associated with the consumption of face during marriage.

Party Secretary Zhao's parents, both low level officials in a township government in northern Zhejiang, had been saving for his marriage ever since he was born. As their only son, they were determined that he marry well, and that his wedding show them to be respectable, prosperous people who had good connections. Zhao agreed to accept his parents' ultimate ruling over any prospective partner, but the wedding was a sticking point. Zhao was dissatisfied with his job in the leather factory and wanted to establish his own business manufacturing clothes. He told his parents he would prefer to have a very simple wedding and use the 40 000 yuan they had saved to set up in business. His parents refused, arguing that no one would do business with a man who had married unceremoniously, and without providing the appropriate banquet for relatives and friends. When I left Hangzhou, Zhao was threatening his parents that he would not marry at all, while they remained adamant that their savings be spent on a splendid wedding:

> They think if I had a cheap wedding it would offend all our friends and relatives. They would lose face. People would get upset because they hadn't been invited. Others would gossip about the family, saying we musn't have enough money for a proper wedding feast, so they would look down on us. It's crazy, spending all that money on one event, when it could be used to invest in my future! (Tape, 19 February 1993)

In contrast, when Aihua's eldest sister's son became engaged at Spring Festival, it was a parent's unwillingness to spend that generated arguments. As the whole family gathered at the dinner table, eldest sister, who had been a contract worker in a Shenzhen garment factory for some years, said she was out of touch with the amounts people in their village were spending on engagement presents. Third younger sister advised her: 'At least ten to twelve cartons of cigarettes and 10 kilograms of candy, then a couple of thousand yuans' worth of gold jewellery and 3 000 in cash before the wedding.' The father, a Shanghai market vendor, objected. They were giving the bride slightly more than the usual sum of gold jewellery, so he wanted to give fewer cartons of cigarettes. The prospective groom was dissatisfied. His complaints against his father's meanness grew in volume and spite with each extra bowl of *gaoliang* he drank:

> It's embarrassing. You're so mean with your money! You've got plenty, but you won't even give as many cartons of cigarettes as the poorest peasants! What will people think of us? Her family is rich! If you are only going to give four cartons, you might as well not give any at all. I don't want to lose face because of your miserliness. (Fieldnotes, 24 January 1993)

The atmosphere heated up. Tempers exploded: bowls were thrown, doors slammed, tears wept. The father stamped out of the house, shouting to the shuttered windows along the village street that the son he had worked hard to raise, educate, and marry was nothing but a lazy, spoilt ingrate. Eldest sister dragged him inside, cautioning that if he made a scene outside the girl's family would be told the whole story by neighbours. Then they would all lose face. Grandmother, the oldest member of the family, berated everyone for arguing, but saved her strongest condemnation for the father. In her opinion, he should have been trying to gain face for the family and a brighter future for the youngsters by giving not only more jewellery, but also more cartons of cigarettes than had ever been presented at a wedding in their district: 'What better way is there to use the money you and eldest sister have brought back?'

As shown in this description of the consumption of dress, food and weddings, irrespective of their position in society, people selectively acquired goods in order to project particular identities. Workers also embraced consumption as a means by which they could manipulate their image and so move up in society, and get information about the identity and social standing of others.

Concurrently, however, consumption functioned as a gate keeping mechanism to restrict entry into the circles of money-power. Certain patterns of consumption signified wealth. Wealth gave face. Face facilitated social connections with the big people in society. Workers lamented that because of the importance placed on the possession, consumption and exchange of material goods, their poverty prevented them from accessing the *guanxi* networks through which flowed resources, capital, and opportunities for the further accumulation of wealth. Thus, whilst consumption appeared as a sphere of open competition in which the prizes were wealth and empowerment, it simultaneously forced workers to acknowledge their penury and disempowerment.

It would, however, be incorrect to conclude that consumption was important just because of the opportunities it afforded for status competition and social inclusion and exclusion. Consumption was also used communicatively as a means of expressing particular attitudes, and evaluating the values and morals of others. State employees and intellectuals condemned the scramble for wealth and its expression in competitive consumption as legitimate principles of identification and hierarchical ordering. It was disparaged as an expression of individualistic materialism, and a negation of the virtues which they themselves possessed. In contrast, many contract and temporary workers thought that conspicuous consumption demonstrated a high level of social competence. The corollary to this was that consumption was utilised a means of enforcing conformity to group norms. Among my Qiushi neighbours, those norms required demonstration of a puritanical socialist ethos. In the case of new recruits at Jinshagang, they demanded feminisation and acceptance of the market as arbiter of image.

As a form of sympathetic magic, consumption worked both as spur and as salve. Economically, psychologically, socially, and ideologically workers were driven to participate in wage labour so as to be able to actualise themselves in dress, food, and weddings. Consumption thereby reinforced capitalist employment relations and systems of social structuration which marked bosses off from their employees. But it was thought that if the magic of consumption proved effective, the things acquired might override the structuring effects of place and power, and release workers from the tedium of wage labour.

I conclude this chapter by recounting an instance of how these contradictory discourses informed a worker's behaviour. In the story of Aihua's house, the experience of being a female, immigrant, temporary worker is transformed into a concrete symbol of security, rootedness, responsibility, capability, and social worth. Aihua's house made sense of her working life, even as it necessitated that life.

AIHUA'S HOUSE: AN IDENTITY PROJECT

I learned about Aihua and her house from several vantage points. There was, first, her own chronicle of her past and the building of her house, as she stood – dripping mop in hand – leaning against a doorway in my apartment, sat in the bakery bagging bread, or bustled about cooking in her room. Second, the story is refracted through conversations with her family and friends, and other outsiders who themselves had built houses in their villages. Third, my neighbours, business people, and officials told me about the 'problems' of unproductive expenditure and runaway construction in the countryside. Finally, I learned about Aihua and her house by studying the policies and practices which were reworking China's proletariat.

Aihua's life is a tale of struggle. She missed out on being sent to school because of the Great Leap Forward and her parents' desperate effort to produce enough food to feed seven children and educate the two who were male. When Aihua turned twenty, she was married into the home of a poor farming family in a village half an hour's bike ride from her natal home on the banks of the Cao'e river, in northern Zhejiang. She and her mother-in-law despised one another. Tired of endless arguments, Aihua, her husband and their two babies moved into his uncle's house. To ease Aihua's solitude and domestic burden, her parents married her younger sister into another family in the same village. In 1980, Aihua and her husband began to farm independently. They grew rice, sugar cane, and cabbages. Three or four times each week Aihua would rise hours before daybreak to cycle more than twenty kilometres to the market in Shaoxing to sell their surplus produce. But as the children grew and prices began to rise, the family could no longer manage on the money earned from farming. Her husband went to Hangzhou to look for work. Two years later, Aihua's sister offered to look after the children so she could follow him.

For the several years she and her husband had spent working in Hangzhou, Aihua planned to build a house. It was Aihua's labour of blood and sweat:

> I did it all myself. Organised the money, materials, got permission. My husband didn't have much to do with it really. He didn't even save nearly as much as I did ... He spends too much on cigarettes! My sister helped a bit, buying things and getting in touch with the builders. (Fieldnotes, 3 February 1993)

Aihua measured her meagre wages from street sweeping, factory labour and cleaning in bags of concrete and kilograms of nails. Each spring festival when she returned to the village, she bought panes of glass, steel reinforcing, and timber, and stored these in her sister's attic. She spoke with pride about the amount of money this foresight had saved her: the prices of nails and glass had tripled in the four years since she purchased them. Her sister and brother-in-law agreed to let Aihua build her house on vacant land adjoining their home. She applied to the village government for formal permission to build on the land, and paid a confusing array of fees and bribes to ensure approval.

In October 1992, Aihua estimated she had managed to accumulate two-thirds of the 30 000 yuan she thought would be required to build the house. None of her savings was kept in a bank:

> We tried that in the beginning. But it was a real hassle. No sooner would we have saved a thousand yuan than someone would write saying they needed to borrow money, and then my husband would have to go and withdraw it from the bank. I couldn't because I can't read the forms. So it was too much trouble. We ended up just keeping it till someone asked for it. People like us never have any cash. We are always either borrowing or lending. (Fieldnotes, 8 February 1993)

Aihua recalled all the money she had lent out, and borrowed another 8000 yuan from her eldest brother and a friend. She disliked the sense of obligation this loan incurred:

> Some people haven't got enough, so they'll have to borrow again to repay us. That always happens. It's good lending, because it gives you face and you know they'll repay you. Borrowing puts a real strain on

your relationships, because you don't feel as though you can speak your mind in front of people you owe money to. You have to be polite and respectful. We'll pay it back as soon as we can. It will be tough, but it's worth it! (Fieldnotes, 8 February 1993)

The house was to be the same as all the other residences that had been put up in the village in the previous few years: a gabled, three storey, concrete-slab construction on a rectangular floor plan, with a single storey kitchen attached to the back by a skillion roof. The builders came from a neighbouring village. They took only a few weeks to finish the house to lock-up stage.

Aihua always explained her desire to build a house by reference to three factors. The first of these was the material insecurity she had experienced as a woman, a peasant, and a temporary migrant worker. The house was a means for gaining some degree of control over, and stability in, her insecure, mobile life. Aihua said that since marrying, she had only ever been an unwelcome or paying guest in other people's homes, and had always had to struggle to provide a bare livelihood for herself and her children. Neither she nor her husband was eligible for any forms of old-age welfare. If they had a house, at least they would have a home of their own to live in when they were too old to continue moving from one temporary job to another. Then, they would represent less of a burden to their children, and would be more likely to be provided with the remainder of their subsistence needs.

The second reason Aihua gave for building her house sprang from her belief that people's opinions of one another were based upon a comparative assessment of their wealth. Given her own manifest poverty, this was a source of considerable anxiety to her: 'That's what it is to be a person. Always comparing yourself with others. People don't care about what is on the inside. They only worry about whether the outside looks good' (Fieldnotes, 2 February 1993). Aihua feared that if she and her husband remained poor and houseless, her son would never be able to find a wife. The house would stand as a universally intelligible material symbol of the family's economic capacity and social value, and the parents' commitment to their son's future:

> The first thing people look at is the house. It shows that we can save money and have face. The more storeys, the more tiled decorations, the better. It's very competitive. No one will let their daughter marry into a family that lives in a dump. It would mean they were incompetent and lacking ambition.[11] (Fieldnotes, 20 February 1993)

Finally, Aihua explained the house as an individual rite of passage, and a mechanism for personal status elevation both in her village and in the city. In building it, she, an illiterate, female, temporary peasant worker, had passed a gruelling test of capability and responsibility. By working to accumulate enough money for the house, she had disproved her mother-in-law's gossip that she was a 'disabled, useless fool'. She demonstrated to the old men of the village that she could participate in complex lending circuits which required honesty, trust, and sophisticated accounting skills, whilst still observing gender conventions: 'We didn't include meals in the builders' contract. But when my sister and I saw that they were having to eat cold rice at lunchtime, we realised we would have to cook for them' (Fieldnotes, 3 February 1993). Building a house simultaneously proved her ability, self-reliance and worth to the people who exploited her in the city. She chuckled as she told me that the Hangzhou boss who abused her for being illiterate and not speaking standard Mandarin, and told her to 'go back to the village to look after your brats', lived in a tiny, publicly owned apartment which would have fitted neatly into one of the three storeys of her house. Aihua's house signified to haughty urbanites that outsiders were independent, respected property-owners in *their* places.

Why did she bother? She would not return to live there for many years to come. She admitted it was likely that by the time her son married, the house would not be considered good enough to attract any desirable mate. In fact, the house was so badly built it might have become uninhabitable within a decade. Window and door frames did not fit tightly, drains did not empty, salt crystals encrusted the concrete walls, and ceilings were patched with damp and cracked plaster. Besides, it was a commonplace in the village that new brides never wanted to live with their mothers-in-law. Aihua said that just as she and her husband had come to Hangzhou, so too would her son and daughter-in-law probably be forced to work in a city.

Clearly, the house was not the point at issue. Instead, it was Aihua, her self and its social identity. Aihua's house was an attempt to compensate for her miserable experiences of hard work, prejudice, and exploitation by reconstructing her past as a martyrdom to her children's material and social well-being, and constructing a sanctuary for her own imagined future. At the same time, Aihua reinvented her identity, drawing upon traditional themes of filiality, landed security and community, as well as new ideas of agency, independent production, and resistance. She fulfilled her obligations towards the future generations. She became a propertied member of a community which was functionally integrated by exchange and lending networks. In her house she appropriated, utilised, and triumphantly objectified symbols of power, wealth and ownership, network and place: those very factors which she saw as having effected her subjugation to business people in Hangzhou. Wage work in the city became the means for self-actualisation in family and village.

The story of Aihua's house answers in summary form questions about the interconnections between work, identity and disposition that were raised at the beginning of this chapter. Participation in capitalist production does inform workers' collective identities, and their determination of the identities of others in the neighbourhoods in which they live. Collective identities are constructed and represented principally by reference to structured relations of place, power and wealth, and consumption. And place, power and wealth, and consumption are considered to be fundamental to the creation of relations of ownership, production, extraction, and accumulation.

That generalisation should not gloss significant points of convergence and divergence. I have detected two specific areas where workers' cognitions and representations of collective identity converge. Workers of all kinds agree that the contemporary synthesis of money-power is a major new source of collective identity. They express a similar understanding of the ways in which networks of money-power are forming, monopolising capital and opportunities, and establishing a common stock of cultural practices. So, too, do they share a negative evaluation of that process of distinction and enrichment, and a resentment about their concurrent exclusion and exploitation. Paradoxically, they also believe in the efficacy of consumption as a means by which people can compete to advance identity claims. Irrespective of their occupational status and place of origin, workers attempt to improve their own and their families' public persona through the acquisition and display of goods.

On the other hand, the story of Aihua's house demonstrates quite clearly that workers' participation in capitalist production does not forge a collective worker-identity. Nor does it unify workers' interpretations and representations of others' identities, or their ideas about which factors order their social system. Workers' identities continue to be differentiated by the structuring effects of place, and the interactive, institutional and ethical aspects of place-based cultures. Their interpretations of how wealth is acquired and their assessments of the moral character of those who are wealthy also diverge markedly. It is hardly surprising that workers' common participation in capitalist has not obliterated differences of identity and disposition for, as this book has shown, the whole system of production in which they participate, the processes by which wealth is accumulated and expressed, and the social organisation of neighbourhoods in China actually are established on, and are sustaining, localism and place of origin identifications, the exercise of power by local bureaucrats, and the competitive activities of exclusive social networks.

9 Conclusion

In the 1990s, China's socialist market economy shows many of the classic hallmarks of capitalism. There is private ownership of some of the means of production and of firms. There are markets for the factors of production, as well as for commodities. The majority of the labour force are propertyless, and rely for a livelihood on wages they earn from producing goods and services which are sold by their employers to realise profit. There is also the promotion by the party-state and entrepreneurs of ideologies, ethics, and values which celebrate private ownership, production for market exchange and capital accumulation.

However, it is evident that there are significant differences between the direction of causality, and the content and consciousness of class relations associated with the rise of capitalism in western Europe, and those which characterise China's emergent capitalism. Rather than the proletariat forming as a consequence of the reorganisation of private production by capitalist employers, in China the party-state has designed policies, laws and institutions specifically with a view to reworking members of the proletariat as individual producers of national and private wealth. Rather than the state evolving as an administrator of processes of industrialisation, or the site of social struggles engendered by the privatisation of property and division of labour, in China local governments and particular officials have joined together with capital to engineer, and benefit from, capitalist relations of production in firms which have a mixture of public and private ownership.

Another departure from the western European experience is that in China territorial bonds and particularistic relations have not been effaced by the advent of a capitalist market economy. On the contrary, local officials and social networks within place-based communities have regulated the allocation of property, resources, funds and opportunities in this economy. These allocations have been normalised and enforced by the deployment of negative stereotypes, patterns of sociability within neighbourhoods, the operation of local institutions, value systems and morals which consolidate and demarcate local communities and networks, and legitimate their exploitation of outsiders and those without *guanxi*. Class relations in China are being built on the basis of pre-existing state, economic, and social structures, and old cultural practices. They bear the imprint of those structures and practices.

Neither has China's proletariat been homogenised and wakened to its common situation by proximity, collaboration in complex labour processes, and the experience and recognition of exploitation. How could it have been, given that labour markets, production processes, and rates of surplus appropriation actually have been keyed to divisions within the work force established by place, power and *guanxi*? Moreover, in the absence of independent, all-inclusive labour unions, institutions mediating relations between workers and employers and facilitating collective action by the contingent work force tend to replicate affiliations and reinforce competitions between groups distinguished by place, power and *guanxi*. The effects of these factors in inhibiting wide-scale labour militancy are compounded by another distinctive feature of China's capitalism: the existence of a massive labour surplus. Contract and temporary workers are sensitive to the ease with which they can be dismissed by employers, and the vast numbers of unemployed people who would willingly to replace them.

The development of capitalism in China is not a unidirectional process in which Chinese workers are the passive objects of change. I have argued in this book that the articulation of capitalist production with place, power and *guanxi* is mutually transformative. Just as capitalism is developing under the aegis of the local state and powerful, place-based networks, so too are all the participants in capitalist production changing the identities, relations, values and practices associated with place, power and *guanxi*. Recall, for example, the various ways in which local workers at Qiushi and Jinshagang attempted to protect their rights to privileged recruitment, promotion and payment as members of place-based communities, and their outrage over the intrusion into urban labour markets and neighbourhoods of a (dis)placed, dangerous population of immigrant workers. Recall, in addition, how recruitment and pay systems within enterprises were changing partly as a consequence of agitation by immigrant employees who represented their (dis)placement as evidence of their independence and sense of responsibility. Then, too, the legitimacy of officials' power was being challenged by all types of workers, who charged that economic reforms had allowed officials and business people to establish *guanxi* networks, collude to privatise public property and firms, and jointly exploit workers' labour for their own benefit. The superior social and moral status once ascribed by position within bureaucratic and intellectual hierarchies was being contested by contract and temporary workers' support for market-determined notions of merit and norms of behaviour, and their embrace of consumption as a form of status competition.

In the course of elucidating these interconnections between place, power and particularism in the creation of capitalist relations of production and the reworking of China's proletariat, I have addressed many of the questions raised in the introductory chapter of this book. Consider the issues of naming and identity. In light of the material presented here, it is clear that contract and temporary workers in China do occupy the positions and experience the working conditions of a classic proletariat. The reasons why they do not identify as a proletariat or as members of the working class are also clear. I have shown that the names workers currently use have real explanatory power. Their categorisation of themselves as small people, outsiders and *da gong* highlights their disempowerment, dispossession and exploitation by place-based networks of officials and business people. Similarly, their description of their employers as big people, city people, locals and clans precisely locates the sources of power and ownership in society, and the agents of their exploitation. Henceforth, any explanation for Chinese workers' rejection of the names proletariat or working class and capitalist class must not only take etymology and the propagation of dominant discourses by political elites into account, but also the discrepancies between workers' perceptions of the roles and relationships which distinguish China's capitalism, and classic models of capitalist class relations.

The self-expressed identities and names used by workers also illuminate a dialectical relationship between the discursive representation of non-class identities and patterns of association, and processes of class structuration. Stereotypes informed by long-standing economic and social competition between bounded communities, the policies of the socialist party-state, contemporary market ideologies and media images of urban modernity and rural primitivism all contribute to the differential positioning and treatment of workers. As the labelling of outsiders as a social problem illustrates, managers' use of a divide-and-rule strategy to govern the shop floor is authorised by state policies, administrative regulations and institutions. It is encouraged by antagonisms between populations which are distinguished by markedly different standards of living and opportunity structures. The notion that *guanxi* is a reflection of social competence similarly helps perpetuate and justify structural inequalities.

A direct consequence of these mutually productive interactions between representation and structuration is that the labels and identities workers bring into, and are given, in the work place are frequently contested in the course of struggles between managers and workers, as well as among various groups of workers. At first glance, it might seem that these struggles further fragment the work force. But workers' affirmation that a name or identity such as production worker, Anhui peasant, or small person is a positive characteristic is a necessary component in a diffuse politic of resistance against hegemonic discourses which encourage lateral competition and workers' emulation of their exploiters. I have described incidents which demonstrate that struggles over names encapsulate complaints about managers' control of workers' bodies, time, and energy, production spaces and processes, and criteria for wage distribution. They dispute issues of equity and exploitation. And they raise the possibility of workers creating more inclusive worker-identities which would permit cooperative action.

So, too, do conflicts in the work place indicate the development of workers' consciousnesses of specific types of social interaction which underpin a general condition which constitutes a class relationship. My use of the clumsy plural form, consciousness*es,* is intentional. It affirms the existence of multiple forms of class consciousness. This book has illuminated several reasons why workers' understandings of the operations of capitalism and the emergence of classes vary. For one thing, while workers are aware that the production system in which they are engaged is based upon unequal ownership and the employment and exploitation of their labour, they know that relations of ownership, employment and exploitation are being mediated by the social connections and activities associated with place, power and *guanxi*. Chinese workers do not share identical experiences of capitalist production. Workers do not share identical relations with their bosses or with other members of their own class. As I have shown, such principles as the necessity to demonstrate social and emotional ties by labouring for others, reciprocity in *guanxi* relations and the pursuit of face for kinship corporations, have been made integral to the recruitment and management of work forces, facilitated business networking and encouraged the consumption of commodities as class signifiers. Nor have workers' consciousnesses of class relations rendered old ethical standards anachronistic. Maoist productivism, socialist collectivism, ideas about regional honour and peasant pride in self-sufficiency continue to provide the moral repertoires by which various groups of workers work, live, think and evaluate 'that-which-does-not-make-sense' in the new capitalist mode of production and in the conduct of class relations.

The proposition that Chinese workers' different class consciousnesses are grounded in real experiences of production and relations structured by capitalism has important implications both for the applicability of Marxist theory, and for future analyses of the political capacity of China's contingent work force. On the one hand, this study lends support to a key tenet of Marxism (Marx, 1954, p. 173; Callinicos, 1985; McCarthy, 1978). Chinese workers' consciousnesses are indeed influenced by their participation in capitalist production. On the other hand, the material presented in this book problematises the Marxist prediction that workers' achievement of class consciousness will be a universalising process. Granted, as

Craig Calhoun (1982, p. 221) points out, this theorisation of workers' awakening to, and organisation as, a unified class incorporates a very long time line. But Marxist scholars tend to assume that a unitary class consciousness will be catalysed by a particular set of circumstances which, in China, either has already taken place, or might never eventuate. The first of these involves workers' recognition of their objective circumstances. Many contract and temporary workers do recognise the objective circumstances of their collective exploitation, and older workers, at least, have been educated in class categorisation and class activism by a revolutionary socialist party. Thus far, the fulfilment of those conditions has resulted neither in homogenisation of workers' understandings, nor in a political coalition.

A second component of the Marxist theorisation of workers' class consciousness posits that this consciousness will be achieved in the course of waging collective struggles against exploitation. That begs the question of whether protests by segments of China's fragmented contingent work force might eventually weld the proletariat into a cohesive, politically effective class. I have pointed out that cohesion is one of the aims of sporadic protests by workers. In attempting to force employers to establish identical conditions of employment for all employees, contract and temporary workers are trying to overturn one of the sources of their division. If they succeed, it will be at the cost of rendering entire work forces vulnerable to intensified productivity pressures and reduced payment. Thus, it is not surprising that activism by the contingent work force has met with opposition not only from employers, but also from urban tenured workers and local employees of TVEs who stand to lose from such a change. In the short term, then, old collectivities centred upon the state, community and network will continue to provide sources of identity, material security and political strength not only to those who are directly benefiting from the development of capitalism, but also to those whose ways of life are immediately threatened by that development.

In conclusion to her study on Chinese labour activism, Elizabeth Perry predicts that the fragmentation of the working class's 'political orientations and activities' is likely to persist (1993, p. 258). My conclusion differs from Perry's. I have argued that even though the non-class identities, circumscribed organisational forms, and ad hoc protests which characterise China's proletariat do not conform with normative Marxist concepts of what the proletariat is, and how it thinks and acts, they are, in Adam Przeworski's (1977, p. 367) words, 'immanent to the practices that (may) result in class formation'. Indeed, I have put forward the idea that, in becoming the focus of workers' 'political orientations and activities', fragmentation actually sharpens workers' class consciousnesses. Three related trends might, in the long term, combine to encourage cooperative political action by China's proletariat. Two of these have already been examined in detail, and need only be touched upon.

There is, first, the effects upon workers' consciousnesses of experiential learning in the capitalist work place. As illustrated throughout this book, the search by employers for ways of increasing productivity and profitability has sometimes led to a reduction of the status and pecuniary entitlements of employees who are urban, members of local communities, or who have useful *guanxi*, and a convergence in production workers' functions and work loads. Over time, the pursuit of profit might prompt such a shift in the identities and affiliations of these workers that they begin to communicate and sympathise with their rural, non-local and unfamiliar colleagues.

Second, and as a corollary of the first trend, there is the potentially transformative effect of workers' own efforts to overturn the sources and expressions of their division, disempowerment, and exploitation. These entail a wide range of activities, from pressures to engage in the patterns of consumption which are described in the previous chapter, to complaints about the circumscribed character of the Chinese nation and neighbourhood gossip about abuses of power, and, at their most extreme, the staging of go-slows and strikes to eliminate discriminatory wage payments. All these diffuse activities indirectly and directly alter the ways workers understand their situation as workers and their relations with employers and officials. In affecting the formation of alliances between segments of the contingent work force and relations between labour and capital, they also become integral to the construction of a class identity and class praxis.

The third, and possibly the most crucial factor which might unite and strengthen China's proletariat has been beyond the purview of this book. The paternalistic relationship China's party-state carefully constructed with the dependent state enterprise work force has broken down. Reforms implemented in state-owned enterprises have adversely affected members of what the party-state has always referred to as China's 'real' working class. In the few months immediately following the September 1997 decision of the CCP's 15th Congress not to further subsidise loss-making state enterprises and to insist that enterprises shed surplus employees, several million state workers did not receive the wages, welfare benefits and pensions due to them, and millions more were made redundant (*FEER*, 2 October 1997; *CND*, 19 January 1998, 23 January 1998, 29 January 1998). The once celebrated, privileged, tenured population of workers is becoming vulnerable to the same material insecurities and productivity pressures that have long been suffered by the contingent work force. Former state employees are having to compete for jobs in local labour markets. They are being employed in collective, joint venture, and privately-owned firms alongside the sort of workers described in this book. There, they too suffer from the absence of formal labour organisations, and are subjected to strict directives, productivity demands, and divide-and-rule strategies for controlling the labour process and extracting surplus. As a consequence, they might become as conscious of the class relations which characterise these enterprises as the old storeman at Sanxian who had once worked in a state-owned printery:

The system was very different in the state enterprise. It had many more activities, the Union was always arranging something or other. And we workers regularly went to meetings. Here, there is just one manager. She is in control of everything. And we workers have to do whatever she tells us. There aren't any activities or even organisations for us temporaries. We temporaries are just here to earn money for them. There is no question of us being involved in decision making. It's not a democratic unit, it's a profit making business! (Fieldnotes, 10 January 1993)

However, unlike other members of the contingent work force, workers cast off from state enterprises may possess the practical knowledge and organisational capacity necessary to give public voice to their grievances against the party-state and employers, and to coordinate class action. State workers have a strong sense of community, have been highly politicised, and share a tradition of large scale protest. They have, in the 1990s, staged massive strikes, besieged government offices, petitioned the National People's Congress, published newspapers and issued radio broadcasts criticising the party-state's abrogation of its responsibilities toward the working class and soliciting broad popular support for the labour movement (Walder, 1991; *Agence France Presse*, 14 March 1996; *FEER*, 26 June, 1997). In addition to their high rate of membership in an increasingly restive ACFTU, state employees also appear to have been disproportionately active in the formation and operation of autonomous trade unions, workers' mutual help societies, and small political associations (Hong Kong Trade Union Education Centre, 1990; Walder, 1991; China Labour Bulletin, no. 39, 1997).

If disaffected workers who have been shed from the state sector join together with the contract and temporary employees of non-state enterprises, China's proletariat may become extremely militant. But will it? The challenge for future researchers is to assess the extent to which these former state employees are prepared to share their political expertise, and extend membership of their formal and informal representative organisations to people against whom they are being pitted in competition, and whom they have reviled as peasants, outsiders, and 'mere' contract and temporary employees. The political future of China's reworked proletariat hinges on these possibilities.

Notes

1   Introduction

1. Craig Calhoun (1982, p.18) gives three conditions under which the vocabulary of class can legitimately be introduced: that class can be used qualitatively or quantitatively as a variable, it is descriptive of the people or sets of relations being analysed, or it is an ideal type.
2. I conceive of ownership as an ensemble of economic rights to control productive resources, capital assets, and corporate forms, and dispose of products and income. See Epstein (1989, pp. 212–15); McDermott (1991, pp. 77–84); Pryor (1973, pp. 2–8).
3. The entry under *wuchan jieji* in Shanghai Shehui Kexueyuan Shehuixue Yanjiusuo, *Shehuixue jianming cidian* (1984, p. 58) says: 'See *gongren jieji* (working class)'.
4. See, for examples, the films *Furong zhen* (Hibiscus Town), and *The Blue Kite*.
5. See, for example, 'Chinese Communist Party Central Committee Document no. 2 (1992): Important Talks by Deng Xiaoping', in *FBIS*, 13 March, 1992.
6. One such example cited by Perry concerned the May 30th movement in 1925, when workers commemorating a factory employee killed by a Japanese foremen were fired upon by police. BAT's unskilled workers were 'not only the first to declare a strike, they were also especially active in the BAT propaganda teams that travelled the city and surrounding countryside to promote public understanding of the strike and solicit monetary contributions for its continuation' (1993, pp. 148–9); see also Chesneaux (1968, pp. 262–89).
7. Workers' protests commonly took the form of laxity on the shop floor, pilfering of state property, ad hoc acts of vandalism and violence, and the display of posters condemning officials and managers, as well as large strikes and street demonstrations. These are illustrated in Howe (1973a); Milton and Milton (1976); Perry (1995); Rofel (1992).

2   Reforming the Proletariat

1. My usage of the term 'central party-state' is intended to distinguish the central Communist Party and government bodies which stand at the apex of policy-making and administration in China and tend not to intervene in the economy from the lower levels and officials of the state which are directly involved in local economies. Provincial governments are increasingly viewed as being, to a greater or lesser degree, autonomous of the central state. For my purpose, however, I categorise provincial governments as part of the 'central party-state' (Shirk, 1990; Chang, 1995). Governments and departments below provincial level, such as municipal, district, county and village governments, are referred to as local government.

2. Rent may be paid in money, negotiable securities, consumer goods, banquets or services. It may be paid in return not only for credit access, permits or licences but also for a favourable judicial outcome (McFarlane, 1990). The extraction of rent by officials has been denounced by government and Chinese Communist Party (CCP) spokespersons as an obstacle to the realisation of the law of value, and contrary to principles of equal exchange and equal competition (*BR*, 16 August 1993).

3. One *Renmin ribao* article dated 19 December 1992 defines nine different ownership categories (*FBIS*, 12 January 1993). For examples of joint ventures between domestic firms, see *HZRB*, 3 June 1992.

4. There is a vast literature on the development and operation of share-holding cooperatives in China. For examples, see *FBIS*, 7 March 1990, 7 June 1991, 1 September 1991, 5 November 1991; Forster (1990–91, pp. 59–60); Tung (1994); Vermeer (1995–6).

5. For clarification of the definition of collective enterprises, see 'Regulations on Collectively Owned City and Town Enterprises', *FBIS*, 27 September 1991; see also *FBIS*, 27 April 1990.

6. These figures vary from those given in *ZJTJNJ*, 1992, p. 18, which indicate that in 1991 state enterprises and collective enterprises produced 29.5% and 60.9% of total industrial output value, respectively. I follow Chi and Rong, first, because as researchers at the Zhejiang Government Centre for Research on Economic Statistics and Social Development, they have access to a wide range of unpublished data sources, and second, because there are discrepancies between the statistics given for the same year in *ZJTJNJ* and *Hangzhou Nianjian*, hereafter *HZNJ*.

7. For studies on attitudes towards private business, see Bruun (1989; 1990, pp. 29–47); Cheng Shu (1992); *FBIS*, 16 February 1990; Young (1991). Workers' attitudes towards employment in different types of enterprises are examined in Leung (1988, pp. 138–40); Lin and Wen (1988, pp. 793–832).

8. For analyses of the links between demographic pressures in the countryside, decollectivisation, and rural–urban migration see Banister and Taylor (1989); Christiansen (1990).

9. The contract system was first promoted on an experimental basis in 1982. See White (1989, pp. 163–4); Zhu Ying (1995, pp. 42–4).

10. Leung (1988, p. 147), cites the conditions under which employees can be dismissed or laid off by joint and foreign ventures in the Guangdong Special Economic Zones. For regulations pertaining to dismissal in state enterprises, see *ZGLDB*, 20 January 1993.

11. For excellent summaries of the formal distinctions made between permanent, contract system, contract, and temporary workers, see Korzec (1992, pp. 28–44); Walder (1986, pp. 40–56).

12. Because contract system workers are partly defined by state planning, this term is not used in the non-state sector.

13. Unfortunately, Alan Gelb (1990) and Meng Xin (1990) do not state whether the 'permanent' workers allocated by local governments to the rural enterprises they surveyed sign employment contracts.

14. Gerard Greenfield, Asia Monitor Resource Centre, personal communication.

15. Although Jean Wilson acknowledges that ACFTU cells operate only in some urban work units and that Union membership does not extend to rural

enterprise employees, she nevertheless glosses over the limited scope of the ACFTU by stating 'union membership is open to all Chinese wage-earners' (1986, pp. 228–9).

3 Placing the Proletariat

1. The analysis of patterns of localism which runs throughout this chapter is influenced by my reading of Agnew (1987); Beynon and Hudson (1993); Ching and Creed (1997); Cox and Mair (1991); Lefebvre (1991); Relph (1976); Paasi (1991); Pred (1985).
2. I am very grateful to Zhang Jian for providing me with up-to-date statistics and information about Xihu, and for dispelling many of the ambiguities which attend the statistical material available in print.
3. The low prices paid for housing by University staff reflects the previous administrative allocation of land use-rights from Yuquan village to the University, and subsidisation of the cost of employee housing by the University.
4. For more information on relationships within state work units, see Lu (1989); Ruan (1993).
5. High rents are supported by the absence of a market in land, the still embryonic state of the real estate market, and a critical shortage of rental accommodation relative to demand.
6. *Waidi ren* refers to any people not born and raised in the locality. Hence the term does not exclusively refer to immigrant workers, but also, for instance, to non-local bureaucrats and self-employed people. Helen Siu (1990) provides a comparative study of the emergence of a discourse about immigrants as 'outsiders' in the Pearl River delta.
7. At the same time the Commission funded similar companies through Universities in Beijing and Shanghai.

4 Recruitment: Segmenting Class

1. Statements from the Labour Ministry suggest that unemployed rural residents are now being taken into account in labour market planning. See *SWB*, 25 January 1994, 8 April 1994.
2. The significance of *hukou* as a social divider is demonstrated by strong patterns of marriage endogamy within urban and rural populations. See, for example, Croll (1984); Potter and Potter (1990, pp. 305–6). A report in *ZJRB* (24 October 1992) found the marriage of a college-educated woman from Hangzhou to a rural male with lower middle school education to be sufficiently unusual to warrant a feature article titled 'Very Special You!' The article noted that the man did possess some redeeming features. He was the manager of a profitable suburban factory, owned a large three storey house, and enjoyed a much higher income than the average urban resident.
3. On the purchase of urban *hukou*, see also *GRRB*, 13 September 1992.
4. The popular image of migrant workers as irrational is strongly contested in journals which attempt more in-depth analyses of sociological issues. See, for example, *SHKXB*, 18 February 1993.

5. According to Item 12 of the national 'Regulations on Labour Management in Rural and Township Enterprises' published by the Agriculture Department on 10 December 1992, recruitment of workers should be carried out on the principle of equal and open competition.

6. In 1992, Hangzhou enterprises had to pay approximately 50 yuan to the Labour Bureau, technical schools, and universities for each staff or worker provided.

7. The utilisation of social resources in job hunting and recruitment is by no means unique to China. A cross-national study by de Graf and Flap (1988) found that in the Netherlands one-third of all males surveyed made use of personal connections to find work, while three-fifths of male job hunters in the USA drew upon their connections. Contacts are also vitally important to job seekers' success in the urban labour markets of India (Holmstrom, 1984).

5 Productive Architecture

1. For examples, see 'Suan, tian, ku, la (1992); Forster (1990/1991); *GRRB*, 9 February 1993; *HZRB*, 12 September 1992; Leung (1988, pp. 116–95); Lin (1991); *SCMP*, 18 March 1993; Smith (1993, pp. 93–5); *ZGLDB*, 15 August 1992.

2. This perception is apparently not exclusive to China: see Ortner (1991, pp. 174–5); Willis (1979, pp. 185–200).

6 Labour Processes

1. For a comparison with communication between management and workers in state enterprises, see Graf *et al.* (1991, pp. 52–3).

2. See also discussions of production planning in *BKWZ*, 3 November 1992; *GRRB*, 26 February 1993; *GMRB*, 11 May 1992.

3. For explanations of these systems, see Sayer and Walker (1992, pp. 170–87); Thompson (1989, pp. 222–4).

4. See comparable reports of workers' exhaustion in Lin (1991); *ZGLDB*, 5 November 1992; 6 February 1993.

5. For a comparative perspective on the similar categorisation of tasks as skilled and unskilled in an American bakery, see Ferguson (1991, pp. 113, 115).

6. In actual fact, because of the high degree of direct supervision in the factory, this model varies quite markedly from the self-regulatory systems of quality control which characterise Japanese 'just-in-time' production methods. See Sayer and Walker (1992, pp. 163–87).

7 A Cipher of Class: The Wage-Labour Bargain

1. It is, thus, consistent with Melvin Lerner's observation that 'As societies and institutions change, so do societally structured bases of entitlement judgement' (1991, pp. 269–70).

2. As mentioned above, the newly introduced national labour law now specifies that the standard working week is 40 hours, with a limit of 36 hours per

month overtime. Minimum wage levels are also being introduced 'in the light of local conditions'.

3. See Gelb (1990, p. 285); Knight and Song (1993, pp. 186, 211); Nolan (1993, p. 304).

4. This relationship is, of course, analysed in detail by Marx (1954, vol. 1, pp. 516–19).

5. Cf. Burawoy (1988); Roy (1972).

6. For a detailed examination of the importance of the ways in which *biaoxian* influenced systems of rewards and punishments in state enterprises during the Maoist era, see Walder (1986, pp. 132–61).

7. The manager declined to tell me exactly how much he had received, saying it was 'more than 20 000 yuan'. Su commented that in fact the monetary income of the manager gives no indication of how much he earns, because almost everything he does and has is paid for by the company. See also Wu, Wang and Xu (1990, pp. 331–2).

8. In 1992–93, municipal regulations stated that temporary employees were eligible for the same period (up to but not exceeding 3 months) of paid sick leave as contract workers, and during this period they should receive 60 per cent of their basic wage. See Item 12, Hangzhou shi renmin zhengfu, *Hangzhou shi wailai linshigong guanli zanxing guiding di 3* (1990). For a comparison of welfare and insurance benefits between tenured and temporary employees in state and collective enterprises in the 1980s, see Walder (1986, pp. 44–5).

9. Kazuhiko Ueno (1994) and Minchuan Yang (1994) have also observed trends for collective rural enterprises to detach themselves from their community obligations and try to establish a contractual relationship between the enterprise and local residents.

8 Neighbourhood Identities, Neighbourhood Dispositions

1. The term 'organised interdependence' is borrowed from Andrew Walder's (1986, pp. 14–21) description of the ways in which workers in China's state industries during the Maoist period became dependent upon their employers for the satisfaction of almost all their needs.

2. Although I conducted this interview in Mandarin, I had to ask a friend whose parents came from villages on opposite sides of Hangzhou for assistance in transcribing sections of the tape. When this assistant said they could not understand some of the old man's replies, I sought the help of another friend from Shaoxing. But even they said they had difficulty understanding some of his earthy vernacular.

3. The convergence of power and money is also central to the theoretical analyses of Gu (1990) and Yu (1990).

4. For an illuminating discussion of ideas about the debilitating consequences of women's exercise of power, see Edwards (1993, pp. 34–59).

5. My use of the term ideology with respect to the exercise of power follows Anthony Giddens' suggestion that ideology is one of the 'systems of signification (which) enter into the existence of sectional forms of domination' (1991, p. 22).

6. These performances of power are beautifully satirised by Liu Binyan (1983a, pp. 1–70).

7. Some studies by western scholars echo these ideas, see Gold (1989, 1990); Young (1991). Interpretations of private business people's conspicuous consumption as status compensation bear many points of resemblance to Ho Ping-ti's classic exposition on the behaviour of eighteenth-century salt merchants. See Ho (1954).

8. For the purposes of this analysis, I interpret face as prestige. However, any comprehensive definition of face would incorporate other meanings. For analyses and illustrations of the concept of face, see *GMRB* 11 July 1992; Lu (1960); Yang (1986, pp. 85–6).

9. In 1992, *renminbi* was not yet convertible in China, and many foreign-invested hotels still required payment either in Foreign Exchange Certificates, or foreign currency.

10 Rural weddings cost considerably less. In 1992–93, marriages in villages near Shangyu generally cost between 6 000 and 15 000 yuan. For comparative accounts of the escalation of wedding costs, see Potter and Potter (1990, pp. 208–10, 214–15); Harrell (1992, pp. 335–6).

11. Sulamith and Jack Potter (1990, p. 219) noted the same motivations for house building among villagers in Zengbu. Sik (1988) and Colloredo-Mansfeld (1994) discuss similarly competitive trends in the building of ever higher, more ornate houses in Hungary and Ecuador.

Bibliography

BOOKS AND ARTICLES

Abercrombie, Nicholas, Stephen Hill and Bryan S. Turner. (1984) *Dictionary of Sociology*. Harmondsworth: Penguin.

Abrams, Dominic and Michael A. Hogg. (1990) *Social Identity Theory: Constructive and Critical Advances*. New York: Harvester.

Agnew, John A. (1987) *Place and Politics: The Geographical Mediation of State and Society*. Boston: Allen & Unwin.

Ajzen, Icek. (1982) 'Equity in Attitude Formation and Change', in *Equity and Justice in Social Behavior*, ed. Jerald Greenberg and Ronald L. Cohen, pp. 161–86. New York: Plenum Press.

All China Federation of Trade Unions. (1989) 'Survey of workers and staff', *Chinese Economic Studies* 22.4: pp. 44–54.

Anagnost, Ann. (1994) 'Who Is Speaking Here? Discursive Boundaries and Representation in Post-Mao China', in *Boundaries in China*, ed. John Hay, pp. 257–79. London: Reaktion Books.

Andors, Phyllis. (1989) 'Women and Work in Shenzhen', *Bulletin of Concerned Asian Scholars* 21.1: pp. 22–41.

Aronowitz, Stanley. (1992) *The Politics of Identity: Class, Culture, Social Movements*. New York: Routledge.

Bagguley, Paul. (1990) *Restructuring: Place, Class and Gender*. London: Sage.

Bakhtin, M. M. (1986) *Speech Genres and Other Late Essays*. Austin: University of Texas.

Balibar, Etienne and Immanuel Wallerstein. (1991) *Race, Nation, Class: Ambiguous Identities*. London: Verso.

Banister, Judith and Jeffrey R. Taylor. (1989) 'China: Surplus Labour and Migration', *Asia-Pacific Population Journal* 4.4: pp. 3–20.

Barmè, Geremie. (1995) 'To Screw Foreigners is Patriotic: China's Avante-Garde Nationalists', *The China Journal* 34: pp. 209–38.

Barnett, A. Doak. (1971) 'Group Indoctrination', in *Education and Communism in China: An Anthology of Commentary and Documents*, ed. Stewart E. Fraser, pp. 281–98. London: Pall Mall Press.

Baudrillard, Jean. (1981) *For a Critique of the Political Economy of the Sign*. St Louis: Telos Press.

Beattie, Hilary J. (1979) *Land and Lineage in China: A study of T'ung-Ch'eng county, Anhwei, in the Ming and Ch'ing Dynasties*. Cambridge: Cambridge University Press.

Becker, Uwe. (1989) 'Class Theory and the Social Sciences: E. O. Wright on classes', *Politics and Society* 7.1: pp. 67–88.

Benson, Douglas and John Hughes. (1983) *The Perspective of Ethnomethodology*. London: Longman.

Berdoulay, Vincent. (1989) 'Place, Meaning and Discourse in French Language Geography', in *The Power of Place: Bringing Together Geographical and Sociological Imaginations*, ed. John A. Agnew and James S. Duncan, pp. 124–39. Boston: Unwin Hyman.

Berger, Roger A. (1993) 'From Text to (Field)work and Back Again: Theorizing a Post (Modern)-Ethnography', *Anthropological Quarterly* 66.4: pp. 174–86.

Beynon, Huw and Ray Hudson. (1993) 'Place and Space in Contemporary Europe: Some Lessons and Reflections', *Antipode* 25.3: pp. 177–90.

Bian, Yanjie. (1994) '*Guanxi* and the Allocation of Jobs in Urban China', *China Quarterly* 140: pp. 971–99.

Bierhoff, Hans-Werner. (1989) *Person, Perception and Attribution*. Berlin: Springer-Verlag.

Billeter, Jean-François. (1985) 'The System of "Class Status"', in *The Scope of State Power in China*, ed. Stuart Schram, pp. 127–69. London: School of Oriental and African Studies.

Blecher, Marc. (1983) 'Peasant Labour for Urban Industry: Temporary Contract Labour, Urban-Rural Balance and Class Relations in Shulu County', *World Development* 11.8: pp. 731–45.

——. (1985) 'Balance and Cleavage in Urban-Rural Relations', in *Chinese Rural Development*, ed. William Parish, pp. 219–45. New York: M. E. Sharpe.

Bodemann, Y. Michal and Wilfried Spohn. (1986) 'The Organicity of Classes and the Naked Proletarian: Towards a New Formulation of the Class Conception', *Insurgent Sociologist* 8.3: pp. 10–19.

Boden, Deidre and Dan H. Zimmerman. (1991) *Talk and Social Structures: Studies in Ethnomethodology and Conversation Analysis*. Cambridge: Polity.

Bondi, Liz. (1993) 'Locating Identity Politics', in *Place and the Politics of Identity*, ed. Michael Keith and Steve Pile, pp. 84–101. London: Routledge.

Bourdieu, Pierre. (1984) *Distinction: A Social Critique of the Judgement of Taste*, translated by Richard Nice. London: Routledge & Kegan Paul.

——. (1987) 'What Makes a Social Class? On the Theoretical and Practical Existence of Groups', *Berkeley Journal of Sociology* 32: pp. 1–17.

——. (1990) *In Other Words: Essays Towards a Reflexive Sociology*. Stanford: Stanford University Press.

——. (1991) *Language and Symbolic Power*. Cambridge: Polity Press.

Bruun, Ole. (1989) 'Business and Bureaucracy in a Chengdu Street: the Ethnography of Individual Business Households in Contemporary China', PhD dissertation, University of Copenhagen.

——. (1990) 'Urban Individual Households and Cultural Change in China: When "Losers" Become "Winners"', *Copenhagen Papers* 5: pp. 29–447.

Buchanan, Allen and Deborah Mathieu. (1986) 'Philosophy and Justice', in *Justice: Views From the Social Sciences*, ed. Ronald L. Cohen, pp. 11–45. New York: Plenum Press.

Burawoy, Michael. (1979) *Manufacturing Consent: Changes in the Labor Process under Monopoly Capitalism*. Chicago: Chicago University Press.

——. (1982) 'Introduction: the resurgence of Marxism in American sociology', in *Marxist Inquiries: Studies of Labor, Class and States*, ed. Michael Burawoy and Theda Skocpol, pp. 1–30. Chicago: University of Chicago.

——. (1984) 'Karl Marx and the satanic mills: factory regimes under early capitalism in England, the U.S.A. and Russia', *American Journal of Sociology* 90.2: pp. 247–81.

Burawoy, Michael. (1985) *The Politics of Production*: *Factory Regimes Under Capitalism and Socialism*. London: Verso.

——. (1988) 'Piece Rates, Hungarian Style', in *On Work*: *Historical, Comparative and Theoretical Approaches*, ed. R. E. Pahl, pp. 210–28. Oxford: Blackwell.

——. (1989) 'Reflections on the Class Consciousness of Hungarian Steelworkers', *Politics and Society* 17.1: pp. 1–34.

Burawoy, Michael and Pavel Krotov. (1993) 'The Soviet Transition from Socialism to Capitalism', in *What About the Workers*? *Workers and the Transition to Capitalism in Russia*, ed. Simon Clarke, Peter Fairbrother, Michael Burawoy and Pavel Krotov, pp. 56–90. London: Verso.

Burawoy, Michael and Erik Olin Wright. (1990) 'Coercion and Consent in Contested Exchange', *Politics and Society* 18.2: pp. 251–66.

Burris, Val. (1990) 'Classes in Contemporary Capitalist Society: Recent Marxist and Weberian Perspectives', in *Organization Theory and Class Analysis*: *New Approaches and New Issues*, ed. Stewart Clegg, pp. 55–74. Berlin: Walter de Gruyter.

Byrd, William A. and Lin Qingsong. (1990) *China's Rural Industry*: *Structure, Development and Reform*. Oxford: Oxford University Press.

Calhoun, Craig. (1982) *The Question of Class Struggle*: *Social Foundations of Popular Radicalism during the Industrial Revolution*. Chicago: University of Chicago Press.

——. (1987) 'Class, Place and Industrial Revolution', in *Class and Space*: *The Making of Urban Society*, ed. Nigel Thrift and Peter Williams, pp. 51–72. London: Routledge & Kegan Paul.

——. (1994) 'Social Theory and the Politics of Identity', in *Social Theory and the Politics of Identity*, ed. Craig Calhoun, pp. 9–36. Oxford: Blackwell.

Callinicos, Alex. (1985) 'Post-modernism, Post-structuralism, Post-Marxism', *Theory and Society* 2.3: pp. 85–101.

Canter, David. (1977) *The Psychology of Place*. London: Architectural Press.

Carver, Terrell. (1987) 'Marx's Political Theory of Exploitation', in *Modern Theories of Exploitation*, ed. Andrew Reeve, pp. 68–79. London: Sage.

Casati, Christine. (1991) 'Satisfying Labor Laws – and Needs', *China Business Review* 18.4: pp. 16–22.

Chan, Anita. (1982) 'Images of China's social structure: the changing perspective of Canton students', *World Politics* 34.4: pp. 295–323.

——. (1985) *Children of Mao*: *Personality Development and Political Activism in the Red Guard Generation*. Seattle: University of Washington Press.

——. (1989) 'The challenge to the social fabric', in *China at Forty*: *Mid-Life Crisis*? eds David S. G. Goodman and Gerald Segal, pp. 66–85. Oxford: Clarendon.

——. (1992) 'Revolution or Corporatism? Chinese Workers in Search of a Solution.' Unpublished paper presented to Towards the year 2000 Conference Murdoch University, Western Australia.

——. (1993) 'Revolution or Corporatism? Workers and Trade Unions in Post-Mao China', *Australian Journal of Chinese Affairs* 29: pp. 31–62.

——. (1995) 'The Emerging Pattern of Industrial Relations in China and the Rise of Two New Labor Movements', *China Information* 9.4: pp. 36–59.

Chan, Anita, Richard Madsen and Jonathan Unger. (1984) *Chen Village*: *the Recent History of a Peasant Community in Mao's China*. University of California Press: Berkeley.

Chan, Ming Kou. (1975) 'Labor and Empire: The Chinese Labor Movement in the Canton Delta 1895–1927', PhD dissertation: Stanford University.

Chang, Ya-chung. (1995) 'Provincial Level Government in Mainland China: Organizational Structure and Central Control', *Issues and Studies* 31.4: pp. 62–77.

Chen Baoming. (1985) 'Getihu dui guannian de tiaozhan' (Private business people's challenge to ideology), *Shehui* 3: pp. 4–7.

Chen Bingshou. (1992) 'Tentative Thoughts on Wages of Enterprise Managers', *JPRS*, 24 November: pp. 22–5. Reprinted from *Jingji guanli* (Economic management) 7.

Chen Binxian and Lu Wenhao. (1991) 'Hangzhou shi xiangzhen gongye heli buju wenti' (The problem of the irrational distribution of Hangzhou's village and township industry), *Zhejiang jingji* 11: pp. 10–12.

Chen Jinquan and Qian Xiaoqiu. (1992) 'Chuli laodong zhengyi yingdang weihu qiye de zizhu quan' (In handling labour disputes it is necessary to uphold enterprise autonomy), *Zhongguo laodong kexue* 7: pp. 10–19.

Chen Qiulin. (1993) 'Yong zhongcai ting de xingshi jiejue laodong zhengyi' (Using the form of an arbitration tribunal to resolve labour disputes), *Zhongguo laodong kexue* 2: pp. 25–7.

Cheng Li. (1996) 'Rediscovering Urban Subcultures: the contrast between Shanghai and Beijing', *The China Journal* 36: pp.139–53.

Cheng Shu. (1992) *Caomang yingxiong: getihu jieceng toushi* (Heroes of the bush: Perspectives on the strata of private business people). Beijing: Zhongguo shehui kexue chubanshe.

'Chengshi liudong renkou wenti tantao: Shanghai "liudong renkou wenti yanjiuhui" zongshu' (The problem of floating population in cities: summary of Shanghai's 'conference on the problem of the floating population'). (1990) *Shanghai shehui kexue* 2: pp. 73–5.

Chesneaux, Jean. (1968) *The Chinese Labor Movement, 1919–1927*, trans. by H. M. Wright. Stanford: Stanford University Press.

Chiang Chen-chang. (1990) 'The Role of Trade Unions in Mainland China', *Issues and Studies* 26.2: pp. 75–98.

Chi Mo and Rong Hua. (1991) 'Lue lun Zhejiang suoyouzhi jiegou de biandong' (A brief introduction to changes in the ownership structure in Zhejiang), *Zhejiang jingji yanjiu* 10: pp. 29–30.

——. (1992) 'Zhejiang suoyouzhi jiegou yanjiu' (An analysis of Zhejiang's ownership structure), *Zhejiang xuekan* 72: pp. 29–30.

'Chinese Communist Party Central Committee, Document no. 2: Important Talks by Deng Xiaoping', in *FBIS*, 13 March 1992.

Chinese Economic System Reform Research Institute. (1987) *Reform in China: Challenges and Choices*, ed. Bruce L. Reynolds. New York: M. E. Sharpe.

Ching, Barbara and Gerald W. Creed. (1997) *Knowing your Place: Rural Identity and Cultural Hierarchy*. London: Routledge.

Ching Kwan-Lee. (1995) 'Engendering the Worlds of Labor: Women Workers, Labor Markets and Production Politics in the South China Miracle', *American Sociological Review* 60.3: pp. 378–97.

Chow, Yung-Teh. (1996). *Social Mobility in China*. New York: Atherton Press.

Christiansen, Flemming. (1990) 'Social Division and Peasant Mobility in Mainland China: the Implications of the *Hu-k'ou* System', *Issues and Studies* 26.4: pp. 23–42.

Christiansen, Flemming. (1992) ' "Market Transition" in China: The Case of the Jiangsu Labor Market', *Modern China* 18.1: pp. 72–93.

Chu Tung Tsu. (1957) 'Chinese Class Structure and its Ideology', in *Chinese Thought and Institutions*, ed. John K. Fairbank, pp. 235–50. Chicago: University of Chicago.

Ci Jiwei. (1994) *Dialectic of the Chinese Revolution: From Utopianism to Hedonism*. Stanford: Stanford University Press.

Clegg, Stewart and Fiona Wilson. (1991) 'Power, Technology and Flexibility in Organisations', in *A Sociology of Monsters: Essays on Power, Technology and Organisation*, ed. John Law, pp. 223–73. London: Routledge.

Clifford, James. (1990) 'Notes on (Field) Notes', in *Fieldnotes: The Makings of Anthropology*, ed. Roger Sanjek, pp. 47–70. Ithaca: Cornell University.

Cochran, Sherman. (1992) 'Three Inroads into Shanghai's Market', in *Shanghai Sojourners*, ed. Frederic Wakeman, Jr. and Wen-hsin Yeh, pp. 56–71. Berkeley: University of California Press.

Cohen, A. P. (1985) *The Symbolic Construction of Community*. Chichester: Ellis Norwood.

Cohen, Myron L. (1993) 'Cultural and Political Inventions in Modern China: The Case of the Chinese "Peasant" ', *Daedalus* 122.2: pp. 151–69.

Cohen, Robin. (1988) *The New Helots: Migrants in the International Division of Labour*. Aldershot: Gower.

Cole, James H. (1986) *Shaohsing: Competition and Cooperation in Nineteenth Century China*. Tucson: University of Arizona.

Collinson, David, David Knights and Margaret Collinson. (1990) *Managing to Discriminate*. London: Routledge.

Colloredo-Mansfeld, Rudolf. (1994) 'Architectural Conspicuous Consumption and Economic Exchange in the Andes', *American Anthropologist* 96.4: pp. 845–65.

Cooke, Phillip. (1985) 'Class Practices as Regional Markers', in *Social Relations and Spatial Structures*, ed. Derek Gregory and John Urry, pp. 213–41. London: Macmillan.

Cooper, Frederic. (1992) 'Colonizing Time', in *Colonialism and Culture*, ed. Nicholas B. Dirks, pp. 209–24. Ann Arbor: University of Michigan.

Coughlan, Reed. (1991) 'Employment Opportunity and Ethnicity in Northern Ireland: The Differential Impact of Industrialization in a Divided Society', in *Economic Dimensions of Social Conflict*, ed. S. W. R. de A. Samarasinghe and Reed Coughlan, pp. 48–73. London: Pinter.

Cox, K. R. and A. Mair. (1991) 'From Localised Social Structures to Localities as Agents', *Environment and Planning A* 23: pp. 197–213.

Croll, Elisabeth. (1984) 'Marriage Choice and Status Groups in Contemporary China', in *Class and Social Stratification in Post-Revolution China*, ed. James L. Watson, pp. 175–97. Cambridge: Cambridge University Press.

Cunliffe, John and Andrew Reeve. (1996) 'Exploitation: the original Saint-Simonian account', *Capital and Class* 59: pp. 61–80.

Dai Yuanchen and Li Hanming. (1992) 'Labor Mobility and Wages Distribution under the Dual-Track Infrastructure', *Social Sciences in China* 13.3: pp. 141–52.

D'Andrade, Roy G. (1984) 'Cultural Meaning Systems', in *Culture Theory: Essays on Mind, Self and Emotion*, ed. Richard A. Shweder and Robert A. LeVine, pp. 88–119. Cambridge: University of Cambridge Press.

Davis, Deborah. (1990) 'Urban Job Mobility', in *Chinese Society on the Eve of Tiananmen: The Impact of Reform*, ed. Deborah Davis and Ezra Vogel, pp. 85–108. Cambridge: Harvard University Press.

——. (1992a) 'Job Mobility in Post-Mao Cities: Increases on the Margins', *China Quarterly* 132: pp. 1062–85.

——. (1992b) ' "Skidding": Downward Mobility Among the Children of the Maoist Middle Class', *Modern China* 18.4: pp. 410–37.

Deetz, Stanley. (1992) 'Disciplinary Power in the Modern Corporation', in *Critical Management Studies*, eds Mats Alvesson and Hugh Willmott, pp. 21–45. London: Sage.

de Graf, Nan Dirk and Hendrik Derk Flap. (1988) ' "With a little help from my friends": Social Resources as an Explanation of Occupational Status and Income in West Germany, the Netherlands and the United States', *Social Forces* 67.2: pp. 452–72.

Deng Liqun. (ed.) (1989) *Dangdai Zhongguo de Zhejiang, shang* (Contemporary China's Zhejiang, volume 1). Beijing: Shehui kexue chubanshe.

Derrida, Jacques. (1994) 'Spectres of Marx', *New Left Review* 205: pp. 31–58.

Deutsch, Morton. (1985) *Distributive Justice: A Social-Psychological Perspective*. New Haven: Yale University Press.

Ding Shuishu. (1989) 'Huji guanli yu shehui kongzhi: xianxing huji guanli zhidu zaiyi.' (Administration of residential registration and social control: further thoughts on the present system of residential registration), *Shehui* 3: pp. 26–9.

Dirlik, Arif. (1989) 'Revolutionary Hegemony and the Language of Revolution: Chinese Socialism Between Present and Future', in *Marxism and the Chinese Experience: Issues in Contemporary Chinese Socialism*, eds Arif Dirlik and Maurice Meisner, pp. 27–39. New York: M. E. Sharpe.

——. (1994) *After the Revolution: Waking to Global Capitalism*. Hanover: Wesleyan University Press.

Dittmer, Lowell. (1978) 'Bases of Power in Chinese Politics: A Theory and an Analysis of the Fall of the Gang of Four', *World Politics* 31.1: pp. 26–60.

Dong Furen. (1989) 'On the Question of the Forms of Socialist Ownership in China', *Chinese Economic Studies* 23.1: pp. 8–23.

Douglas, Mary. (1975) *Implicit Meanings: Essays in Anthropology*. London: Routledge & Kegan Paul.

——. (1983) *Sociology, Ethnomethodology and Experience: A Phenomenological Critique*. Cambridge: Cambridge University Press.

Durkheim, Emile. (1933) *The Division of Labor in Society*. New York: Free Press.

Eberhard, Wolfram. (1962) *Social Mobility in Traditional China*. Leiden: E. J. Brill.

Eder, Klaus. (1989) 'The Cognitive Representations of Social Inequality: A Sociological Account of the Cultural Basis of Modern Class Society', in *Social Structure and Culture*, ed. Hans Haferkamp, pp. 125–46. Berlin: Walter de Gruyter.

Edmonds, Richard Louis. (1990) 'History: Historical Perspectives on the Current Geography of China', in *The Geography of Contemporary China: The Impact of Deng Xiaoping's Decade*, ed. Terry Cannon and Alan Jenkins, pp. 61–79. London: Routledge.

Edwards, Louise. (1993) 'Representations of Women and Social Power in Eighteenth Century China: the Case of Wang Xifeng', *Late Imperial China* 14.1: pp. 34–59.

Edwards, P. K. (1990) 'Understanding Conflict in the Labour Process: The Logic and Autonomy of Struggle', in *Labour Process Theory*, ed. David Knights and Hugh Willmott, pp. 125–52. London: Macmillan.

Elejabarrieta, Fran. (1994) 'Social Positioning: A Way to Link Social Identity and Social Representations', *Social Science Information* 33.2: pp. 241–53.

Engels, Friedrich. (1987) *The Condition of the Working Class in England*. Harmondsworth: Penguin.

Engen, John R. (September 1994) 'Training Chinese Workers', *Training*: pp. 79–83.

Epstein, Edward J. (1989) 'The Theoretical System of Property Rights in China's "General Principles of Civil Law": Theoretical Controversy in the Drafting Process and Beyond', *Law and Contemporary Problems* 52.2: pp. 177–216.

Esherick, Joseph. (1979) 'On the "Restoration of Capitalism": Mao and Marxist Theory', *Modern China* 5.1: pp. 41–78.

Evans, Sara M. and Barbara J. Nelson. (1989) *Wage Justice: Comparable Worth and the Paradox of Technocratic Reform*. Chicago: University of Chicago Press.

Eyraud, François. (1993) 'Equal Pay and the Value of Work in Industrialised Countries', *International Labour Review* 132.1: pp. 33–48.

Fabian, Johannes. (1990) 'Presence and Representation: The Other and Anthropological Writing', *Critical Inquiry* 16: 753–72.

Fan Qimiao and Peter Nolan. (1994) *China's Economic Reforms: The Costs and Benefits of Incrementalism*. New York: St Martin's Press.

Faure, David. (1990) 'What made Foshan a Town? The Evolution of Rural and Urban Identities in Ming-Qing China', *Late Imperial China* 11.2: pp. 1–31.

Fei Xiaotong. (1983) *Chinese Village Close-up*. Beijing: New World Press.

Feng Lanyu and Jiang Weiyu. (1987) 'Nongye shengyu laodongli zhuangyi moshi de bijiao yanjiu' (A comparative study of the pattern of transfer of the surplus agricultural labour force) *Zhongguo shehui kexue* 5: pp. 43–52.

Ferguson, Ann Arnett. (1991) 'Managing Without Managers: Crisis and Resolution in a Collective Bakery', in *Ethnography Unbound: Power and Resistance in the Modern Metropolis*, ed. Michael Burawoy *et al.*, pp. 108–32. Berkeley: University of California Press.

Fewsmith, Joseph. (1985) *Party, State and Local Elites in Republican China: Merchant Organizations and Politics in Shanghai, 1890–1930*. Honolulu: University Hawaii Press.

——. (1994) *Dilemmas of Reform in China: Political Conflict and Economic Debate*. New York: M. E. Sharpe.

Foley, Douglas E. (1989) 'Does the Working Class have a Culture in the Anthropological Sense?', *Cultural Anthropology* 4.2: pp. 137–62.

Forster, Keith. (1990/1991) 'The Wenzhou Model for Economic Development', *China Information* 5.3: pp. 53–64.

Foucault, Michel. (1980) *Power/Knowledge: Selected Interviews and Other Writings 1972–1977*, ed. Colin Gordon. Brighton: Harvester Press.

Frank, Arthur W. (1991) 'For a Sociology of the Body: An Analytical Review', in *The Body: Social Process and Cultural Theory*, ed. Mike Featherstone, Mike Hepworth and Bryan S. Turner, pp. 36–102. London: Sage.

Friedman, Andrew L. (1977) *Industry and Labour: Class Struggle at Work and Monopoly Capitalism*. London: Macmillan.

——. (1990) 'Managerial Strategies, Activities, Techniques and Technology: Towards a Complex Theory of the Labour Process', in *Labour Process Theory*, ed. David Knights and Hugh Willmott, pp. 177–208. London: Macmillan.

Friedman, Jonathan. (1992) 'The Past in the Future: History and the Politics of Identity', *American Anthropologist* 94.4: pp. 837–59.

Friedrich, Paul. (1989) 'Language, Ideology, and Political Economy', *American Anthropologist* 91.2: pp. 295–312.

Gallino, Luciano. (1989) 'The Interplay of Culture and Social Structure in the Mind: The Social Actor as a Tangled Decision-Maker', in *Social Structure and Culture*, ed. Hans Haferkamp, pp. 201–15. Berlin: Walter de Gruyter.

Gamberg, Ruth. (1977) *Red and Expert: Education in the People's Republic of China*. New York: Schocken Books.

Gao Shangquan. (1996) *China's Economic Reform*. London: Macmillan.

Gao Xiching. (1989) 'Today's Legal Thinking and its Economic Impact in China', *Law and Contemporary Problems* 52.2: pp. 89–116.

Gartman, David. (1991) 'Culture as Class Symbolization or Mass Reification? A Critique of Bourdieu's *Distinction*', *American Journal of Sociology* 97.2: pp. 421–47.

Gates, Hill. (1979) 'Dependency and the Part-time Proletariat in Taiwan', *Modern China* 5.3: pp. 381–407.

——. (1987) *Chinese Working Class Lives: Getting By in Taiwan*. Ithaca: Cornell University Press.

Geertz, Clifford. (1973) *The Interpretation of Cultures: Selected Essays by Clifford Geertz*. New York: Basic Books.

——. (1983) *Local Knowledge: Further Essays in Interpretive Anthropology*. London: Fontana.

——. (1988) *Works and Lives: The Anthropologist as Author*. Cambridge: Polity.

Gelb, Alan. (1990) 'TVP Workers' Incomes, Incentives and Attitudes', in *China's Rural Industry: Structure, Development and Reform*, ed. William A. Byrd and Lin Qingsong, pp. 280–98. Oxford: Oxford University Press.

'General Principles of Civil Law of the People's Republic of China' (1989) *Law and Contemporary Problems* 52.2: pp. 27–57.

Giddens, Anthony. (1987) 'Structuralism, Post-structuralism and the Production of Culture', in *Social Theory Today*, ed. Anthony Giddens and Jonathon H. Turner, pp. 195–223. Cambridge: Polity.

——. (1991) 'Four Theses on Ideology', *Canadian Journal of Political and Social Theory* 15.1–2&3: pp. 21–4.

Gilmore, David D. (1991) 'Subjectivity and Subjugation: Fieldwork in the Stratified Community', *Human Organisation* 50.3: pp. 215–24.

Gledhill, John. (1994) *Power and its Disguises: Anthropological Perspectives on Politics*. London: Pluto Press.

Godkin, Michael A. (1980) 'Identity and Place: Clinical Applications Based on Notions of Rootedness and Uprootedness', in *The Human Experience of Space and Place*, ed. Anne Buttimer and David Seaman, pp. 73–85. London: Croom Helm.

Gold, Thomas B. (1985) 'After Comradeship: Personal Relations in China Since the Cultural Revolution', *China Quarterly* 104: pp. 657–75.

——. (1989) 'Guerilla Interviewing Among the Getihu', in *Unofficial China: Popular Culture and Thought in the People's Republic*, ed. Perry Link, Richard Madsen and Paul G. Pickowicz, pp. 175–92. Boulder: Westview.

Gold, Thomas B. (1990) 'Urban Private Business and Social Change', in *Chinese Society on the Eve of Tiananmen: The Impact of Reform*, ed. Deborah Davis and Ezra F. Vogel, pp. 157–80. Cambridge: Harvard University Press.

Gordon, David M., Richard Edwards and Michael Reich. (1982) *Segmented Work, Divided Workers: The Historical Transformation of Labour in the United States.* Cambridge: Cambridge University.

Gorz, André. (1966) 'Sartre and Marx', *New Left Review* 37: pp. 33–52.

Gough, A. J. (1992) 'Workers' Competition, Class Relations and Space', *Society and Space* 10.3: pp. 265–86.

Graf, Lee A., Masoud Hammasi, John A. Lust and Yuhua Liang. (1991) 'Perceptions of Desirable Organizational Reforms in Chinese State Enterprises', in *Organization and Management in China 1979–1990*, ed. Oded Shankar, pp. 47–56. New York: M. E. Sharpe.

Gramsci, Antonio. (1957) *The Modern Prince and Other Writings.* New York: International Publishers.

———. (1971) *Selections from the Prison Notebooks.* New York: International Publishers.

Granet, Marcel. (1958) *Chinese Civilization.* New York: Meridian.

Granick, David. (1991) 'Multiple Labour Markets in the Industrial State Enterprise Sector', *China Quarterly* 126: pp. 269–89.

Greenberg, Jerald. (1982) 'Approaching Equity and Avoiding Inequality in Groups and Organizations', in *Equity and Justice in Social Behaviour*, ed. Jerald Greenberg and Ronald L. Cohen, pp. 389–435. New York: Academic Press.

Greenhalgh, Susan. (1988) 'Families and Networks in Taiwan's Economic Development', in *Contending Approaches to the Political Economy of Taiwan*, ed. Edwin A. Winckler and Susan Greenhalgh, pp. 224–45. New York: M. E. Sharpe.

Grieco, Margaret. (1987) 'Family Networks and the Closure of Employment', in *The Manufacture of Disadvantage*: *Stigma and Social Closure*, ed. Gloria Lee and Ray Loveridge, pp. 33–44. Milton Keynes: Open University.

Griffin, Keith and Zhao Renwei. (1993) *The Distribution of Income in China.* New York: St Martins Press.

Groves, Theodore, Yongmiao Hong, John Macmillan and Barry Naughton. (1995) 'China's Evolving Managerial Market', *Journal of Political Economy* 103.4: pp. 873–92.

Guangdong shi laodong ju zhongcai chu. (1993) 'Laodong zhengyi chuli zhong de ruo gan zhengce xing wenti tantao', (A discussion of some questions of a policy nature in the handling of labour disputes), *Zhongguo laodong kexue* 2: pp. 37–8.

Guest, David. (1992) 'Employee Commitment and Control', in *Employment Relations: The Psychology of Influence and Control at Work*, ed. Jean F. Hartley and Geoffrey M. Stephenson, pp. 111–35. Oxford: Blackwell.

Gu Jieshan. (1990) 'Shehui liyi qunti lilun he liyi qunti fenxi fangfa jianlun' (A theory and methodology for the analysis of social interest groups), *Shehuixue yanjiu* 3: pp. 9–16.

Guo Jiyan. (ed.) (1997) 'Changes in Urban Residents' Personal Incomes in China and Regulatory Measures', Report of the Research Team of the Social Development Research Institute, State Planning Commission. *Social Sciences in China* 18.1: pp. 79–87.

Gu Shengzu, Zhu Nong and Deng Banglin. (1989) 'Renkou liudong ji qi houguo tanwei' (A tentative exploration of population mobility and its consequences), *Renkou xuekan* 4: pp. 1–5.

Haber, Honi Fern. (1994) *Beyond Postmodern Politics.* New York: Routledge.

Hagendoorn, Louk. (1993) 'Ethnic Categorization and Outgroup Exclusion', *Ethnic and Racial Studies* 16.1: pp. 26–51.

Hall, Stuart. (1991a) 'The Local and the Global: Globalization and Ethnicity', in *Culture, Globalization and the World System: Contemporary Conditions for the Representation of Identity*, ed. Anthony D. King, pp. 19–39. London: Macmillan.

——. (1991b) 'Old and New Identities: Old and New Ethnicities', in *Culture, Globalization and the World System: Contemporary Conditions for the Representation of Identity*, ed. Anthony D. King, pp. 41–68. London: Macmillan.

Hammersley, Martin. (1990) 'What's Wrong with Ethnography? The Myth of Theoretical Description', *Sociology* 24.4: pp. 597–615.

Hangzhou nianjian 1991. (Hangzhou Yearbook 1991). (1991) Hangzhou: Hangzhou daxue chubanshe.

Hangzhou shi dangqian shiyong nongmingong xianzhuang yu duice (The present employment of peasant workers in Hangzhou and strategies for dealing with the situation). (1989) Unpublished essay presented to Zhejiang Province Economic Society's 1989 essay competition, Hangzhou.

Hangzhou shi jingji tizhi gaige bangongshi. (1991) 'Fenlei zhidao, wanshan tigao, zhuangda hexin ceng, fazhan jinmi ceng' (Breakdown directives, perfect improvements, strengthen the core, develop integration), *Zhejiang jingji yanjiu* 6: pp. 21–3.

Hangzhou shi laodong ju. (1990) 'Hangzhou shi wailai linshigong guanli zanxing guiding' (Provisional regulations on the management of outside temporary workers in Hangzhou). Hangzhou.

Hannan, Kate. (1995) *China, Modernization and the Goal of Prosperity: Government Administration and Economic Identity in the Late 1980s*. Cambridge: Cambridge University Press.

Han Xiya. (1986) 'Gaige kaifang zhong woguo jieji jiegou yanbian de chubu yuce' (A preliminary forcast of changes in China's class structure during reform and opening up) *Shehuixue yanjiu* 5: pp. 75–78.

Harré, Rom. (1978) 'Accounts, Actions, Meanings – the Practice of Participatory Psychology', in *The Social Contexts of Method*, ed. Michael Brenner, Peter Marsh and Marylin Brenner, pp. 44–66. London: Croom Helm.

——. (1981) 'Philosophical Aspects of the Macro-Micro Problem', in *Advances in Social Theory and Methodology: Towards an Integration of Micro- and Macro-Sociologies*, ed. K. Knorr-Cetina and A. V. Cicourel, pp. 139–60. Boston: Routledge & Kegan Paul.

Harrell, Stevan. (1992) 'Aspects of Marriage in Three South Western Villages', *China Quarterly* 130: pp. 323–37.

Helliwell, Christine. (1996) 'Space and Sociality in a Dayak Longhouse', in *Things as They Are: New Directions in Phenomenological Anthropology*, ed. Michael Jackson, pp. 128–48. Bloomington: Indiana University Press.

Henriques, Julian, Wendy Hollaway, Cathy Urwin, Couze Venn and Valerie Walkerdine. (1984) *Changing the Subject: Psychology, Social Regulation and Subjectivity*. London: Methuen.

Hepple, Bob. (1992) 'Labour Law and the New Labour Force', in *Labour Relations in a Changing Environment*, ed. Alan Gladstone *et al.*, pp. 287–96. Berlin: Walter de Gruyter.

Heritage, John C. (1987) 'Ethnomethodology' in *Social Theory Today*, ed. Anthony Giddens and Jonathan Turner, pp. 224–72. Cambridge: Polity Press.

Hermkens, Piet and David van Kreveld. (1991) 'Social Justice, Income Distribution, and Social Stratification in the Netherlands: A Review', in *Social Justice in Human Relationships: Volume 2*, ed. Herman Steensma and Riel Vermunt, pp. 119–38. New York: Plenum Press.

Hershatter, Gail Brook. (1986) *The Workers of Tianjin, 1900–1949*. Stanford: Stanford University Press.

He Xin. (1992) (no title) in *New Ghosts, Old Dreams: Chinese Rebel Voices*, ed. Geremie Barmè and Linda Jaivan, p. 135. New York: Random House, Trans. from 'Tongzhang ehua ji jinggai shibaide yuanyin', *Mingbao yuekan* 2, 1989.

Hindess, Barry. (1986) 'Interests in Political Analysis', in *Power, Action and Belief: A New Sociology of Knowledge*, ed. John Law, pp. 112–25. London: Routledge.

——. (1990) 'Classes, Collectives and Corporate Actors', in *Organisation Theory and Class Analysis: New Approaches and New Issues*, ed. Stewart R. Clegg, pp. 157–74. Berlin: Walter de Gruyter.

Hinton, William. (1966) *Fanshen: A Documentary of Revolution in a Chinese Village*. Harmondsworth: Penguin.

Hoffman, Charles. (1974) *The Chinese Worker*. Albany: The State University of New York.

Holmstrom, Mark. (1984) *Industry and Inequality: The Social Anthropology of Indian Labour*. Cambridge: Cambridge University Press.

Holubenko, M. (1975) 'The Soviet Working Class: Discontent and Opposition', *Critique* 4: pp. 5–24.

Hong Fenglin and Shao Daoshang. (1989) 'Workers' Assessment of Party Spirit and Interpersonal Relations', *Chinese Economic Studies* 22.4: pp. 44–54. Trans. from *Weidinggao* 1 (1987).

Hong Kong Trade Union Education Centre. (1990) *A Moment of Truth: Workers' Participation in China's 1989 Democracy Movement and the Emergence of Independent Trade Unions*. Hong Kong: Asia Monitor Centre.

Honig, Emily. (1986) *Sisters and Strangers: Women in the Shanghai Cotton Mills, 1919–1949*. Stanford: Stanford University Press.

——. (1989) 'Pride and Prejudice: Subei People in Contemporary Shanghai', in *Unofficial China: Popular Culture and Thought in the People's Republic*, ed. Perry Link, Richard Madsen and Paul Pickowicz, pp. 138–55. Boulder: Westview.

——. (1992) *Creating Chinese Ethnicity: Subei People in Shanghai, 1850–1980*. New Haven: Yale University Press.

Ho Ping-ti. (1954) 'The Salt Merchants of Yang-chou: a Study of Commercial Capitalists in Eighteenth Century China', *Harvard Journal of Asiatic Studies* 2.17: pp. 154–67.

——. (1976) *The Ladder of Success in Imperial China: Aspects of Social Mobility, 1368–1911*. New York: Da Capo Press.

Hormuth, Stefan E. (1990) *The Ecology of Self: Relocation and Self-Concept Change*. Cambridge: Cambridge University Press.

Howe, Christopher. (1973a) 'Labour Organisation and Incentives in Industry', in *Authority, Participation and Cultural Change in China*, ed. Stuart R. Schram, pp. 233–56. London: University of London.

——. (1973b) *Wage Patterns and Wage Policy in Modern China, 1919–1972*. Cambridge: Cambridge University Press.

'Huang Kangsheng interviews Yu Hongren', *FBIS*, 16 May 1990: p. 2. Trans. from *Renmin ribao*, 3 May.

Huang Xiaojing and Yang Xiao. (1987) 'From Iron Ricebowls to Labor Markets', in *Reform in China: Challenges and Choices*, ed. Bruce L. Reynolds, pp. 147–60. New York: M. E. Sharpe.

Huang Yasheng. (1990) 'Web of Interests and Patterns of Behaviour of Chinese Local Economic Bureaucracies and Enterprises During Reforms', *China Quarterly* 123: pp. 431–58.

Hudson, Ray and David Sadler. (1986) 'Contesting Work Closures in Western Europe's Old Industrial Regions: Defending Place or Betraying Class?', in *Production, Work, Territory: The Geographical Anatomy of Industrial Capitalism*, ed. Allen J. Scott and Michael Storper, pp. 172–93. Boston: Allen & Unwin.

Hu Hanmin. (1960) 'Six Principles of the People's Report', in *Sources of Chinese Tradition*, Volume 2, ed. W. Theodore de Bary, Wing-tsit Chan and Chester Tan, p. 104. New York: Columbia University Press.

Humphrey, Caroline. (1989) ' "Janus-Faced Signs" – the Political Language of a Social Minority Before Glasnost', in *Social Anthropology and the Politics of Language*, ed. Ralph Grillo, pp. 145–75. London: Routledge.

——. (1994) 'Remembering an "Enemy": the Bogd-Khaan in Twentieth Century Mongolia', in *Memory, History and Opposition under State Socialism*, ed. Rubie S. Watson, pp. 21–44. Santa Fe: School of American Research.

Huspek, Michael. (1994) 'Oppositional Codes and Social Class Relations', *British Journal of Sociology* 45.1: pp. 79–102.

Jackson, Michael. (1996) 'Introduction: Phenomenology, Radical Empiricism, and Anthropological Critique', in *Things as They Are: New Directions in Phenomenological Anthropology*, ed. Michael Jackson, pp. 1–50. Bloomington: Indiana University Press.

Jackson, Sukhan. (1990) *Post-Mao Wage Policy and Trends in the People's Republic of China*. University of Queensland Department of Economics, Discussion Paper no. 32. Brisbane: University of Queensland.

——. (1992) *Chinese Enterprise Management Reforms in Economic Perspective*. Berlin: Walter de Gruyter.

Jefferson, Gary H. and Thomas G. Rawski. (1992) 'Unemployment, Underemployment and Employment Policy in China's Cities', *Modern China* 18.1: pp. 42–71.

Jenkins, Richard. (1986) *Racism and Recruitment: Managers, Organisations and Equal Opportunity in the Labour Market*. Cambridge: Cambridge University Press.

Jenkins, Richard and Gary Parker. (1987) 'Organisational Politics and the Recruitment of Black Workers', in *The Manufacture of Disadvantage: Stigma and Social Closure*, ed. Gloria Lee and Ray Loveridge, pp. 58–70. Milton Keynes: Open University.

Jenner, W. J. F. (1992) *The Tyranny of History: The Roots of China's Crisis*. London: Allen Lane.

Jia Nianfeng. (1989) 'Taiyuan laodongli shichang fazhan zhanlue yanjiu' (Research on strategies for developing the market for labour power in Taiyuan), *Chengshi yanjiu* 2: pp. 2–8.

Jiang Yiwei. (1990) 'Enterprise Reform', in *The Chinese Economy and its Future: Achievements and Problems of Post-Mao Reforms*, ed. Peter Nolan and Dong Fureng, pp. 151–60. Cambridge: Polity.

Joll, Caroline, Chris McKenna, Robert McNabb and John Shorey. (1983) *Developments in Labour Market Analysis*. London: Allen & Unwin.

Kane, Daniel. (1992) 'The Chinese Political and Intellectual Elite in the Year 2000', Unpublished paper presented to Towards the Year 2000 Conference, Murdoch University, Western Australia.

Kannappan, Subbiah. (1985) 'Urban Employment and the Labor Market in Developing Nations', *Economic Development and Cultural Change* 33.4: pp. 699–730.

Katznelson, Ira. (1986) 'Working Class Formation: Constructing Cases and Comparisons', in *Working Class Formation: 19th Century Patterns in Western Europe and the United States*, ed. Ira Katznelson and Aristide R. Zolberg, pp. 3–44. New Jersey: Princeton University Press.

Kelley, Jonathan and M. D. R. Evans. (1993) 'The Legitimation of Inequality: Occupational Earnings in Nine Nations', *American Journal of Sociology* 99.1: pp. 75–125.

Kellner, Douglas. (1992) 'Popular Culture and the Construction of Post-modern Identity', in *Modernity and Identity*, ed. Scott Lash and Jonathan Friedman, pp. 141–77. Oxford: Blackwell.

King, Timothy and Zhang Jiping. (1992) *Case Studies of Chinese Economic Reform*. Washington: World Bank.

Kirkby, R. J. R. (1985) *Urbanisation in China*. London: Croom Helm.

Knight, John and Song Lina. (1993) 'Why Urban Wages Differ in China', in *The Distribution of Income in China*, ed. Keith Griffin and Zhao Renwei, pp. 215–84. New York: St Martins Press.

Knights, David. (1990) 'Subjectivity, Power and the Labour Process' in *Labour Process Theory*, ed. David Knights and Hugh Willmott, pp. 297–335. London: Macmillan.

Kondo, Dorinne K. (1990) *Crafting Selves: Power, Gender and Discourses of Identity in a Japanese Workplace*. Chicago: University of Chicago Press.

Korzec, Michael (1992) *Labour and the Failure of Reform in China*. London: Macmillan.

Kouzmin, Alexander. (1980) 'Control and Organization: Towards a Reflexive Analysis', in *Work and Inequality Volume 2: Ideology and Control in the Capitalist Labour Process*, ed. Paul Boreham and Geoff Dow, pp. 130–162. Melbourne: Macmillan.

Kraus, Richard. (1981) *Class Conflict in Chinese Socialism*. New York: Columbia University Press.

——. (1983) 'Bureaucratic Privilege as an Issue in Chinese Politics', *World Development* 11.8: pp. 673–82.

Kruse, Lenelis and Susanne Schwarz. (1992) 'Who Pays the Bill? The Language of Social Representation', in *Social Representations and the Social Bases of Knowledge*, ed. Mario von Cranach, Willem Doise and Gabriel Mugny, pp. 23–9. Lewiston, NY: Hogrefe & Huber.

Kueh, Y. Y. (1992) 'Foreign Investment and Economic Change in China', *China Quarterly* 161: pp. 637–90.

Kuhn, Philip A. (1984) 'Chinese Views on Social Stratification', in *Class and Social Stratification in Post-Revolutionary China*, ed. James L. Watson, pp. 16–28. Cambridge: Cambridge University Press.

Kwong, Julia. (1997) *The Political Economy of Corruption in China*. New York: M. E. Sharpe.

Laaksonen, Oiva. (1988) *Management in China During and After Mao in Enterprises, Government and Party*. Berlin: Walter de Gruyter.

Lakoff, George. (1987) *Women, Fire and Dangerous Things: What Categories Reveal about the Mind*. Chicago: University of Chicago Press.

Lang, Alfred. (1992) 'On the Knowledge in Things and Places', in *Social Representations and the Social Bases of Knowledge*, ed. Mario von Cranach, Willem Doise and Gabriel Mugny, pp. 112–19. Lewiston, NY: Hogrefe & Huber.

Langman, Lauren. (1992) 'Neon Cages: Shopping for Subjectivity', in *Lifestyle Shopping: The Subject of Consumption*, ed. Rob Shields, pp. 40–82. London: Routledge.

Lardy, Nicholas. (1992) 'The Role of Foreign Trade and Investment in China's Economic Transformation', *China Quarterly* 161: 1065–82.

Lee, Ching Kwan. (1995) 'Engendering the Worlds of Labor: Women Workers, Labor Markets, and Production Politics in the South China Economic Miracle', *American Sociological Review* 60.3: pp. 378–97.

Lee, Kuen. (1993) 'Property Rights and the Agency Problem in China's Enterprise Reform', *Cambridge Journal of Economics* 17: pp. 179–94.

Lee, Martyn. (1993) *Consumer Culture Reborn: The Cultural Politics of Consumption*. London: Routledge.

Lefebvre, Henri. (1976) 'Reflections on the Politics of Space', *Antipode* 8.2: pp. 30–7.

——. (1991) *The Production of Space*, trans. Donald Nicholson Smith. Oxford: Blackwell.

Lenin, V. I. (1971) *Selected Works*. Moscow: Progress Publishers.

Lerner, Melvin J. (1991) 'Integrating Societal and Psychological Rules of Entitlement', in *Social Justice in Human Relations: Volume 1*, ed. Riel Vermunt and Herman Steensma, pp. 13–32. New York: Plenum Press.

Leung Wing-Yue. (1988) *Smashing the Iron Rice Pot: Workers and Unions in China's Market Socialism*. Hong Kong: Asia Monitor Centre.

LeVine, Robert A. (1973) *Culture, Behavior and Personality*. Chicago: Aldine.

Leys, Simon. (1977) *Chinese Shadows*. New York: Viking Press.

Liang Heng and Judith Shapiro. (1983) *Son of the Revolution*. London: Chatto & Windus.

Liao Shuhui. (1990) 'Perfection of the system of property rights of incorporated state enterprises', *FBIS*, 26 April 1991: pp. 34–7. Reprinted from *Jingji guanli* 12.

Li Cheng and Lynn White. (1991) 'China's Technocratic Movement and the World Economic Herald', *Modern China* 17.3 (111): pp. 342–88.

Li Cheng and Lynn White. (1992) 'Elite transformation and modern change in mainland China and Taiwan: empirical data and the theory of technocracy', *China Quarterly* 121: pp. 1–35.

Li, David. (1996) 'A Theory of Ambiguous Property Rights in Transitional Economies: The Case of the Chinese Non-State Sector', *Journal of Comparative Economics* 23: pp. 1–19.

Li Hua. (1989) 'The Democratic Management of Enterprises and Workers' Awareness of Democracy', *Chinese Economic Studies* 22.4: pp. 69–80.

Li Jianguo. (1991) 'Xiandaihua: Zhongguo shehui jieceng jiegou de tiao shi' (Modernisation: the appropriate form of transformation of the structure of social strata in China), *Shehui kexue* 6: pp. 40–3.

248   *Bibliography*

Lindbeck, Assar and Dennis J. Snower. (1988) *The Insider-Outsider Theory of Employment and Unemployment.* Cambridge: MIT Press.

Lin Gen. (1991) ' "Linshigong wangguo" you xi lu' (A chronicle of care and joy in the kingdom of temporary workers), *Shehui* 12: pp. 2–7.

Lin Nan and Yanjie Bian. (1991) 'Getting Ahead in Urban China', *American Journal of Sociology* 97.3: pp. 657–88.

Lin Nan and Wen Xie. (1988) 'Occupational Prestige in Urban China', *American Journal of Sociology* 93.4: pp. 793–832.

Lin Yimin. (1992) 'Between Government and Labor: Managerial Decision making in Chinese Industry', *Studies in Comparative Communism* 25.4: pp. 381–403.

Littek, Wolfgang and Ulrich Heisig. (1990) 'Work Organisation under Technological Change', in *Class Analysis: New Approaches, New Issues*, ed. Stewart R. Clegg, pp. 299–314. Berlin: Walter de Gruyter.

Liu Binyan. (1983a) 'Inside News', in *Fragrant Weeds: Chinese Short Stories Once Labelled as Poisonous Weeds*, ed. W. J. F. Jenner, pp. 1–70. Hong Kong: Joint Publishing Company.

——. (1983b) 'People or Monsters?' trans. Madelyn Ross with Perry Link, in *People or Monsters? And other Stories and Reportage from China*, ed. Perry Link, pp. 11–68. Bloomington: Indiana University Press.

Liu Chunbin. (1989) 'Lun Zhongguo de eryuan shehui jiegou' (A discussion of China's dual social structure), *Shehui* 8: pp. 20–5.

Liu Jisheng. (1992) 'The Reform of State-Owned Enterprises', in *Case Studies in Chinese Economic Reform*, ed. Timothy King and Zhang Jiping, pp. 80–109. Washington: World Bank.

Liu Pinan. 'Guangzhou "sanzi" qiye wenti toushi ji duice, 1' ('A Perspective on problems in Guangzhou's "joint venture" firms, and countermeasures, Part 1'), *Neibu wenzhai* 25 April 1992: pp. 23–8.

Livingstone, David and J. Marshall Mangan. (eds) (1996) *Recast Dreams: Class and Gender Consciousness in Steeltown.* Ontario: Garamond Press.

Li Yuanjian. (1991) 'Hangzhou shi qiye zuzhi jiegou de diaocha he sikao' (A survey and reflections upon Hangzhou enterprises' organisational structure), *Zhejiang jingji yanjiu* 8: pp. 2–5.

Lo, C. P. and Xiao-di Song. (1992) 'Ningbo', in *China's Coastal Cities: Catalysts for Modernization*, ed. Yue-man Yeung and Xu-wei Hu, pp. 153–77. Honolulu: University of Hawaii Press.

Lockwood, David. (1966) 'Sources of Identity in Working-Class Images of Society', *Sociological Review* 14.3: pp. 249–67.

Lou Jiwei and Zhou Xiaochuan. (1989) 'On the Direction of Reform in the Price System', *Chinese Economic Studies* 22.3: pp. 14–23.

Lovell, David W. (1988) *Marx's Proletariat: The Making of a Myth.* London: Routledge.

Lowenthal, Richard. (1970) 'Development Versus Utopia in Communist Policy', in *Change in Communist Systems*, ed. Chalmers Johnson, pp. 33–116. Stanford: Stanford University Press.

Lu Feng. (1989) 'Dan wei – A Special Form of Social Organisation', *Social Sciences in China* 10.3: pp. 100–22.

Lu Jianhua. (1991) 'Chinese Workers' High Expectations of Managers', *International Sociology* 6.1: pp. 37–49.

Luo Guifeng. (1989) 'Gongye zhong de fei zhengshi qunti yu zhigong de renji jiaowang' (Informal groups in industrial enterprises and relations between employees), *Shehuixue yanjiu* 6: pp. 71–82.

Luo Ruiqing. (1988) 'An Explanation of the Draft Resolutions on the Regulations Concerning Household Registration in the Peoples' Republic of China', in Zhang Qingwu, 'Basic Facts on the Household Registration System', Appendix 1B, *Chinese Economic Studies* 22.1: pp. 93–102.

Luo Xiaopeng. (1994) 'Rural Reform and the Rise of Localism', in *Central-Local Relations in China: Reform and State Capacity*, ed. Jia Hao and Lin Zimin, pp. 113–33. Boulder: Westview.

Lu Renyuan. 'Why Private Entrepreneurs Constitute a Capitalist Class', *JPRS*, 9 August 1991: p. 18. Trans. from *Zhengli de zhuiqiu*, 15 April.

Lu Xun. (1960) 'On Face', *Lu Xun Selected Works, vol. 4.* Trans. Yang Xianyi and Gladys Yang, pp. 131–4. Beijing: Foreign Languages Press.

Maas, Anne and Luciano Arcuri. (1992) 'The Role of Language in the Persistence of Stereotypes', in *Language, Interaction and Social Cognitio*, ed. Gun R. Semin and Klaus Fiedler, pp. 129–43. London: Sage.

McAll, Christopher. (1990) *Class, Ethnicity and Social Inequality.* Montreal: McGill-Queens University Press.

McCarthy, Timothy. (1978) *Max and the Proletariat: A study in Social theory.* Westport: Greenwood.

McDermott, John. (1991) *Corporate Society: Class, Property and Contemporary Capitalism.* Boulder: Westview.

——. (1991–1992) 'Free Enterprise and Socialized Labor', *Science and Society* 55.4: pp. 388–416.

Macdonald, Sharon. (1993) 'Identity Complexes in Western Europe: Social Anthropological Perspectives', in *Inside European Identities: Ethnography in Western Europe*, ed. Sharon Macdonald, pp. 1–26. Providence: Berg.

McDonough, Roisin. (1977) 'Ideology as False Consciousness: Lukacs', in *On Ideology*, ed. Centre For Contemporary Cultural Studies, University of Birmingham, pp. 33–44. London: Hutchinson.

McFarlane, Bruce. (1990) 'Market Socialism and Democracy', in *The Chinese Economy and its Future: Achievements and Problems of Post-Mao Reform*, ed. Peter Nolan and Dong Fureng, pp. 72–95. Cambridge: Polity.

McKracken, Grant. (1990) *Culture and Consumption: New Approaches to the Symbolic Character of Consumer Goods and Activities.* Bloomington: Indiana University Press.

McLellan, David. (1977) *Karl Marx: Selected Writings.* Oxford: Oxford University Press.

Mallee, Hein. (1988) 'Rural-Urban Migration in the People's Republic of China', *China Information* 1.4: pp. 12–23.

Mao Tse-Tung. (1965) *Selected Works of Mao Tse-Tung.* Beijing: Foreign Languages Press.

Marcus, George E. (1986) 'Contemporary Problems of Ethnography in the Modern World System', in *Writing Culture: The Poetics and Politics of Ethnography*, ed. James Clifford and George E. Marcus, pp. 165–94. Berkeley: University of California.

——. (1989) 'Imagining the Whole: Ethnography's Contemporary Efforts to Situate Itself', *Critique of Anthropology* 9.3: pp. 7–30.

Marshall, Gordon. (1988) 'Some Remarks on the Study of Working-Class Consciousness', in *Social Stratification and Economic Change*, ed. David Rose, pp. 98–126. London: Hutchinson.

Marx, Karl. (1954) *Capital*: *A Critique of Political Economy*, vols *1*, *3*. Moscow: Progress Publishers.

Marx, Karl and Frederic Engels. (1947) *The German Ideology*. London: Lawrence & Wishart.

——. (1968) 'Value, Price and Profit', in *Classes, Power and Conflict*: *Classical and Contemporary Debates*, ed. Anthony Giddens and David Held, pp. 30–5. London: Macmillan, 1982. Reprinted from Karl Marx and Friedrich Engels, *Selected Works*. New York: International Publishers.

——. (1986) *Manifesto of the Communist Party*. Moscow: Progress Publishers.

Mathews, R. H. (1931) *Mathews' Chinese-English Dictionary*, rev. edn. Shanghai: China Inland Mission and Presbyterian Mission Press.

Meng Chen and Zou Nongjian. (1985) 'Xin de chanye, xin de jieceng, xin de bianhua: Jianggang zhen xin gongren jieceng de diaocha yanjiu', (New production, new strata, new variations: Analysing a survey of the new working strata of Jianggang town), *Shehui* 3: pp. 13–16.

Meng Xin. (1990) 'The Rural Labour Market', in *China's Rural Industry*: *Structure, Development and Reform*, ed. William A. Byrd and Lin Qingsong, pp. 299–322. Oxford: Oxford University Press.

Mennell, Steven. (1994) 'The Formation of We-Images: A Process Theory', in *Social Theory and the Politics of Identity*, ed. Craig Calhoun, pp. 175–97. Oxford: Blackwell.

Merriman, John M. (1979) *Consciousness and Class Experience in Nineteenth Century Europe*. New York: Holmes Meier.

Metcalfe, Andrew. (1988) *For Freedom and Dignity*: *Historical Agency and Class Structures in the Coalfields of New South Wales*. Sydney: Allen & Unwin.

——. (1990) 'The Demonology of Class: The Iconography of the Coalminer and the Symbolic Construction of Political Boundaries', *Critique of Anthropology* 10.1: pp. 39–63.

Miliband, Ralph. (1991) *Divided Societies*: *Class Struggle in Contemporary Capitalism*. Oxford: Oxford University Press.

Miller, Daniel. (1994) *Acknowledging Consumption*. London: Routledge.

Miller, Peter and Nikolas Rose. (1993) 'Governing Economic life', *Economy and Society* 19.1: 75–105.

Milton, David and Nancy Milton. (1976) *The Wind Will Not Subside*: *Years in Revolutionary China 1964–1969*. New York: Pantheon.

Mommaas, Hans. (1996) 'Modernity, Postmodernity and the Crisis of Social Modernization: A Case Study In Urban Fragmentation', *International Journal of Urban and Regional Research* 20.2: pp. 196–216.

Moore, Barrington, Jr. (1978) *Injustice* : *the Social Bases of Obedience and Revolt*. London: MacMillan.

MOW International Research Team. (1987) *The Meaning of Working*. London: Academic Press.

Murray, Geoffrey. (1994) *Doing Business in China*. Sydney: Allen & Unwin.

Murray, Kevin. (1989) 'The Construction of Identity in the Narratives of Romance and Comedy', in *Texts of Identity*, ed. John Shotter and Kenneth Gergen, pp. 176–205. London: Sage.

Nader, Laura and Andree Sursock. (1986) 'Anthropology and Justice', in *Justice*: *Views from the Social Sciences*, ed. Ronald L. Cohen, pp. 205–33. New York: Plenum Press.

Nash, June. (1989) 'Cultural Resistance and Class Consciousness in Bolivian Tin-mining Communities', in *Power and Popular Protest*: *Latin American Social Movements*, ed. Susan Eckstein, pp. 182–202. Berkeley: University of Caslifornia Press.

Nee, Victor. (1989) 'Peasant Entrepreneurship and the Politics of Regulation in China', in *Remaking the Institutions of Socialism*: *China and Eastern Europe*, ed. Victor Nee and David Stark, pp. 169–207. Stanford: Stanford University Press.

——. (1991) 'Social Inequalities in Reforming State Socialism', *American Sociological Review* 56.3: pp. 267–82.

——. (1992) 'Organizational Dynamics of Market Transition', *Administrative Science Quarterly* 37.1: pp. 1–27.

Ning Hongbao. (1992) 'Yingdang zhongshi laodong zhengyi de fei chengxu chuli' (Need to stress the non-procedural handling of labour disputes), *Zhongguo laodong kexue* (Labour Science in China) 7: pp. 21–2.

Nolan, Peter. (1993) *State and Market in the Chinese Economy*: *Essays on Controversial Issues*. London: Macmillan.

Nolan, Peter and Gordon White. (1984) 'Urban Bias, Rural Bias or State Bias? Urban-Rural Relations in Post-Revolutionary China', *Journal of Development Studies* 20.3: pp. 52–81.

O'Brien, Gordon E. (1992) 'Changing Meanings of Work', in *Employment Relations*: *The Psychology of Influence and Control at Work*, ed. Jean F. Hartley and Geoffrey M. Stephenson, pp. 44–66. Oxford: Blackwell.

Odgaard, Ole. (1992) *Private Enterprises in Rural China*. Aldershot: Avebury.

Oi, Jean. (1989a) 'Market reforms and corruption in rural china', *Studies in Comparative Communism* 22.2/3: 221–233.

——. (1989b) *State and Peasant in Contemporary China*: *the Political Economy of Village Government*. Berkeley: University of California Press.

——. (1990) 'The Fate of the Collective after the Commune', in *Chinese Society on the Eve of Tiananmen*: *The Impact of Reform*, ed. Deborah Davis and Ezra F. Vogel, pp. 15–36. Cambridge: Harvard University Press.

——. (1992) 'Fiscal Reform and the Economic Foundations of Local State Corporatism in China', *World Politics* 45: pp. 99–126.

Ollman, Bertell. (1987) 'How to Study Class Consciousness and Why We Should', *Insurgent Sociologist* 14.1: pp. 57–98.

Ong, Aihwa. (1987) *Spirits of Resistance and Capitalist Discipline*: *Factory Women in Malaysia*. Albany: State University of New York.

Ortner, Sherry B. (1991) 'Reading America: Preliminary Notes on Class and Culture', in *Recapturing Anthropology*: *Working in the Present*, ed. Richard G. Fox, pp. 163–89. Santa Fe: School of American Research Press.

Ossowski, Stanislaw. (1963) *Class Structure in the Social Consciousness*. New York: Free Press.

Paasi, A. (1991) 'Deconstructing Regions: Notes on the Scale of Spatial Life', *Environment and Planning A* 23: pp. 239–56.

Pahl, R. E. and C. D. Wallace. (1988) 'Neither Angels in Marble nor Rebels in Red: Privatization and Working Class Consciousness', in *Social Stratification and Economic Change*, ed. David Rose, pp. 127–52. London: Hutchinson.

Pan Kuang-tan and Fei Hsiao-tung. (1963) 'City and Village; The Inequality of Opportunity', in *The Chinese Civil Service: Career Open to Talent?* ed. Johanna Menzel, pp. 9–21. Lexington: D. C. Heath.

Parker, Robert. (1993) 'The Labor Force in Transition: the Growth of a Contingent Workforce in the United States', in *The Labor Process and Control of Labor*, ed. Berch Berberoglu, pp. 116–36. Westport: Praeger.

Patton, Paul. (1988) 'Marxism and Beyond: Strategies of Reterritorialization', in *Marxism and the Interpretation of Culture*, ed. Cary Nelson and Lawrence Grossberg, pp. 123–36. London: Macmillan.

Pearson, Margaret M. (1992) 'Breaking the Bonds of "Organized Dependence": Managers in China's Foreign Sector', *Studies in Comparative Communism* 25.1: pp. 57–77.

Perry, Elizabeth J. (1992a) 'Casting a Chinese "Democracy" Movement: The Roles of Students, Workers, and Entrepreneurs', in *Popular Protest and Political Culture in Modern China*, ed. Jeffrey N. Wasserstrom and Elizabeth J. Perry, pp. 146–64. Boulder: Westview.

——. (1992b) 'Strikes Among Shanghai Silk Weavers, 1927–1937', in *Shanghai Sojourners*, ed. Frederic Wakeman, Jr and Wen-hsin Yeh, pp. 305–41. Berkeley: University of California Press.

——. (1993) *Shanghai on Strike: The Politics of Chinese Labor*. Stanford: Stanford University Press.

——. (1994) 'Shanghai's Strike Wave of 1957', *China Quarterly* 137: 1–27.

——. (1995) 'Labor's battle for political space: the role of worker associations in contemporary China' in *Urban Spaces in Contemporary China*, ed. Deborah S. Davis, Richard Kraus, Barry Naughton and Elizabeth J. Perry, pp. 302–325. Cambridge: Cambridge University Press.

Phizacklea, Annie and Robert Miles. (1980) *Labour and Racism*. London: Routledge & Kegan Paul.

Pieke, Frank Nikolaas. (1992) "The Ordinary and the Extraordinary: An Anthropological Study of Chinese Reform and Political Protest in Beijing, 1989", PhD dissertation: University of California, Berkeley.

Potter, Sulamith Heins. (1983) 'The Position of Peasants in Modern China's Social Order', *Modern China* 9.4: pp. 465–500.

Potter, Sulamith Heins and Jack M. Potter. (1990) *China's Peasants: The Anthropology of a Revolution*. Cambridge: Cambridge University Press.

Poulantzas, Nicos. (1974) *Classes in Contemporary Capitalism*. London: Verso.

Pred, Allan. (1985) 'The Social Becomes the Spatial: The Spatial Becomes the Social', in *Social Relations and Spatial Structures*, ed. Derek Gregory and John Urry, pp. 337–65. London: Macmillan.

Price, R. F. (1970) *Education in Modern China*. London: Routledge & Kegan Paul.

Prybla, Jan. (1997) 'China as an Asian Economic Power', *Issues and Studies* 33.1: pp.1–22.

Pryor, Frederic L. (1973) *Property and Industrial Organization in Capitalist and Communist Nations*. Bloomington: Indiana Press.

Przeworski, Adam. (1977) 'Proletariat into a Class: The Process of Class Formation form Karl Kautsky's *The Class Struggle* to recent Controversies', *Politics and Society* 7.4: pp. 343–402.

Qian Yingyi and Joseph Stiglitz. (1996) 'Institutional Innovations and the Role of Local Governments in Transitional Economies: the Case of Guangdong

Province in China', in *Reforming Asian Socialism: the Growth of Market Institutions*, ed. John Macmillan and Barry Naughton, pp. 175–93. Ann Arbor: University of Michigan.

Qie Jianwei. (1992) 'Shixing quanyuan laodong hetong zhi shi qiye laodong zhidu gaige de fangxiang' (The wholescale implementation of the labour contract system is the trend for reform of the enterprise labour system), *Zhongguo laodong kexue* 8: pp. 16–19.

Qin Shaoxiang. (1989) 'Thoughts on the development of the individual and private economy', *FBIS*, 12 January 1990: pp. 51–3. Trans. from *Zhongguo jingji tizhi gaige* 23.

Rankin, Mary Backus. (1971) *Early Chinese Revolutionaries: Radical Intellectuals in Shanghai and Chekiang, 1902–1911*. Cambridge: Harvard University Press.

Rebel, Hermann. (1989) 'Cultural Hegemony and Class Experience: a Critical Reading of Recent Ethnological-Historical Approaches', *American Ethnologist* 16.1: pp. 117–36.

Reis, Harry T. (1987) 'The Nature of the Justice Motive: Some Thoughts on Operation, Internalization, and Justification', in *Social Comparison, Social Justice, and Relative Deprivation*, ed. John C. Masters and William P. Smith, pp. 131–50. Hillsdale: Lawrence Erlbaum.

Relph, E. (1976) *Place and Placelessness*. London: Pion.

Roberts, Bryan. (1978) *Cities of Peasants: The Political Economy of Urbanisation in the Third World*. London: Edward Arnold.

Rodgers, Mary F. (1975) *Implicit Meanings: Essays in Anthropology*. London: Routledge & Kegan Paul.

——. (1983) *Sociology, Ethnomethodology and Experience: A Phenomenological Critique*. Cambridge: Cambridge University Press.

Rodman, Margaret. (1992) 'Empowering Place: Multilocality and Multivocality', *American Anthropologist* 94.3: pp. 640–56.

Rofel, Lisa. (1989a) "Eating Out of One Big Pot: Hegemony and Resistance in a Chinese Factory", PhD dissertation: Stanford University.

——. (1989b) 'Hegemony and Productivity: Workers in Post-Mao China', in *Marxism and the Chinese Experience: Issues in Contemporary Chinese Socialism*, ed. Arif Dirlik and Maurice Meisner, pp. 235–52. New York: M. E. Sharpe.

——. (1992) 'Rethinking Modernity: Space and Factory Discipline in China', *Cultural Anthropology* 7.1: pp. 93–114.

Rothbart, Myron and Marjorie Taylor. (1992) 'Category Labels and Social Reality: Do We View Social Categories as Natural Kinds?', in *Language, Interaction and Social Cognition*, ed. Gun R. Semin and Klaus Fiedler, pp. 11–36. London: Sage.

Rowe, William T. (1989) *Hankow: Conflict and Community in a Chinese City, 1796–1895*. Stanford: Stanford University Press.

Roy, Donald. (1972) 'Quota Restriction and Goldbricking in a Machine Shop', in *Payment Systems: Selected Readings*, ed. Tom Lupton, pp. 35–63. Harmondsworth: Penguin.

Ruan Danching. (1993) 'Interpersonal Networks and Workplace Controls in Urban China', *Australian Journal of Chinese Affairs* 29: pp. 89–106.

Ruccio, David, Stephen Resnick and Richard Wolff. (1991) 'Class Beyond the Nation State', *Capital and Class* 43.1: pp. 25–36.

Sabel, Charles F. (1982) *Work and Politics: The Division of Labour in Industry*. Cambridge: Cambridge University Press.

Sabin, Lora. (1994) 'New Bosses in the Workers' State: The Growth of Non-State Sector Employment in China', *China Quarterly* 140: pp. 944–70.

Sacks, Karen. (1989) 'Toward a Unified Theory of Class, Race and Gender', *American Anthropologist* 16.3: pp. 534–50.

Said, Edward. (1993) *Culture and Imperialism*. London: Vintage.

——. (1989) 'Representing the Colonized: Anthropology's Interlocutors', *Critical Inquiry* 15.2: pp. 205–25.

Sangren, P. Steven. (1995) ' "Power" against Ideology: A Critique of Foucaultian Usage', *Cultural Anthropology* 10.1: pp. 3–40.

Sanjek, Roger. (1990) 'A Vocabulary for Fieldnotes', in *Fieldnotes: The Makings of Anthropology*, ed. Roger Sanjek, pp. 92–121. Ithaca: Cornell University Press.

Sargeson, Sally and Zhang Jian. (1997) *The Market in Service of the Local State? Property Rights Reform in Xihu*. Asia Research Centre Working Paper no. 68. Perth: Murdoch University.

Sawer, Marion. (ed.) (1978) *Socialism and the New Class: Towards the Analysis of Structural Inequality Within Socialist Societies*. Adelaide: Flinders University Press.

Sayer, Andrew and Richard Walker. (1992) *The New Social Economy: Reworking the Division of Labour*. Oxford: Blackwell.

Schmidt, Charles G. and Yuk Lee. (1987) 'Residential Preferences in China,' *Geographical Review* 77: pp. 318–27.

Schoppa, R. Keith. (1982) *Chinese Elites and Political Change: Zhejiang Province in the Early Twentieth Century*. Cambridge: Harvard University Press.

Schram, Stuart. (1989) *The Thought of Mao Tse-Tung*. Cambridge: Cambridge University Press.

Schurmann, Franz. (1960) *Ideology and Organization in Communist China*. Berkeley: University of California Press.

Scott, James C. (1990) *Domination and the Arts of Resistance: Hidden Transcripts*. New Haven: Yale.

Selden, Mark and Patti Eggleston. (1979) *The People's Republic of China: A Documentary History of Revolutionary Change*. New York: Monthly Review.

Senenscher, Michael. (1989) *Work and Wages: Natural Law, Politics and the eighteenth-century French Trades*. Cambridge: Cambridge University Press.

Sennett, Richard and Jonathon Cobb. (1972) *The Hidden Injuries of Class*. Cambridge: Cambridge University Press.

Shanghai shehui kexue yuan, Shehuixue yanjiusuo. (1984) *Shehuixue jianming cidian*. (Concise Dictionary of Sociology). Shanghai.

Shen, J. and N. A. Spence. (1993) 'Population Trends, Labour Supply and the Employment Problem in China', Paper presented at Annual Conference of the Institute of British Geographers, 5–8 January. Royal Holloway and Bedford New College, University of London.

Shirk, Susan L. (1984) 'The Decline of Virtuocracy in China', in *Class and Social Stratification in Post-Revolutionary China*, ed. James L. Watson, pp. 56–83. Cambridge: Cambridge University Press.

——. (1990) ' "Playing to the Provinces": Deng Xiaoping's Political Strategy of Economic Reform', *Studies in Comparative Communism* 3.4: pp. 227–58.

Shotter, John. (1989) 'Social Accountability and the Construction of 'You', in *Texts of Identity*, ed. John Shotter and Kenneth J. Gergen, pp. 133–51. London: Sage.

——. (1990) 'The Social Construction of Remembering and Forgetting', in *Collective Remembering*, ed. David Middleton and Derek Edwards, pp. 120–38. London: Sage.

——. (1993) *Cultural Politics of Everyday Life*: *Social Constructionism, Rhetoric and Knowing of the Third Kind*. Buckingham: Open University Press.

Sider, Gerald M. (1986) *Culture and Class in Anthropology and History*: *A Newfoundland Illustration*. Cambridge: Cambridge University Press.

Sik, Endre. (1988) 'Reciprocal Exchange of Labour in Hungary', in *On Work*: *Historical, Comparative and Theoretical Approaches*, ed. R. E. Pahl, pp. 527–47. Oxford: Blackwell.

Silverman, Sydel. (1981) 'Rituals of Inequality', in *Social Inequality*: *Comparative and Developmental Approaches*, ed. Gerald D. Berreman and Kathleen M. Zaretsky, pp. 163–81. New York: Academic Press.

Siskind, Janet. (1991) 'Class Discourse in an Early 19th Century New England Factory', *Dialectical Anthropology* 16: pp. 35–48.

Siu, Helen F. (1989) *Agents and Victims in South China*: *Accomplices in Rural Revolution*. New Haven: Yale University Press.

——. (1990) 'The Politics of Migration in a Market Town', in *Chinese Society on the Eve of Tiananmen*: *The Impact of Reform*, ed. Deborah Davis and Ezra Vogel, pp. 61–82. Cambridge: Harvard University Press.

Skinner, G. William. (1965) 'Marketing and Social Structure in Rural China: Part 3', *Journal of Asian Studies* 24.3: pp. 363–400.

Smart, Alan and Josephine Smart. (1992) 'Capitalist Production in Socialist Society: The Transfer of Manufacturing from Hong Kong to China', in *Anthropology and the Global Factory*: *Studies of the New Industrialisation in the Late Twentieth Century*, ed. Frances Abrahamer Rothstein and Michael L. Blim, pp. 47–61. New York: Bergin & Garvey.

——. (1993) 'Obligation and Control: Employment of Kin in Capitalist Labour Management in China', *Critique of Anthropology* 13.1: pp. 7–31.

Smith, Dennis. (1987) 'Knowing Your Place: Class, Politics and Ethnicity in Chicago and Birmingham 1890–1983', in *Class and Space*: *The Making of Urban Society*, ed. by Nigel Thrift and Peter Williams, pp. 276–305. London: Routledge.

Smith, Neil. (1992) 'Contours of a Spatialized Politics', *Social Text* 33: pp. 54–81.

Smith, Raymond T. (1984) 'Anthropology and the concept of social class', *Annual Review of Anthropology* 13: pp. 467–94.

Smith, Richard. (1993) 'The Chinese Road to Capitalism', *New Left Review* 199: pp. 55–99.

So, Alvin Y. and Suwarsono. (1990) 'Class Theory or Class Analysis? A Reexamination of Marx's Unfinished Chapter on Class', *Critical Sociologist* 17.2: pp. 35–56.

Soja, Edward W. (1989) *Postmodern Geographies*: *The Reassertion of Space in Critical Social Theory*. London: Verso.

Solinger, Dorothy J. (1989) 'Capitalist Measures with Chinese Characteristics', *Problems of Communism* 38.1: pp. 19–33.

——. (1991) *China's Transients and the State*: *A Form of Civil Society?* Hong Kong: Chinese University of Hong Kong, Institute of Asia-Pacific Studies.

——. (1993) *China's Transition From Socialism*: *Statist Legacies and Market Reform 1980–1990*. New York: M. E. Sharpe.

——. (1995) 'The Chinese Work Unit and Transient Labour in the Transition from Socialism', *Modern China* 21.2: pp. 155–83.

Somers, Margaret and Gloria D. Gibson. (1994) 'Reclaiming the Epistemological "Other": Narrative and the Social Constitution of Identity', in *Social Theory and the Politics of Identity*, ed. Craig Calhoun, pp. 37–99. Oxford: Blackwell.

Song Qiang, Zhang Cangcang, Qiao Bian. (1996) *Zhongguo keyi shuo bu* (China can say no) Beijing: Zhongguo gongshang lianhe chubanshe.

Stark, David. (1986) 'Rethinking Internal Labor Markets: New Insights from a Comparative Perspective', *American Sociological Review* 51: pp. 492–504

——. (1989) 'Coexisting Organisational Forms in Hungary's Emerging Mixed Economy', in *Remaking the Economic Institutions of Socialism: China and Eastern Europe*, ed. Victor Nee and David Stark, pp. 137–68. Stanford: Stanford University Press.

——. (1990) 'Privatization in Hungary: From Plan to Market or from Plan to Clan?', *East-European Politics and Society* 4.3: pp. 351–91.

Stedman Jones, Gareth. (1983) *Languages of Class: Studies in English Working Class History 1832–1982*. Cambridge: Cambridge University Press.

Steinberg, Marc W. (1991a) 'The Remaking of the English Working Class', *Theory and Society* 20: pp. 173–97.

——. (1991b) 'Talkin' Class: Discourse, Ideology, and Their Roles in Class Conflict', in *Bringing Class Back In: Contemporary and Historical Perspectives*, eds Scott G. McNall, Rhonda F. Levine, Rick Fantasia, pp. 261–84. Boulder: Westview.

'Suan, tian, ku, la: "dagong chao"' (The joys and sorrows of life: 'the labouring tide'), (1992) *Dadi* 10: pp. 48–52.

Sundstrom, Eric and Mary Graehl Sundstrom. (1986) *Work Places: The Psychology of the Physical Environment in Offices and Factories*. Cambridge: Cambridge University Press.

Svejnar, Jan. (1990) 'Productive Efficiency and Employment', in *China's Rural Industry: Structure, Development and Reform*, ed. William A. Byrd and Lin Qingsong, pp. 243–54. Oxford: Oxford University Press.

Szirmai, A. (1991) 'Explaining Variations in Attitudes Towards Income Equality', in *Social Justice in Human Relations: Volume 2*, ed. Herman Steensma and Riel Vermunt, pp. 229–68. New York: Plenum Press.

Taussig, Michael. (1980) *The Devil and Commodity Fetishism in South America*. Chapel Hill: University of North Carolina.

Taylor, Romeyn. (1989) 'Chinese Hierarchy in Comparative Perspective', *Journal of Asian Studies* 48.3: pp. 490–511.

Tedlock, Dennis. (1987) 'Questions Concerning Dialogical Anthropology', *Journal of Anthropological Research* 43: pp. 325–37.

Thireau, Isabelle. (1991) 'From Equality to Equity: An Exploration of Changing Norms of Distribution in Rural China', *China Information* 5.4: pp. 42–57.

Thomas, Nicholas. (1991) 'Against Ethnography', *Cultural Anthropology* 6.3: pp. 306–22.

Thomas, Robert J. (1982) 'Citizenship and Gender in Work Organization: Some Considerations for Theories of the Labor Process', in *Marxist Inquiries: Studies of Labor, Class and States*, ed. Michael Burawoy and Theda Skocpol, pp. 86–112. Chicago: Chicago University Press.

Thomas, W. A. (1993) 'Emerging Securities Markets: The Case of China', *Journal of Asian Business* 9.4: pp. 90–109.

Thompson, E. P. (1978) *The Poverty of Theory and Other Essays*. London: Merlin Press.
——. (1980) *The Making of the English Working Class*. Harmondsworth: Penguin.
——. (1980) *Customs in Common*. Harmondsworth: Penguin.
Thompson, Paul. (1989) *The Nature of Work*: An Introduction to Debates on the *Labour Process*. London: Macmillan.
Tien, H. Yuan. (1973) *China's Population Struggle*: Demographic Decisions of the *Peoples Republic of China*. Columbus: Ohio University Press.
Torgovnick, Marianna. (1990) *Gone Primitive*: Savage Intellects, Modern Lives. Chicago: University of Chicago Press.
Trouillot, Michel-Rolph. (1991) 'Anthropology and the Savage Slot: The Poetics and Politics of Otherness', in *Recapturing Anthropology*: Working in the Present, ed. Richard G. Fox, pp. 17–44. Santa Fe: School of American Research Press.
Tung, Ricky. (1994) 'Transforming the Management of Mainland China's State-Owned Enterprises', *Issues and Studies* 29.12: pp. 1–17.
Turner, Bryan S. (1986) *Equality*. London: Tavistock.
——. (1991) 'Recent Developments in the Theory of the Body', in *The Body*: Social *Process and Cultural Theory*, ed. Mike Featherstone, pp. 1–35. London: Sage.
Turner, John C. (1987) *Rediscovering the Social Group*: A Self-Categorization *Theory*. Oxford: Blackwell.
Turton, Andrew. (1984) 'Limits of Ideological Domination and the Formation of Social Consciousness', in *History and Peasant Consciousness in South-East Asia*, ed. A. Turton and S. Tanabe, pp. 19–71. Osaka: National Museum of Ethnology.
Ueno, Kazuhiko. (1994) 'The Dynamism of Rural Enterprises in China', *China Newsletter* 108: pp. 8–13.
Vermeer, Eduard B. (1996) 'Experiments with Rural Industrial Shareholding Cooperatives: The Case of Zhoucun District, Shandong Province', *China Information* 10.3/4: pp. 75–107.
Volosinov, V. N. (1973) *Marxism and the Philosophy of Language*. New York: Seminar Press.
Walder, Andrew G. (1983) 'Organized Dependency and Cultures of Authority in Chinese Industry', *Journal of Asian Studies* 43.1: pp. 51–72.
——. (1984) 'The Remaking of the Chinese Working Class 1949–1981', *Modern China*, 10.1: pp. 3–48.
——. (1985) 'The Political Dimension of Social Mobility in Communist States: Reflections on the Soviet Union and China', *Research in Political Sociology* 1: pp. 101–17.
——. (1986) *Communist Neo-Traditionalism*: Work and Authority in Chinese *Industry*. Berkeley: University of California Press.
——. (1989a) 'Factory and Manager in an Era of Reform', *China Quarterly* 118: pp. 242–64.
——. (1989b) 'The Political Sociology of the Beijing Upheaval of 1989', *Problems of Communism* 38.5: pp. 30–40.
——. (1990) 'Economic Reform and Income Distribution in Tianjin, 1976–1986', in *Chinese Society on the Eve of Tiananmen*: The Impact of Reform, eds Deborah Davis and Ezra Vogel, pp. 135–56. Cambridge: Harvard University Press.
——. (1991) 'Popular Protest in the Chinese Democracy Movement of 1989', working paper presented to workshop on Comparative Social Analysis, University of California, Berkeley.

——. (1992) 'China's Evolving Property Rights and their Consequences for Social Stratification and Politics', Paper presented to Towards the Year 2000 Conference, Murdoch University, Perth.

——. (1995) 'Local Governments as Industrial Firms: An Organizational Analysis of China's Transitional Economy', *American Journal of Sociology* 101.2: pp. 263–301.

Walder, Andrew and Gong Xiaoxiao. (1990) 'Workers in the Beijing Democracy Movement: Reflections on the Brief History of the Beijing Workers Autonomous Union', Paper presented to Berkeley China Seminar, University of California, Berkeley.

Walker, James. (1985) 'Social Problems in Shiftwork', in *Hours of Work: Temporal Factors in Work Scheduling*, ed. Simon Folkard and Timothy H. Monk, pp. 211–25. Chichester: John Wiley.

Wang Ge. (1990) 'Ze, quan, li de chabie yu laodongzhe he chengbaoren de chongtu' (Disparities in responsibility, authority, and benefits, and conflict between workers and contractors), *Shehuixue yanjiu* 2: pp. 74–83.

Wang Jie. (1987) 'Gaige zhong de jieji jiegou de bianhua he duice zhi wo jian', (My views on changes in the class structure during reform, and countermeasures), *Shehuixue yanjiu* 2: pp. 1–13.

——. (1991) '1991 nian Zhejiang jingji shikuang fenxi', (An on the spot analysis of Zhejiang's 1991 economy), *Zhejiang jingji* 12: pp. 3–7, 31.

Wang Liming and Liu Zhaonan. (1989) 'On the Property Rights System of State Enterprises in China', *Law and Contemporary Problems* 52.3: pp. 19–42.

Wang Renzhi. 'On Opposing Bourgeois Liberalization', *FBIS*, 23 February (1990): pp. 12–27. Trans. from *Qiushi* 3.

Wang Shaoguang. (1994) 'Central-Local Fiscal Politics in China', in *Changing Central-Local Relations in China: Reform and State Capacity*, ed. Jia Hao and Lin Zhimin, pp. 91–112. Boulder: Westview.

Wang Zhen. (1991) 'Township Enterprises and the National Distribution of Resources', *JPRS*, 10 December 1991: pp. 26–31. Trans. from *Zhongguo nongcun jingji* 8.

Wang Zhongming. (1989) 'Participation and Skill Utilization in Organisational Decisionmaking in Chinese Enterprises', in *Advances in Industrial Organizational Psychology*, ed. Barry J. Fallon, H. Peter Pfister and John Brebner, pp. 19–26. Amsterdam: Elsevier Science Press.

——. (1994) 'The Patterns of Human Resource Management: 8 Cases of Chinese-Japanese Joint Ventures and 2 Cases of Wholly Japanese Ventures', *Journal of Managerial Psychology* 9.4: pp.12–21.

Wank, David. (1995) 'Bureaucratic Patronage and Private Business: Changing Networks of Power in Urban China', in *The Waning of the Communist State: Economic Origins of Political Decline in China and Hungary*, ed. Andrew G. Walder, pp. 153–81. Berkeley: University of California.

Warminski, Ardrzej. (1995) 'Hegel/Marx: Consciousness and Life', in *Depositions: Althusser, Balibar, Machey and the Labor of Reading*, ed. Jacques Lezra, pp. 118–41. New Haven: Yale.

Watson, Rubie S. (1985) *Inequality Among Brothers: Class and Kinship in South China*. Cambridge: Cambridge University Press.

Weber, Max. (1968) *Economy and Society*. New York: Bedminster Press.

Webster, Juliet. (1991) 'Advanced Manufacturing Technologies: Work Organisation and Social Relations Crystallised', in *A Sociology of Monsters: Essays on Power, Technology and Domination*, ed. John Law, pp. 192–222. London: Routledge.

Webster, Murray and Martha Foschi. (1992) 'Social Referencing and Theories of Status Interaction', in *Social Referencing and the Social Construction of Reality in Infancy*, ed. Saul Feinman, pp. 269–94. New York : Plenum Press.

Whitaker, Mark P. (1996) 'Ethnography as Learning: A Wittgensteinian Approach to Writing Ethnographic Accounts', *Anthropological Quarterly*, 69.1: pp. 1–13.

White, Gordon. (1976) *The Politics of Class and Class Origins: The Case of the Cultural Revolution*. Canberra: Australian National University, Contemporary China Papers 9.

——. (1982) 'Urban Employment and Labour Allocation Policies in Post-Mao China', *World Development* 10.8: pp. 613–32.

——. (1987) 'The Politics of Economic Reform in Chinese Industry', *China Quarterly* 111: pp. 365–89.

——. (1989) 'Restructuring the Working Class: Labor Reform in Post-Mao China', in *Marxism and the Chinese Experience: Issues in Contemporary Chinese Socialism*, eds Arif Dirlik and Maurice Meisner, pp. 152–68. New York: M. E. Sharpe.

——. (1993) *Riding the Tiger: The Politics of Economic Reform in Post-Mao China*. Stanford: Stanford University Press.

White, Lynn T. III. (1978) *Careers in Shanghai: The Social Guidance of Personal Energies in a Developing Chinese City 1949–1966*. Berkeley: University of California Press.

——. (1984) 'Bourgeois Radicalism in the "New Class" in Shanghai 1949–1969', in *Class and Social Stratification in Post-Revolutionary China*, ed. James L. Watson, pp. 142–74. Cambridge: Cambridge University Press.

Williams, Raymond. (1973) *The Country and the City*. New York: Oxford University Press.

——. (1976) *Keywords: A Vocabulary of Culture and Society*. London: Fontana.

Willis, Paul E. (1978) *Learning to Labour: How Working Class Kids Get Working Class Jobs*. Westmead: Saxon House.

——. (1979) 'Shop Floor Culture, Masculinity and the Wage Form', in *Working Class Culture: Studies in History and Theory*, ed. J. Clarke, C. Critcher, R. Johnson, pp. 185–200. New York: St Martins Press.

Willmott, Hugh. (1987) 'Racism, Politics and Employment Relations', in *The Manufacture of Disadvantage: Stigma and Social Closure*, ed. Gloria Lee and Ray Loveridge, pp. 128–43. Milton Keynes: Open University.

——. (1990) 'Subjectivity and the Dialectics of Praxis: Opening up the Core of Labour Process Theory', in *Labour Process Theory*, ed. David Knights and Hugh Willmott, pp. 336–79. London: Macmillan.

Wilson, Jean. (1986) 'The People's Republic of China', in *Trade Unions in Communist States*, ed. Alex Pravda and Blair A. Ruble, pp. 219–52. Boston: Allen & Unwin.

Wilson, Richard W. (1991) 'Rethinking Universalism and Relativism in Political Culture', *Journal of Asian Studies* 50.1: pp. 53–60.

Wolf, Margery. (1968) *The House of Lim*. Englewood Cliffs: Prentice-Hall.

Wortzel, Larry M. (1987) *Class in China: Stratification in a Classless Society.*
New York: Greenwood Press.

Wright. E. O. (1982a) 'Proletarianization in the changing American class structure', in *Marxist Inquiries: Studies of Labor, Class and States*, ed. Michael
Burawoy and Theda Skocpol, pp. 176–209. Chicago: University of Chicago.

——. (1982b) 'The Status of the Political in the Concept of Class Structure',
Politics and Society 11.3: pp. 321–41.

——. (1984) 'A General Framework for the Analysis of Class Structure', *Politics
and Society* 13.4: pp. 383–423.

——. (1987) 'Reflections on *Classes*', *Berkeley Journal of Sociology* 32: pp. 19–50.

Wu Gang. (1991) 'Hangzhou shimin jiuye xingwei piancha ji qi jiaozheng'
(Rectifying deviations in the occupational behaviour of Hangzhou residents),
Zhejiang jingji 7: pp. 41–4.

Wu Jiaxing and Jin Lizuo. (1988–1989) 'Sharing Enterprises: an Approach to
Further Reform', *Chinese Economic Studies* 22.2: pp. 24–37. Reprinted from
Jingji fazhan yu tizhi gaige 12 (1985).

Wu Quhui, Wang Hansheng and Xu Xinxin. (1990) 'Noneconomic Determinants
of Workers' Incomes', in *China's Rural Industry: Structure, Development and
Reform*, ed. William A. Byrd and Lin Qinsong, pp. 323–37. Oxford: Oxford
University Press.

Wu Shouhui and Guo Jinhua. (1989) 'Workers' Evaluation of and Hopes for Trade
Unions', *Chinese Economic Studies* 22.4: pp. 56–68.

Xia Jizhi. (1992) 'Shixing laodong hetong zhi shi Zhongguo laodong zhidu gaige
de biyou zhi lu' (Implementation of the labour contract system is the only way
to reform China's labour system), *Zhongguo laodong kexue* 1: pp. 13–15.

Xiao Wentao. (1989) 'Woguo yanhai kaifang diqu shehui jieceng de fenhua zuhe
qingkuang yu liyi xietiao' (The polarisation and convergence between social
strata in China's open coastal regions and the problem of coordinating their
interests), *Shehui kexue* 9: pp. 35–9.

Xiao Yingzhi and Qin Shaoxiang. 'Study of changes in the structure of class and
strata in China – Interview with He Jianzhang', *FBIS*, 25 September (1990):
pp. 17–19. Trans. from *Zhongguo jingji tizhi gaige* 8.

Xihu qu jingji tongji nianjian 1992 (1992) (Economic Statistical Yearbook of Xihu
District 1992). Hangzhou: Xihu qu tongji ju.

Xihu qu tongji nianjian 1990 (1990) (Statistical Yearbook of Xihu District 1990).
Hangzhou: Xihu qu tongji bumen.

Xi Shutao. (1990) 'Guanyu shehui liudong ruo gan wenti de tantao' (An inquiry
into some questions regarding social mobility), *Xueshu jiaoliu* 3: pp. 115–18.

Xu Haibo. 'Guanyu pingjunzhuyi fenpei qingxiang de jidian fenxi' (An Analysis
of Some Aspects of Trends in Egalitarian Distribution), *Neibu Wenzhai* 25
February 1992: pp. 3–6.

Yabuki, Susumu. (1995) *China's New Political Economy: The Giant Awakes.*
Translated by Stephen M. Harner. Boulder: Westview.

Yang Guan. (1991) 'Qiye "jiazu" xianxiang' (The phenomena of 'clannishness' in
enterprises), *Shehui* 4: pp. 42–5.

Yang, Mayfair Mei-hui. (1986) 'The Art of Social Relationships and Exchange in
China', PhD dissertation: University of California, Berkeley.

——. (1988) 'The Modernity of Power in the Chinese Socialist Order', *Cultural
Anthropology* 3.4: pp. 408–27.

——. (1989a) 'Between State and Society: The Construction of Corporateness in a Chinese Socialist Factory', *Australian Journal of Chinese Affairs* 22: pp. 31–62.

——. (1989b) 'The Gift Economy and State Power in China' *Comparative Studies in Society and History* 31.1: pp. 25–54.

Yang, Minchuan. (1994) 'Reshaping Peasant Culture and Community', *Modern China* 20.2: pp. 157–79.

Yan Yunxiang. (1996) *The Flow of Gifts: Reciprocity and Social Networks in a Chinese Village*. Stanford: Stanford University Press.

Yates, Robin D. S. (1994) 'Body, Space, Time and Bureaucracy: Boundary Creation and Control Mechanisms in Early China', in *Boundaries in China*, ed. John Hay, pp. 56–80. London: Reaktion Books.

Young, Iris. (1990) *Justice and the Politics of Difference*. Princeton: Princeton University Press, .

Young, Susan. (1991) 'Wealth but not security: attitudes towards private business in China in the 1980s', *Australian Journal of Chinese Affairs* 25: pp. 115–38.

Yu Zhen. (1990) 'Dui yi ge shequ de liyi qunti de pouxi – jian lun ruhe juti renshi shehui de liyi guanxi yu maodun' (An analysis of interest groups in one urban community – a theory on how to concurrently recognise society's interest relations and contradictory interests), *Shehuixue yanjiu* 3: pp. 17–28.

Zan Baoyi. (1987) 'Shehui diwei yu juese.' (Social status and social roles), *Shehui* 1: pp. 5–7.

Zhang Gang. (1993) 'Government Intervention versus Marketization in China's Rural Industries', *China Information* 8.1–2: pp. 45–73.

Zhang Qingwu. (1988) 'Basic Facts on the Household Registration System', *Chinese Economic Studies* 22.1: pp. 3–21.

Zhang Weiguo. 'Losing Chains, Gaining Freedom', *JPRS*, 16 February 1992: pp. 17–20. Trans. from *Jing bao* 8.

Zhang Wenhong. 'Cursory Analysis of Elements of Instability in Reform and Opening to the Outside World', *JPRS*, 23 December 1991: pp. 76–80. Trans. from *Shehui* 8.

Zhang Yonghuo and Pan Weiliang. (1993) 'Laodong bumen zhuanhuan zhineng de zhuanti' (The special topic of the transformation of the Labour Bureau's functions), *Zhongguo laodong kexue* 2: pp. 22–5.

Zhang Yunqiu. (1996) 'The Entrepreneurial Role of Local Bureaucracy in China: A Case Study of Shandong Province', *Issues and Studies* 32:12: pp. 89–110.

Zhang Zhiguang. (1991a) 'Kaichu, chuming, citui deng laodong zhengyi qianyi' (A brief discussion of discharge, removal from [personnel] list, dismissal, etc. in labour disputes), *Beijing gongren* 11: pp. 8–9.

——. (1991b) 'Quanyi zai zheli dedaole weihu, zhengyi zai zheli dedaole jiejue' (Here, rights and interests are safeguarded: here, disputes are resolved), *Beijing Gongren* 7: pp. 16–17.

Zhao Minghua and Theo Nichols. (1996) 'Management Control of Labour in State-Owned Enterprises: Cases from the Textile Industry', *The China Journal* 36: pp. 1–21.

Zhejiang jingji nianjian 1990 (1990) (Economic Yearbook of Zhejiang 1990). Hangzhou: Zhejiang renmin chubanshe.

Zhejiang sheng renmin zhengfu. (1991) 'Zhejiang sheng quanmin suoyouzhi qiye linshigong guanli zanxing guiding' (Zhejiang province provisional regulations on the management of temporary workers in enterprises owned by the whole people). Hangzhou.

Zhejiang tongji nianjian 1992, 1993. (1992/1993) (Statistical Yearbook of Zhejiang 1992, 1993). Hangzhou: Zhongguo tongji chubanshe.

Zhongguo chengshi tongji nianjian 1991. (1991) (Statistical Yearbook of Chinese Cities 1991). Beijing: Zhongguo tongji chubanshe.

Zhongguo gongchandang di shisi jie zhongyang weiyuan hui di san ci quanti huiyi. *Zhonggong zhongyang guanyu jianli shehuizhuyi shichang jingji tizhi ruogan wenti de jueding* (Chinese Communist Party Central Committee's decisions on several questions relating to the foundation of a socialist market economic system). Beijing, 14 November 1993.

Zhongguo laodong tongji nianjian 1991, 1996 (1991/1996) (*ZGLDTJNJ*: Statistical Yearbook of Chinese Labour 1991, 1996) Beijing: Zhongguo tongji chubanshe.

Zhongguo nongcun chanye jiegou yanjiu ketizu. (1987) '1986–2000 nian Zhongguo nongcun chanye jiegou yanjiu baogao (lianyi)' (Part 1: report on research into China's rural production structure), *Zhongguo nongcun jingji* (China's Rural Economy) 8: p. 25.

Zhongguo renmin gongheguo guowuyuan. (1989) 'Quanmin suoyouzhi qiye lin-shigong guanli zanxing guiding' (Provisional regulations on the management of temporary workers in enterprises owned by the whole people). Beijing.

Zhongguo tongji nianjian 1993, 1995, 1996 (1993/1995/1996) (*ZGTJNJ*: Statistical Yearbook of China 1993, 1995, 1996). Beijing: Zhongguo tongji chubanshe.

Zhou Enlai. (1979) 'On Classes, Customs and Cultural Revolution', in *The Peoples' Republic of China: A Documentary History of Revolutionary Change*, ed. Mark Selden, with Patti Eggleston, pp. 564–71. New York: Monthly Review.

Zhou Fuxiang. 'Correctly Assess Changes in Patterns of National Income Distribution', *JPRS*, 9 November 1992: pp. 4–8. Trans. from *Gaige* 5.

Zhu Qingfang. (1988) 'Gaige zhong de Zhongguo shehui liudong zhuangkuang' (The conditions of social mobility in China during reform), *Shehuixue yanjiu* 3: pp. 1–6.

——. (1990) 'Shinian lai woguo ge jieji, jieceng jiegou yanbian de fenxi' (An analysis of the structural changes in China's social classes and strata over the past ten years) *Shehuixue yanjiu* 3: pp. 1–8.

Zhu Ying. (1995) 'Major changes underway in China's industrial relations', *International Labour Review* 134.1: pp. 37–49.

Zhuo Yongliang. (1989) 'Chengshi (zhen) laodongli duanque de shenyuan yingxi-ang' (The profound effects of shortage in the urban labour force), *Zhejiang xuekan* 1: pp. 32–37, 43.

Zimmerman, Don H. and Deidre Boden. (1991) 'Structure-in-Action: An Introduction', in *Talk and Social Structure: Studies in Ethnomethodology and Conversation Analysis*, ed. Deidre Boden and Don H. Zimmerman, pp. 3–21. Cambridge: Polity Press.

Zou Ji. (1992) 'The Assignment of Jobs to College Graduates', in *Case Studies of Chinese Economic Reform*, ed. Timothy King and Zhang Jiping, pp. 51–79. Washington, DC: World Bank.

Zou Nongjian. (1991a) 'Dangqian jieji, jieceng yanjiu zhong ruogan lundian bianxi' (An examination of a number of theories in contemporary research on classes and strata), *Yunnan shehui kexue* 3: pp. 43–49.
——. (1991b) 'Shehui jiegou de chongzu, maodun jiqi tiaozheng' (Reorganization and contradiction within the social structure, and its adjustment), *Shehui kexue* 8: pp. 46–50.

NEWSPAPERS AND NEWS SERVICES

Agence France Presse, http://open.academic.n2k.com/p/P0614AAhtm 1996
Asian Labour Update, Hong Kong 1995–96
Baokan wenzhai *BKWZ* (News Digest), Beijing 1990–93
Beijing Gongren *BJGR* (Beijing Worker), Beijing 1992–93
Beijing Review *BR*, Beijing 1987–97
China Daily *CD*, Beijing 1987–97
China Labour Bulletin, Hong Kong 1997
China News Digest *CND*, http://www.cnd.org/CND-Global/ 1997–98
Dangdai gongren *DDGR* (Contemporary Worker), Beijing 1991–92
Economic Intelligence Unit *EIU*, http://www.eiu.com/ 1995–96
Fazhi ribao *FZRB* (Law Daily), Beijing 1992–93
Gongren ribao *GRRB* (Workers' Daily), Beijing 1992–93
Guangming ribao *GMRB* (Guangming Daily), Beijing 1992–93
Hangzhou ribao *HZRB* (Hangzhou Daily), Hangzhou 1992–93
Nanfang zhoumou (Southern weekend) Guangzhou 1998
Qianjiang wanbao *QJWB* (Qianjiang Evening News), Hangzhou 1992–93
Shehui kexue bao *SHKXB* (Social Sciences Bulletin), Beijing, 1992–93
South China Morning Post *SCMP*, Hong Kong 1992–95
Wen hui bao (Wen hui Daily), Shanghai 1995
Xin wenhua bao *XWHB* (New Culture News), Beijing 1992
Xinhua (New China News Service), Beijing 1996
Yangcheng wanbao *YCWB* (Yangcheng Evening News), Guangzhou 1993
Zhejiang ribao *ZJRB* (Zhejiang Daily), Hangzhou 1992–93
Zhongguo gongshang bao *ZGGSB* (China Industry and Commerce News), Beijing 1992–93
Zhongguo laodong bao *ZGLDB* (China Labour News), Beijing 1992–93

TELEVISION STATIONS

Hangzhou shi dianshi tai, Hangzhou 1992–93
Zhejiang dianshi tai, Hangzhou 1992–93

Index